BARBAROUS MEXICO

Portion of a mural by David Alfaro Siqueiros in Chapultepec Castle. John Kenneth Turner can be seen over the left shoulder of Karl Marx, who is holding out a book.

Barbarous Mexico

By JOHN KENNETH TURNER

Introduction by Sinclair Snow

UNIVERSITY OF TEXAS PRESS, AUSTIN

International Standard Book Number 0–292–70737–1
Library of Congress Catalog Card Number 76–84627
Copyright © 1969 by Sinclair Snow

Printed in the United States of America

Third Paperback Printing, 1990

Requests for permission to reproduce material from this
work should be sent to Permissions, University of Texas
Press, Box 7819, Austin, Texas 78713–7819.

⊗ The paper used in this publication meets the mini-
mum requirements of American National Standard for
Information Sciences—Permanence of Paper for Printed
Library Materials, ANSI Z39.48–1984.

CONTENTS

The Texas Pan American Series

ACKNOWLEDGMENTS

I wish to express my appreciation for aid given me by Ethel Duffy Turner, historian, novelist, and widow of John Kenneth Turner; Fredericka Martin, historian and translator; Kimberley H. M. S. Snow, graduate student at the University of North Dakota; and the Faculty Research Grant Committee of the University of North Dakota. Mrs. Turner furnished a great part of the biographical information in the Introduction and lent a number of valuable photographs from her collection; Mrs. Martin aided in obtaining additional photographs; Mrs. Snow wrote the captions; and the Research Grant Committee furnished the funds to purchase photographs.

SINCLAIR SNOW

Barbarous Mexico, the classic indictment of the tyrannical regime of Porfirio Díaz, has been called the *Uncle Tom's Cabin* of the Mexican Revolution of 1910. The comparison is a valid one if the molding of public opinion by a literary work is the basis for judgement, for both books caused untold numbers of complacent Americans to take a new look at their immediate neighbors and to revise their opinions of their leaders and their social and economic institutions. In both cases the fundamental issue was slavery, open in the one case and disguised in the other. Mrs. Stowe's book was a novel, a story of what could be happening south of the Potomac; Mr. Turner's book was an exposé of what was actually taking place south of the Rio Grande. And both books contributed greatly to the advancement of human freedom in the conflicts that followed their appearance. Not that either book was widely read in the area criticized; on the contrary, both were banned and it was not until years later that *Uncle Tom's Cabin* was read in the South or that *Barbarous Mexico* was translated and allowed to circulate in Mexico.

By the early 1900's reform leadership in the United States had in many cases passed into the hands of militant socialists, many of them of the muckraking variety. John Kenneth Turner was one of these muckraking socialists, and although polite society then as today condemned socialism as foreign, Turner himself was eminently American. He was born in Portland, Oregon, on April 5, 1879, of old American stock. His maternal grandfather, a Methodist minister, had led a wagon train of pioneers across the continent from Kentucky to Oregon in 1849. Turner's father was a printer on the Portland *Oregonian* and later had his own printing shop in Stockton, California. There Turner passed his youth and learned the printer's trade. At sixteen he became interested in socialism and at seventeen he was publishing his own newspaper, a muckraking weekly called the *Stockton Saturday Night*, which was devoted to exposing corrupt politicians and businessmen. He drifted into schoolteaching and eventually into his proper field, journalism. While a special student at the University of California, he met his future wife, Ethel E. Duffy, a senior at the university. They were married in 1905 and made their home in San Francisco until driven out by the earthquake of 1906. For a while they lived in Portland but soon moved to Los Angeles, California, where Turner obtained a position as a reporter on the Los Angeles *Express*.

Los Angeles was at this time the headquarters of the Organizing Junta of the Mexican Liberal Party, an anti-Díaz group formed by Camilo Arriaga in San Luis Potosí in 1900. By 1906 the movement had assumed a revolutionary character under the leadership of Ricardo Flores Magón, an anarchist and one of the charter members of the Mexican Liberal Party. He and three of his colleagues—Antonio I. Villarreal, Librado Rivera, and Manuel Sarabia—after years of evading United States and Mexican agents of various kinds, had finally been run to earth and jailed in Los Angeles following several abortive uprisings in Mexico which the Liberal Party had sponsored. They were formally charged with conspiracy to violate the neutrality laws of the United States, but the real reason for their arrest was the desire of the Taft administration to please Porfirio Díaz. They were being defended by Job Harriman, a young Socialist lawyer who had devoted his life to the cause of labor and who was many years later to become the cofounder of a noted worker's school, Commonwealth College, in Arkansas. The Socialist Party of Los Angeles, of which Harriman and the Turners were members, had taken an interest in the plight of the Liberal Party leaders since their arrest, and it was through Harriman that Turner arranged to interview the prisoners for the *Express*. Turner's interview convinced him that Díaz was a monster who should be driven from Mexico and he immediately determined to expose him in the press.

Porfirio Díaz was immensely popular in the United States up to the eve of the Mexican Revolution. Middle-class Americans thought of him as the man who had brought order out of chaos in Mexico after half a century of turmoil following the wars for independence from Spain. Under his presumably benevolent rule, Mexico had made astonishing economic progress: railroads had been built, mines opened, and factories established. The peso was solid as the dollar and Mexican credit had been soundly established in the financial centers of the world. The Mexican Army, small but believed to be more than adequate for any emergency, had been trained by Prussian officers, and the countryside was efficiently policed by the famed *rurales*.

But Mexican peace and prosperity were superficial. The upper classes and foreign interests in Mexico had prospered at the expense of the lower classes, and while the gross national product was rising, the standard of living of the great majority of people was falling. And the peace that reigned was the peace of fear, not of contentment. As the Liberal Party organ *Regeneración* put it:

The quietness of death reigns in Mexico because of the fear of punishment so prodigally administered by Porfirio Díaz. Before even whispering an opinion it is necessary to look around carefully to make sure that no one is listening. The press is silent, newsmen have been imprisoned or murdered in the shadows of the jail; those persons who have shown opposition to the government are dragged from their beds at night to be killed in some secluded spot; the courts are in the hands of government lackeys; the peace that reigns is the peace of death.[1]

The first problem in the exposure of Díaz by Turner and his colleagues was to obtain unimpeachable evidence of the truthfulness and accuracy of the charges made by the Liberal Party leaders

[1] Rafael Romero Palacios, "Inédito," *Regeneración*, No. 100 (July 27, 1912), 1; translation by the editor.

against the Díaz dictatorship. This task was assigned to John Murray, a prominent Socialist who was to become the leading spirit in the formation of the Pan-American Federation of Labor in 1918, its first Spanish-language secretary, and a trusted lieutenant of Samuel Gompers until his death several years later. Born in New York of the old Quaker family for which Murray Hill in New York City had been named, Murray had been influenced in his youth by the writings of Tolstoy and had renounced his patrimony to become a crusader for human betterment. He had played a leading role in Los Angeles labor and radical movements since his arrival in California and had been especially active in aiding Mexican refugees and immigrants, the "wetbacks" of his day. On May 8, 1908, he left Los Angeles for Mexico and eventually traveled as far south as the Valle Nacional in Oaxaca, where debt slavery was rampant, although he did not for a number of reasons enter the notorious valley itself. Before he returned to Los Angeles he had collected a substantial body of information on conditions in Mexico but not enough to make an effective exposé of Porfirio Díaz.

John Murray's trip to Mexico had been financed by an affluent member of the Los Angeles Socialist Party, Elizabeth Darling Trowbridge, a native of Boston. A former Radcliffe student, Miss Trowbridge had rebelled against conventional upper-middle-class life and the unattractive possibility of a middle-class marriage and had thrown in her lot with the Socialists. Unlike John Murray, however, she had not renounced her patrimony and in the years to come was to spend her entire fortune in promoting humanitarian causes. In 1909 she married Manuel Sarabia, one of the Liberal Party Junta defendants, and shortly thereafter she and her husband fled to London to avoid further persecution of Sarabia by Díaz. There Sarabia became the spokesman for the fight against Díaz both in the press and on the lecture platform.

Soon after the return of John Murray, Turner himself decided on a fact-finding trip into Mexico. But since he did not at this time speak Spanish well it was necessary for him to take along an interpreter. The person chosen for this task was Lázaro Gutiérrez de Lara, one of the most trusted members of the Liberal Party. De Lara had come to Los Angeles in 1906 from Sonora, where he had been jailed for making speeches in support of the striking miners at Cananea. He was of an outstanding Mexico City family and had been trained for the law. Before becoming active in the labor movement he had been a practicing attorney, an official in the Mexican State Department, and the judge of a minor court. He was a radical of many years' standing who had been associated with Ricardo Flores Magón while living in Mexico City. He had been released from jail in Sonora through the efforts of his brother, a prominent physician in Mexico City who had Díaz connections. Soon after arriving in Los Angeles he became editor of *Revolución*, a short-lived Liberal Party newspaper. In August 1908 he and Turner left Los Angeles for Mexico, the money for the trip having been contributed by Elizabeth Trowbridge. Their chief object was to gather information on the fate of the thousands of Yaqui Indians who were being deported from Sonora to Yucatan and the Valle Nacional as forced laborers. This was an extremely hazardous undertaking for Turner and De Lara and they were forced to keep their identity a secret. Turner posed as a wealthy American businessman who wanted to invest heavily in Mexican henequen and tobacco, while De Lara acted the part of his intimate friend, interpreter, and advisor. Luckily enough, they were apparently never suspected, although they penetrated deep into the slave labor areas of both Yucatan and the Valle Nacional. The big planters were more than happy to talk business with a well-heeled gringo, for the depression of 1907 had left many of them in straitened circumstances. In many cases the planters made no effort to hide the brutality of their operations from Turner and De Lara, who had ample opportunity to see for themselves what it was like to be a forced laborer on a large hacienda. And what they saw was not pretty: it was a confirmation of what Turner had been told by the Liberal Party leaders when he had interviewed them in jail in Los Angeles. The experiences of Turner and De Lara and the horrors that they witnessed are told in the first chapters of *Barbarous Mexico*.

While Turner and De Lara were in Mexico, Elizabeth Trowbridge bought out a printing shop in Tucson, Arizona, and there
the *Border*, a magazine devoted to the defense of Mexican refugees
and the exposure of Porfirio Díaz, was established under the joint
management of John Murray, Ethel Turner, and Elizabeth Trowbridge. The shop also printed a Liberal Party periodical in Spanish called *El Defensor del Pueblo*, which was edited by Manuel
Sarabia, now out on bail after having developed tuberculosis while
in prison. The establishment immediately came under the sur-
veillance of local police and Díaz agents. Turner joined the staff
of the *Border* soon after returning from Mexico but in a few weeks
left for New York to find a publisher for several articles on slave
labor in Mexico that he had completed. Shortly after his depar-
ture the printing shop was entered at night, presumably by Díaz
agents, and the printing press wrecked. The project was abandoned
soon thereafter.

Turner's articles were accepted by the *American Magazine*,
formerly *Leslie's*, which had been established by a group of prominent muckrakers including Lincoln Steffens, Ida Tarbell, Ray
Stannard Baker, and Finley Peter Dunne, who had "seceded" from
McClure's in 1906 because of its growing conservatism. The circulation of the *American Magazine* by 1909 was approximately
300,000 but it was laboring under a debt of $400,000 and its own-
ers were hard put to meet the interest payments. The "Barbarous
Mexico" series would undoubtedly increase circulation, for the
exposure of Díaz would be a revelation that would attract wide
attention. But before proceeding with the series it was necessary
that Turner do further research into the matter, that he make a
thorough investigation into the political nature of the Díaz regime.

Turner, accompanied by his wife, returned to Mexico late in
January 1909. Because of his skill as a tennis player he was able
to obtain a position as sports editor on an English-language newspaper, the *Mexican Herald*, in Mexico City, and soon gained ac-
ceptance into sports circles by umpiring the Mexican-United States
tennis tournament held at the Country Club in Churubusco. In his
spare time he collected information on the Díaz machine. By late

April he had completed his investigation and was soon back in New York, where he turned over his latest articles to the *American Magazine.*

The September 1909 issue of the *American Magazine* carried a full-page announcement that the "Barbarous Mexico" series would begin in October. The magazine praised Turner as the one American who had seen Mexico as it really was and compared him to George Kennan, who "saw Russia and Siberia twenty years ago, and in some ways that which he [Turner] saw and reports is even more terrible than that which Mr. Kennan told us about." The author of the announcement commented on the great American ignorance of Mexico and blamed it on doctored "news" from that country and on the success of Díaz in suppressing publications critical of his government.

The October issue, which inaugurated the series, carried in 14-point type a two-page editorial introduction to "Barbarous Mexico" which concluded as follows:

A great Díaz-Mexico myth has been built up through skilfully applied influence upon journalism. It is the most astounding case of the suppression of truth and the dissemination of untruth and half-truth that recent history affords. But Mr. Turner has by long and often hazardous journeys and investigations got at the truth. As you read the articles one after another, follow the author in his adventures, and see with his eyes how things really are, you will be forced to admit that Mexico the "Republic" is a pretence and a sham. Díaz is an able autocrat who has policed the country well, used his power for the benefit of the few and neglected the welfare of the great body of the people. In Mexico they say "after him the deluge, if indeed he is not swept away by it."

With this introduction, "Barbarous Mexico" got off to a good start. The first installment, entitled "Slaves of Yucatan" and appropriately illustrated with carefully chosen photographs and excellent drawings by George Varian, set the tone for what promised to be a shocking series of revelations of conditions in Díaz' Mexico. The November issue carried "The Tragic Story of the Yaqui In-

dians," and the December number dealt with "The Contract Slaves
of the Valle Nacional." The articles were written with skill and
passion and they carried conviction; they were calculated not only
to inform but to create a highly emotional response in the reader.

   "Barbarous Mexico" created a sensation in Mexico, in the United
States, and in England, where the series was reprinted in a London newspaper. Protests from Mexico were prompt; in fact, soon
after the *American Magazine* had announced its intention to publish the series, there were sharp denials in the Mexican press of the
truth of the forthcoming articles. Some persons linked the series
with the Madero movement, while others saw the attack on Díaz
as simply a manifestation of continuing Yankee aggression. To
many conservative Mexicans, "Barbarous Mexico" was unques-
tionably part of an insidious campaign against Mexico that had
begun only recently with the publication in the United States of
Herman Whitaker's *The Planter* and Carlo de Fornaro's *Díaz,
Czar of Mexico*, the former a novel telling of some of the horrors
related by Turner and the latter a muckraking exposé of such violence as to result in a prison sentence for the author.[2] And not only
Mexicans but also United States citizens living in Mexico were
bitterly opposed to "Barbarous Mexico." One E. S. Smith, speaking
unofficially for the American colony in Mexico City—so he alleged—stated his intention in the Mexico City *Record* of asking for
a writ of mandamus compelling the *American Magazine* to sub-
stantiate its charges against Díaz. Smith was the most vociferous
of the Díaz supporters and attempted to prevent delivery of the
magazine to subscribers by sending the following wire to President
Taft:

Please prohibit use of the United States mails to the American Magazine
proposing publication of "Barbarous Mexico" in October number. The

---

   [2] According to Turner in the *Appeal to Reason* (June 4, 1910), Fornaro was an
Italian newspaperman who had been the Sunday editor of Mexico City's *El
Diario*. He wrote his book on Díaz while in the United States and was convicted
of criminal libel and sent to prison in the United States. He was still in prison in
1910, serving a one-year term.

foreword threatens libel against the whole Mexican people, and its circulation here or elsewhere is a disgrace and injury to American citizens in Mexico.[3]

Smith's appeal to Taft was ineffective, but he continued his efforts in behalf of Díaz by publishing an article entitled "The Truth About Mexico" in the November issue of *Bankers Magazine*, an eminently conservative publication which devoted this entire issue to "selling" Díaz to its readers. Díaz himself took action in Mexico against the circulation of the "Barbarous Mexico" articles and the publishers were forced to protest to the United States State Department and the Postoffice Department that copies of the November issue of the *American Magazine* destined for Mexico were being detained or confiscated by Díaz authorities.

The "Barbarous Mexico" series was enthusiastically received in the United States. The articles were given scores of favorable reviews and comments in the American press beginning with the first article in October. The New York *Sun* spoke approvingly of the "heart-rending installment" in the November issue. The Rochester *Times* said, "The Abolitionists in our own ante bellum days did not formulate an indictment as repulsive as that brought against Mexico by this impassioned writer." The Milwaukee *Journal* in an article headed "More Power to the American" commented that "the horror of the thing grows, and the guilt, not of the American people but of their dollars, begins to come into view." The San Diego *Sun*, as Christmas approached, called the series "a fit thing for you to think about in that season of the year when 'peace on earth and good will to men' is on every lip." The Socialist and labor reviews were especially favorable; in England the *Labour Leader* in an article headed "The Henequen Hells of Mexico" called Turner "an American humanitarian who deserves the thanks of civilisation." More staid publications were noncommittal in their observations but their reviews were of respectable length and included many long and telling quotations. The *Literary Digest* headed its review "The Slave Trade of Mexico" and the *Review of*

---

[3] San Francisco *Bulletin*, September 4, 1909.

Reviews discussed the series in its column "Leading Articles of the Month." The first three installments of "Barbarous Mexico" had been a magnificent success.

But something went wrong and the December installment was the last of Turner's articles to appear in the *American Magazine*. The January 1910 issue continued the series but made no mention of John Kenneth Turner. Instead, there was an editorial on Mexico which began: "We wish to affirm what we said at the beginning of these articles—that Mexico as a civilized government is a farce and a failure; as a republic it is a mockery. It is still barbarous in that it permits and indulges in barbarities." The editorial continued in this vein and ended by stating: "There is slavery at this moment. . . . There is barbarous political persecution at this moment. . . . There is imprisonment for free speaking at this moment. . . . There is suppression of personal and political liberty at this moment." The editorial was followed by an unsigned article dealing with debt slavery entitled "Moving Pictures of Mexico in Ferment." In February the series was continued with an article by Herman Whitaker of *The Planter* on debt slavery in the rubber-producing areas of Mexico, the March number had a short anonymous piece by a former debt slave whom the magazine called "a responsible German now living in California," and the April issue carried the personal observations of two Englishmen on forced labor in Yucatan, in the form of an open letter to Díaz. But the May, June, and July numbers made no mention of "Barbarous Mexico." In the meantime, there was much speculation in liberal and radical circles regarding the suppression of the Turner articles. In the June 4, 1910, issue of the *Appeal to Reason*, Turner himself charged that the editors of *American Magazine* had been intimidated by Díaz: "The editors of The American Magazine imagined that they were strong, but they found themselves pitifully weak. They thought themselves brave men, but they discovered that they were only cowards. Weak and cowardly were they, but only in the face of a power whose might they had misjudged and which threatened to crush them." This charge was answered by *American Magazine* in its August 1910 issue:

It will come as a complete surprise to at least nineteen out of twenty of our readers that an attack has been made in certain socialistic newspapers on the honesty and integrity of THE AMERICAN MAGAZINE.

We have been charged with having stopped publication of our "Barbarous Mexico" articles because "Wall Street has got us," and so on.

We should not take notice of this absurd piece of folly were it not for the fact that we are humble enough to realize that a few of our friends, far away, may hear these ridiculous stories and put some measure of faith in them if we wholly ignore them, as we are inclined to do. It seems to us that it is simpler, more direct, and more human, to stand up quietly and say, once for all, that this periodical is as free as the air, that it is devoted to the truth, that the Mexican government or anybody else outside this office does not and cannot control it....

The September issue carried nothing on Mexico, but in the October number there was an article on Díaz by E. Alexander Powell, an English traveler, which Turner in the October 8, 1910, issue of the *Appeal to Reason* effectively exposed as a paraphrase of an article which he, Turner, had written for *American Magazine* some months before. The November issue carried nothing and in that of December there was only a very short anonymous article, said to be the translation of an unpublished document, which was called in English "I Also Accuse." This was the end of the "Barbarous Mexico" series that had started out so bravely fourteen months before.

What had happened? No one knows for sure. Upton Sinclair in the *Brass Check* wrote close to a decade later:

The magazine had begun the publication of a sensational series of articles, "Barbarous Mexico," by John Kenneth Turner. These articles, since published in book form, and a second time suppressed,[4] gave an intimate, firsthand account of the ferocities of the Díaz regime, under which American "dollar diplomats" were coining enormous fortunes. The "American" began the publication with a grand hurrah; it published two or three of the articles, and then suddenly it quit, with a

---

[4] Mr. Sinclair is incorrect in stating that the book was suppressed.

feeble and obviously dishonest excuse—and poor Turner had to take
his articles to that refuge of the suppressed muckraker, the "Appeal to
Reason."

There must have been a crisis in the office of the magazine. Somebody
had evidently had a "show-down", the editors had been "taught their
place." Ever since they have been a theme for tears. . . .

Be that as it may, one thing is certain: *American Magazine* was
no longer interested in Mexico and when the Revolution began in
the fall of 1910 it had no comment to make.

After his series had been dropped by the *American Magazine*,
Turner began publishing the remainder of the articles in other
periodicals. By the end of 1910 seven chapters of the book had
been published in the *Appeal to Reason*, one chapter had appeared
in the *International Socialist Review*, and the *Pacific Monthly* had
carried another.

It is not clear exactly when Turner decided to publish his articles in book form, but it must have been during the summer of
1910. Unable to find a standard publisher in the United States, he
turned to Charles H. Kerr and Company, an old Socialist firm of
Chicago, which announced in the December 3, 1910, issue of the
Appeal that *Barbarous Mexico* would be off the press in the very
near future. Publication in England was by the standard firm of
Cassell and Company.

During the months immediately preceding the publication of
Barbarous Mexico, Turner created a sensation in the press by
charging that local, state, and national officials as well as private
detective agencies in the United States were cooperating with Díaz
agents in persecuting Mexican political refugees. These charges
were made before a joint committee of the House of Representatives
in Washington during June 1910. The witnesses were John Kenneth Turner, John Murray, Lázaro Gutiérrez de Lara, and Mother
(Mrs. Mary) Jones, probably the most noted female Socialist agi-
tator of this time. The published proceedings of these hearings run
to ninety-five printed pages and contain a wealth of information
on the persecution of anti-Díaz Americans and Mexicans in the

United States on the eve of the Mexican Revolution. News of the
hearings, including portions of the testimony, was carried by the
United Press and by major American dailies such as the New York
Times, the Baltimore *Sun*, and the San Francisco *Daily News*. The
publicity given these hearings—despite efforts of the pro-Díaz fac-
tion on the committee to keep the testimony secret—enhanced the
fame of Turner as a fighter for justice and created sympathy for
the Mexican rebels in the approaching conflict.

Early in August 1910, Ricardo Flores Magón, Antonio I. Villarreal, and Librado Rivera were released from prison. They immediately established the headquarters of the Junta of the Mexican
Liberal Party in Los Angeles and began the republication of its
official organ, *Regeneración*. Turner acted as a confidential purchasing agent for the Liberal Party Junta and bought all the rifles,
revolvers, and ammunition available in the local stores. These mu-
nitions were packed in cases marked "farm machinery" and shipped
to Jim Wilson, a friendly farmer living near Holtville, California.
Wilson then hauled them in his wagon to the border, where they
were slipped into Mexico at night and hidden in the brush. After
the Revolution began in November, Liberal Party members par-
ticipated in various engagements, sometimes in alliance with the
maderistas, but the Junta had an objective of its own: the capture
of Baja California. Plans were made by the Junta for the conquest
of Mexicali and Tijuana; Mexicali was taken without difficulty on
January 29, 1911.

While the Revolution was getting under way, *Barbarous Mexico*
came off the press, first in the United States and shortly thereafter in England. The first reviews appeared in February 1911.
Like the magazine articles, the book was well received. The Portland *Telegram* headed its review "The Book That Caused a Civil
War" and called it "an epoch in Mexican history." The London
Daily Mail reviewed it in its Book of the Day column and declared:
"If Mexico is half as bad as she is painted by Mr. Turner, she is
covered with the leprosy of a slavery worse than that of San Thome
or Peru, and should be regarded as unclean by all the free peoples
of the world." The Chicago *Daily Tribune* discussed it at great

length and with numerous long quotations, along with the recent
laudatory Díaz biography by James Creelman, *Díaz, Master of
Mexico.* The New York *Times* reviewer remarked of Turner: "For
many of his charges there is only too much ground." Some publications were less favorable, a minority ranging from mildly to
bitterly hostile. The *Spectator* said that "the facts may be exaggerated." The *Saturday Review* saw the book as "full of prejudice and
altogether unfair to Díaz." *Outlook* said that it lost its effectiveness
"because of the sensational, rhetorical, and feverish methods employed." Years later the book was still being commented on. Henry
Baerling in *Mexico: The Land of Unrest* wrote in 1914: "The
worst one can say of Mr. Turner is that he is pretty full of truth."
Edith O'Shaughnessy, an American diplomat's wife in Mexico City
during Victoriano Huerta's term in power, spoke of it as "that
depressing book, *Barbarous Mexico.*" Herbert Ingram Priestley,
writing in the *Hispanic American Historical Review* in 1919, says
that it "was hotly discussed" in both the United States and Mexico. Timothy Turner, an American newspaperman who reported
the Mexican Revolution, wrote in *Bullets, Bottles, and Gardenias*
in 1935: "Turner's book, *Barbarous Mexico*, was the 'Mother India' of the time and caused a great sensation; some said it had much
to do with bringing on the revolution."

Turner, acting as the confidential agent of the Liberal Party
Junta and as chief advisor to the rebels in Baja California, was in
and out of Mexico during the early months of the Revolution, but
he took no part in the actual fighting. He had two major tasks: to
reconcile differences between rival factions in the Liberal fighting
forces and to handle Liberal publicity in such a manner as to fore-
stall United States intervention in the conflict. He was suspected
by United States authorities of violating the neutrality laws and
was threatened with arrest by the United States District Attorney,
but the federal government was wary of attempting to indict Turner because of his international reputation as a fighter for justice.
Other Liberal Party leaders were arrested but Turner remained
free. By late May 1911 Tijuana had fallen to the Liberals, Ciudad
Juárez had been taken by the *maderistas*, and Porfirio Díaz had

fled to Europe. The first phase of the Mexican Revolution had come to an end and Turner retired unmolested to Carmel, California, to relax and write.

The writers' and artists' colony in Carmel was in its infancy in 1911 and still retained its primitive attractiveness. Reminiscing half a century later, Ethel Turner wrote:

We gathered wild blackberries. We hunted pine cones for our fireplaces. We lay on the white sand dunes among the fragrant sand verbena. We found agates on the beach. We saved abalone blisters . . . to make into jewelry. Sometimes we bathed in the ocean, but the surf was rough and dangerous. The river mouth was better. Every year on Bech's birthday he gave a roast pig party. He tended the pig all afternoon, and when it was ready we ate on plank tables out of doors. There was plenty of wine and gaiety.[5]

While the Turners' house was being built, they lived in the home of the poet George Sterling, their closest associate in Carmel. They were active in the Forest Theater—Turner made a big hit as Shylock—and they became friends of many noted literary figures who lived in or wandered in and out of Carmel: Robinson Jeffers, Upton Sinclair, Jack London, Sinclair Lewis.

Turner was by no means satisfied with the course that events had taken in Mexico following the fall of Díaz. The Liberal Party had split and several members of the Junta had joined the *maderistas*, the Liberal revolt in Baja California had been crushed by Madero, and in the south Zapata was forced to continue his fight for agrarian reform. Turner did not believe that Madero intended to make a serious effort to solve the agrarian problem by giving land to the landless peasants and he decided to talk to Madero in an effort to determine his intentions. He left for Mexico in late December 1912 and upon his arrival in Mexico City he arranged to write for the newspaper *El País* to defray expenses. On January 27, 1913, he had an interview with Madero and wrote his wife the following day:

[5] Ethel Duffy Turner, "Notes on Early Literary Carmel," an unpublished manuscript in Bancroft Library, University of California, Berkeley.

Big news! Last night El Señor Presidente received me, sending various personages away in order to talk to me. He greeted me with: "You are a very famous man." We talked for 45 minutes, walking up and down the same balcony where Creelman had his highfalutin interview with Díaz. I haven't time to tell you what he said at all, though I might say he said that "Barbarous Mexico" had helped him very much in the revolution of 1910, as it gave the American people the knowledge that he was fighting for liberty. But he told me many things, showed me a map of Lower California with the various concessions, told me a good deal about the land question, outlined most of his policies, and in the end gave me the thing I wanted—a sweeping letter ordering all the authorities, military and civil, in the republic, to give me all the data I asked for. Of course the flattering reception did not warp my judgement at all. I finally left at my own suggestion, as I didn't want to overdo the thing. In parting he told me to come back later if I wanted anything, and if any official failed to give me the information I wanted, to complain direct to him.[6]

Turner took full advantage of the carte blanche given him by Madero and was on the streets of Mexico City during the Tragic Ten Days, February 9 to 19, which resulted in the downfall of Madero and his murder by Victoriano Huerta. His news items on the revolt were cabled to the New York press. On February 16 he was arrested by a member of the anti-Madero forces, allegedly as a suspected spy. His story was carried in the March 8 issue of the New York *World*:

I was taken to the Ciudadela. After General Mondragon had seen me, I was thrown into a hole, with drunken soldiers for fellow prisoners, and kept there for seven hours.

I sent for Ambassador [Henry Lane] Wilson, who came and promised to get me out that night. Then he said he had lost a great deal of time and would let me stay there over night, but I would be perfectly safe, he said.

[6] John Kenneth Turner to Ethel Duffy Turner, January 28, 1913, the original in the possession of Ethel Duffy Turner, Cuernavaca, Morelos, Mexico.

Up to that time I had given a false name, but when Ambassador Wilson said he would have to look up some of my friends, I told him my right name. He took umbrage at this and brusquely asked me why I had given a false name. I told him I had done so because my life would not be worth the purchase price if the Díaz people knew I was the man who wrote *Barbarous Mexico,* describing the atrocities of Porfirio Díaz.

Ambassador Wilson practically compelled me to give my right name to the lieutenants of Felix Díaz.

In so many words, Mr. Wilson told me that the only thing that in any way made me deserving of the punishment they intended for me was the fact that I had criticized the policy of the American administration.

Felix Díaz afterwards accused me of plotting to assassinate him. Fortunately, after my arrest and before reaching the arsenal, I had destroyed a letter from President Madero which I had been carrying. It commended me to all his officers, assuring them that they could give me with safety any information at their disposal, and informing them that I was criticizing the administration of President Taft. If this letter had been found upon me, I should have been summarily put to death.

Three times I was sentenced to be shot, but each time something happened to prevent the execution. Notwithstanding the Ambassador's promise, I was three days in the arsenal.

News of Turner's predicament was carried by the Hearst newspapers in the United States and a campaign was immediately begun by his friends and colleagues, including Richard Harding Davis, to obtain his release. But before the campaign could get well under way, he was suddenly and mysteriously set free. He stayed in Mexico for a few days, but upon learning that he was to be arrested again he fled to Veracruz, where he took ship for New York. Back in the United States he exposed Henry Lane Wilson in the press and in letters to President Woodrow Wilson and Secretary of State William Jennings Bryan.

After this adventure Turner did not visit Mexico for close to two years. During this period he wrote for the press on the Revolution and on strikes in the United States. He had a contract with the Scripps-McRae chain of newspapers and in addition wrote much for the Socialist New York *Call*, the *Appeal to Reason*, and various other periodicals. In the spring of 1915 he returned to Mexico to report on the United States occupation of Veracruz, a move which he bitterly condemned. On this trip he had an exclusive interview with Venustiano Carranza. Shortly thereafter he published two books on Mexico: *Quién es Pancho Villa?* and *La intervención en México y sus nefandos factores.* The following year he made two more trips to Mexico and wrote articles opposing the Pershing Punitive Expedition.

In April 1917, as a guest of Senator Robert M. LaFollette, Turner heard President Wilson deliver his war message to Congress. From this time on he opposed United States participation in the war. His views on Wilson were expressed in his highly critical book *Shall It Be Again?*

Following the war, when there was still danger of United States intervention in Mexico, the Rand School of Social Science published Turner's *Hands Off Mexico.* He was greatly interested in agrarian reform and in 1921 went to Cuernavaca where he interviewed Genevevo de la O, a noted *zapatista* general.

This was Turner's last visit to Mexico. He continued to make his home in Carmel but the reaction of the 1920's discouraged him profoundly and he did little writing. His last book came after a lapse of many years in 1941, when he published his *Challenge to Karl Marx.* He died in 1948.

There has been a renewal of interest in Turner and *Barbarous Mexico* in recent years. This is no doubt due in part to the reappraisal of Ricardo Flores Magón and the Mexican Liberal Party that is presently taking place. In 1955 the first Spanish translation of *Barbarous Mexico* was published in Mexico, with numerous illustrations, in *Problemas agrícolas e industriales de México.* The second Spanish edition appeared in 1964 under the auspices of the Instituto Nacional de la Juventud Mexicana, and the third Spanish edition was issued by "Cordemex" in 1965. David Alfaro Siqueiros included Turner in his Chapultepec Castle mural along with the great Mexican heroes of the Revolution. The central figure in this famous mural is Fernando Palomárez, a Liberal Party member who was one of Turner's advisors while he was writing *Barbarous Mexico.* (Palomárez had the distinction of having emptied his revolver at Porfirio Díaz while the latter was making a speech, and living to tell the tale.) More recently, in 1967, the book was used as the basis of a two-hour experimental motion picture entitled *El Periodista Turner*, which was directed by Oscar Menéndez. The movie was certainly a worthwhile project, but the well-fed amateur actors who play the parts of debt slaves in Yucatan bear little resemblance to the original debt slaves of *Barbarous Mexico.*

SINCLAIR SNOW

University of North Dakota
Grand Forks

PREFACE TO THE FIRST EDITION (1910)

The bulk of the material embodied in this volume was gathered during two trips through Mexico made in 1908 and 1909; the rest of it was gleaned from a reading of various writings of Mexico, both in English and Spanish, and from other sources. My purpose is to give the reader a correct impression of Diaz and his political and economic system, of the character of the Mexican people, and of the Diaz-American partnership which has helped to enslave the Mexican nation, on the one hand, and kept the American public in ignorance of the real facts of Diaz and Mexico, on the other. Current illusions of Mexico and Porfirio Diaz are exploded and the American defenders of slavery and autocracy are made to appear in their true light. The term "barbarous" which I use in my title is intended to apply to Mexico's form of government rather than to its people.

NOTE

In this second edition the text is faithfully given as
Turner published it, with his spelling of certain words
and without accents and other diacritical marks. However, the obvious typographical errors have been silently
corrected.

BARBAROUS MEXICO

The Slaves of Yucatan

What is Mexico?

Americans commonly characterize Mexico as "Our Sister Republic." Most of us picture her vaguely as a republic in reality much like our own, inhabited by people a little different in temperament, a little poorer and a little less advanced, but still enjoying the protection of republican laws—a free people in the sense that we are free.

Others of us, who have seen the country through a car window, or speculated a little in Mexican mines or Mexican plantations, paint that country beyond the Rio Grande as a benevolent paternalism in which a great and good man orders all things well for his foolish but adoring people.

I found Mexico to be neither of these things. The real Mexico I found to be a country with a written constitution and written laws in general almost as fair and democratic as our own, but with neither constitution nor laws in operation. Mexico is a country without political freedom, without freedom of speech, without a free press, without a free ballot, without a jury system, without political parties, without any of our cherished guarantees of life, liberty and the pursuit of happiness. It is a land where there has been no contest for the office of president for more than a generation, where the executive rules all things by means of a standing army, where political offices are sold for a fixed price. I found Mexico to be a land where the people are poor because they have no rights, where peonage is the rule for the great mass, and where actual chattel slavery obtains for hundreds of thousands. Finally, I found that the people do not idolize their president, that the tide of opposition, dammed and held back as it has been by army and secret police, is rising to a height where it must shortly overflow that dam. Mexicans of all classes and affiliations agree that their country is on the verge of a revolution in favor of democracy; if not a revolution in the time of Diaz, for Diaz is old and is expected soon to pass, then a revolution after Diaz.

My special interest in political Mexico was first awakened early in 1908, when I came in contact with four Mexican revolutionists who were at that time incarcerated in the county jail at Los Angeles, California. Here were four educated, intelligent Mexicans, college men, all of them, who were being held by the United States authorities on a charge of planning to invade a friendly nation—Mexico—with an armed force from American soil.

Why should intelligent men take up arms against a republic? Why should they come to the United States to prepare for their military maneuvers? I talked with those Mexican prisoners. They assured me that at one time they had peacefully agitated in their own country for a peaceful and constitutional overthrow of the persons in control of their government.

But for that very thing, they declared, they had been imprisoned and their property had been destroyed. Secret police had dogged their steps, their lives had been threatened, and countless methods had been used to prevent them from carrying on their work. Finally, hunted as outlaws beyond the national boundaries, denied the rights of free speech, press and assembly, denied the right peaceably to organize to bring about political changes, they had resorted to the only alternative—arms. Why had they wished to overturn their government? Because it had set aside the constitution, because it had abolished those civic rights which all enlightened men agree are necessary for the unfolding of a nation, because it had dispossessed the common people of their lands, because it had converted free laborers into serfs, peons, and some of them even into—slaves.

"Slavery? Do you mean to tell me that there is any real slavery left in the western hemisphere?" I scoffed. "Bah! You are talking like an American socialist. You mean 'wage slavery,' or slavery to miserable conditions of livelihood. You don't mean chattel slavery."

But those four Mexican exiles refused to give ground. "Yes, slavery," they said, "chattel slavery. Men, women and children bought and sold like mules—just like mules—and like mules they belong to their masters. They are slaves."

"Human beings bought and sold like mules in America! And in the twentieth century. Well," I told myself, "if it's true, I'm going to see it."

So it was that early in September, 1908, I crossed the Rio Grande bound for my first trip through the back yards of Old Mexico.

Upon this first trip I was accompanied by L. Gutierrez De Lara, a Mexican of distinguished family, whose acquaintance I had made also in Los Angeles. De Lara was opposed to the existing government in Mexico, which fact my critics have pointed out as evidence of bias in my investigations. On the contrary, I did not depend on De Lara or any other biassed source for my information, but took every precaution to arrive at the exact truth, and by as many different avenues as practicable. Every essential fact which I put down here in regard to the slavery of Mexico I saw with my own eyes or heard with my own ears, and heard usually from those individuals who would be most likely to minimize their cruelties—the slave-drivers themselves.

Nevertheless, to the credit of De Lara I must say that he gave me most important aid in gathering my material. By his knowledge of the country and the people, by his genius as a "mixer," and, above all, through his personal acquaintance with valuable sources of information all over the country—men on the inside—I was enabled to see and hear things which are practically inaccessible to the ordinary investigator.

Slavery in Mexico! Yes, I found it. I found it first in Yucatan. The peninsula of Yucatan is an elbow of Central America, which shoots off in a northeasterly direction almost half way to Florida. It belongs to Mexico, and its area of some 80,000 square miles is almost equally divided among the states of Yucatan and Campeche and the territory of Quintana Roo.

The coast of Yucatan, which comprises the north-central part of the peninsula, is about a thousand miles directly south of New Orleans. The surface of the state is almost solid rock, so nearly solid that it is usually impossible to plant a tree without first blasting a hole to receive the shoot and make a place for the roots. Yet this naturally barren land is more densely populated than is our own United States. More than that, within one-fourth of the territory three-fourths of the people live, and the density of the population runs to nearly seventy-five per square mile.

The secret of these peculiar conditions is that the soil and the climate of northern Yucatan happen to be perfectly adapted to the production of that hardy species of century plant which produces *henequen*, or sisal hemp. Hence we find the city of Merida, a beautiful modern city claiming a population of 60,000 people, and surrounding it, supporting it, vast henequen plantations on which the rows of gigantic green plants extend for miles and miles. The farms are so large that each has a little city of its own, inhabited by from 500 to 2,500 people, according to the size of the farm. The owners of these great farms are the chief slave-holders of Yucatan; the inhabitants of the little cities are the slaves. The annual export of henequen from Yucatan approximates 250,000,000 pounds. The population of Yucatan is about three hundred thousand. The slave-holders' club numbers 250 members, but the vast majority of the lands and the slaves are concentrated in the hands of fifty henequen kings. The slaves number more than one hundred thousand.

In order to secure the truth in its greatest purity from the lips of the masters of the slaves I went among them playing a part. Long before I put my feet upon the white sands of Progreso, the port of Yucatan, I had heard how visiting investigators are bought or blinded, how, if they cannot be bought, they are wined and dined and filled with falsehood, then taken over a route previously pre-pared—fooled, in short, so completely that they go away half be-lieving that the slaves are not slaves, that the hundred thousand half-starving, overworked, degraded bondsmen are perfectly happy and so contented with their lot that it would be a shame indeed to yield to them the freedom and security which, in all humanity, is the rightful share of every human being born upon the earth.

The part I played in Yucatan was that of an investor with much money to sink in henequen properties, and as such I was warmly welcomed by the henequen kings. I was rather fortunate in going to Yucatan when I did. Until the panic of 1907 it was a well-under-stood and unanimously approved policy of the "Camara de Agri-cola," the planters' organization, that foreigners should not be al-lowed to invade the henequen business. This was partly because the profits of the business were huge and the rich Yucatecos wanted to "hog it all" for themselves, but more especially because they feared that through foreigners the story of their misdeeds might become known to the world.

But the panic of 1907 wiped out the world's henequen market for a time. The planters were a company of little Rockefellers, but they needed ready cash, and they were willing to take it from anyone who came. Hence my imaginary money was the open ses-ame to their club, and to their farms. I not only discussed every phase of henequen production with the kings themselves, and while they were off their guard, but I observed thousands of slaves under their normal conditions.

Chief among the henequen kings of Yucatan is Olegario Molina, former governor of the state and Secretary of Fomento (Public Promotion) of Mexico. Molina's holdings of lands in Yucatan and Quintana Roo aggregate 15,000,000 acres, or 23,000 square miles —a small kingdom in itself. The fifty kings live in costly palaces in Merida and many of them have homes abroad. They travel a great deal, usually they speak several different languages, and they and their families are a most cultivated class of people. All Merida and all Yucatan, even all the peninsula of Yucatan, are dependent on the fifty henequen kings. Naturally these men are in control of the political machinery of their state, and naturally they operate that machinery for their own benefit. The slaves are 8,000 Yaqui Indians imported from Sonora, 3,000 Chinese (Koreans), and between 100,000 and 125,000 native Mayas, who formerly owned the lands that the henequen kings now own.

The Maya people, indeed, form about ninety-five per cent of the population of Yucatan. Even the majority of the fifty henequen kings are Mayas crossed with the blood of Spain. The Mayas are Indians—and yet they are not Indians. They are not like the Indians of the United States, and they are called Indians only because their homes were in the western hemisphere when the Europeans came. The Mayas had a civilization of their own when the Europeans "discovered" them, and it was a civilization admittedly as high as that of the most advanced Aztecs or the Incas of Peru.

The Mayas are a peculiar people. They look like no other people on the face of the earth. They are not like other Mexicans; they are not like Americans; they are not like Chinamen; they are not like East Indians; they are not like Turks. Yet one might very easily imagine that fusion of all these five widely different peoples might produce a people much like the Mayas. They are not large in stature, but their features are remarkably finely chiselled and their bodies give a strong impression of elegance and grace. Their skins are olive, their foreheads high, their faces slightly aquiline. The women of all classes in Merida wear long, flowing white gowns, unbound at the waist and embroidered about the hem and perhaps also about the bust in some bright color—green, blue or purple. In the warm evenings a military band plays and hundreds of comely women and girls thus alluringly attired mingle among the fragrant flowers, the art statues and the tropical greenery of the city plaza.

The planters do not call their chattels slaves. They call them "people," or "laborers," especially when speaking to strangers. But when speaking confidentially they have said to me: "Yes, they are slaves."

But I did not accept the word slavery from the people of Yucatan, though they were the holders of the slaves themselves. The proof of a fact is to be found, not in the name, but in the conditions thereof. Slavery is the ownership of the body of a man, an ownership so absolute that the body can be transferred to another, an ownership that gives to the owner a right to take the products of that body, to starve it, to chastise it at will, to kill it with impunity. Such is slavery in the extreme sense. Such is slavery as I found it in Yucatan.

The masters of Yucatan do not call their system slavery; they call it enforced service for debt. "We do not consider that we own our laborers; we consider that they are in debt to us. And we do not consider that we buy and sell them; we consider that we transfer the debt, and the man goes with the debt." This is the way Don Enrique Camara Zavala, president of the "Camara de Agricola de Yucatan," explained the attitude of the henequen kings in the matter. "Slavery is against the law; we do not call it slavery," various planters assured me again and again.

But the fact that it is not service for debt is proven by the habit of transferring the slaves from one master to another, not on any basis of debt, but on the basis of the market price of a man. In figuring

on the purchase of a plantation I always had to figure on paying
cash for the slaves, exactly the same as for the land, the machinery
and the cattle. Four hundred Mexican dollars apiece was the prevailing price, and that is what the planters usually asked me. "If
you buy now you buy at a very good time," I was told again and
again. "The panic has put the price down. One year ago the price
of each man was $1,000."

The Yaquis are transferred on exactly the same basis as the
Mayas—the market price of a slave—and yet all people of Yucatan
know that the planters pay only $65 apiece to the government for
each Yaqui. I was offered for $400 each Yaquis who had not been
in the country a month and consequently had had no opportunity
of rolling up a debt that would account for the difference in price.
Moreover, one of the planters told me: "We don't allow the Yaquis
to get in debt to us."

It would be absurd to suppose that the reason the price was uniform was because all the slaves were equally in debt. I probed this
matter a little by inquiring into the details of the selling transaction.
"You get the photograph and identification papers with the man,"
said one, "and that's all." "You get the identification papers and
the account of the debt," said another. "We don't keep much account of the debt," said a third, "because it doesn't matter after
you've got possession of the man." "The man and the identification
papers are enough," said another; "if your man runs away, the
papers are all the authorities require for you to get him back again."
"Whatever the debt, it takes the market price to get him free again,"
a fifth told me.

Conflicting as some of these answers are, they all tend to show
one thing, that the debt counts for nothing after the debtor passes
into the hands of the planter. Whatever the debt, it takes the market price to get the debtor free again!

Even then, I thought, it would not be so bad if the servant had
an opportunity of working out the price and buying back his free-

dom. Even some of our negro slaves before the Civil War were permitted—by exceptionally lenient masters—to do that.

But I found that such was not the custom. "You need have no fear in purchasing this plantation," said one planter to me, "of the laborers being able to buy their freedom and leave you. They can never do that."

The only man in the country whom I heard of as having ever permitted a slave to buy his freedom was a professional man of Merida, an architect. "I bought a laborer for $1,000," he explained to me. "He was a good man and helped me a lot about my office. After I got to liking him I credited him with so much wages per week. After eight years I owed him the full $1,000, so I let him go. But they never do that on the plantations—never."

Thus I learned that the debt feature of the enforced service does not alleviate the hardships of the slave by making it easier for him to free himself, neither does it affect the conditions of his sale or his complete subjection to his master. On the other hand, I found that the one particular in which this debt element does play an actual part in the destiny of the unfortunate of Yucatan militates against him instead of operating in his favor. For it is by means of debt that the Yucatan slave-driver gets possession of the free laborers of his realm to replenish the overworked and underfed, the overbeaten, the dying slaves of his plantation.

How are the slaves recruited? Don Joaquin Peon informed me that the Maya slaves die off faster than they are born, and Don Enrique Camara Zavala told me that two-thirds of the Yaquis die during the first year of their residence in the country. Hence the problem of recruiting the slaves seemed to me a very serious one. Of course, the Yaquis were coming in at the rate of 500 per month, yet I hardly thought that influx would be sufficient to equal the tide of life that was going out by death. I was right in that surmise, so I was informed, but I was also informed that the problem of recruits was not so difficult after all.

"It is very easy," one planter told me. "All that is necessary is that you get some free laborer in debt to you, and then you have him. Yes, we are always getting new laborers in that way."

The amount of the debt does not matter, so long as it is a debt, and the little transaction is arranged by men who combine the functions of money lender and slave broker. Some of them have offices in Merida and they get the free laborers, clerks and the poorer class of people generally into debt just as professional loan sharks of America get clerks, mechanics and office men into debt—by playing on their needs and tempting them. Were these American clerks, mechanics and office men residents of Yucatan, instead of being merely hounded by a loan shark, they would be sold into slavery for all time, they and their children and their children's children, on to the third and fourth generation, and even farther, on to such a time as some political change puts a stop to the conditions of slavery altogether in Mexico.

These money-lending slave brokers of Merida do not hang out signs and announce to the world that they have slaves to sell. They do their business quietly, as people who are comparatively safe in their occupation, but as people who do not wish to endanger their business by too great publicity—like police-protected gambling houses in an American city, for example. These slave sharks were mentioned to me by the henequen kings themselves, cautiously by them, as a rule. Other old residents of Yucatan explained their methods in detail. I was curious to visit one of these brokers and talk with him about purchasing a lot of slaves, but I was advised against it and was told that they would not talk to a foreigner until the latter had established himself in the community and otherwise proved his good faith.

These men buy and sell slaves. And the planters buy and sell slaves. I was offered slaves in lots of one up by the planters. I was told that I could buy a man or a woman, a boy or a girl, or a thousand of any of them, to do with them exactly as I wished, that the police would protect me in my possession of those, my fellow beings. Slaves are not only used on the henequen plantations, but in the city, as personal servants, as laborers, as household drudges, as prostitutes. How many of these persons there are in the city of Merida I do not know, though I heard many stories of the absolute power exercised over them. Certainly the number is several thousand.

So we see that the debt element in Yucatan not only does not palliate the condition of the slave, but rather makes it harder. It increases his extremity, for while it does not help him to climb out of his pit, it reaches out its tentacles and drags down his brother, too. The portion of the people of Yucatan who are born free possess no "inalienable right" to their freedom. They are free only by virtue of their being prosperous. Let a family, however virtuous, however worthy, however cultivated, fall into misfortune, let the parents fall into debt and be unable to pay the debt, and the whole family is liable to pass into the hands of a henequen planter. Through debt, the dying slaves of the farms are replaced by the unsuccessful wage-workers of the cities.

Why do the henequen kings call their system enforced service for debt instead of by its right name? Probably for two reasons— because the system is the outgrowth of a milder system of actual service for debt, and because of the prejudice against the word slavery, both among Mexicans and foreigners. Service for debt in a milder form than is found in Yucatan exists all over Mexico and is called peonage. Under this system, police authorities everywhere recognize the right of an employer to take the body of a laborer who is in debt to him, and to compel the laborer to work out the debt. Of course, once the employer can compel the laborer to work, he can compel him to work at his own terms, and that means that he can work him on such terms as will never permit the laborer to extricate himself from his debt.

Such is peonage as it exists throughout all Mexico. In the last analysis it is slavery, but the employers control the police, and the fictional distinction is kept up all the same. Slavery is peonage carried to its greatest possible extreme, and the reason we find the extreme in Yucatan is that, while in some other sections of Mexico a fraction of the ruling interests are opposed to peonage and consequently exert a modifying influence upon it, in Yucatan all the ruling interests are in henequen. The cheaper the worker the higher the profits for all. The peon becomes a chattel slave.

The henequen kings of Yucatan seek to excuse their system of slavery by denominating it enforced service for debt. "Slavery is against the law," they say. "It is against the constitution." When a thing is abolished by your constitution it works more smoothly if called by another name, but the fact is, service for debt is just as unconstitutional in Mexico as chattel slavery. The plea of the henequen king of keeping within the law is entirely without foundation. A comparison of the following two clauses from the Mexican constitution will show that the two systems are in the same class.

"Article I, Section 1. In the Republic all are born free. Slaves who set foot upon the national territory recover, by that act alone, their liberty, and have a right to the protection of the laws."

"Article V, Section 1 (Amendment). No one shall be compelled to do personal work without just compensation and without his full consent. The state shall not permit any contract, covenant or agreement to be carried out having for its object the abridgment, loss or irrevocable sacrifice of the liberty of a man, whether by reason of labor, education or religious vows. * * * Nor shall any compact be tolerated in which a man agrees to his proscription or exile."

So the slave business in Yucatan, whatever name may be applied to it, is still unconstitutional. On the other hand, if the policy of the present government is to be taken as the law of the land, the slave business of Mexico is legal. In that sense the henequen kings "obey the law." Whether they are righteous in doing so I will leave to hair-splitters in morality. Whatever the decision may be, right or wrong, it does not change, for better or for worse, the pitiful misery in which I found the hemp laborers of Yucatan.

The slaves of Yucatan get no money. They are half starved. They are worked almost to death. They are beaten. A large percentage of them are locked up every night in a house resembling a jail. If they are sick they must still work, and if they are so sick that it is impossible for them to work, they are seldom permitted the services of a physician. The women are compelled to marry, compelled to marry men of their own plantation only, and sometimes are compelled to marry certain men not of their choice. There are no schools for the children. Indeed, the entire lives of these people are ordered at the whim of a master, and if the master wishes to kill them, he may do so with impunity. I heard numerous stories of slaves being beaten to death, but I never heard of an instance in which the murderer was punished, or even arrested. The police, the public prosecutors and the judges know exactly what is expected of them, for the men who appoint them are the planters themselves. The *jefes politicos*, the rulers of the political districts corresponding to our counties, who are as truly czars of the districts as Diaz is the Czar of all Mexico, are invariably either henequen planters or employes of henequen planters.

The first mention of corporal punishment for the slaves was made to me by one of the members of the Camara, a large, portly fellow with the bearing of an opera singer and a white diamond shining at me like a sun from his slab-like shirt front. He told a story, and as he told it he laughed. I laughed, too, but in a little different way. I could not help feeling that the story was made to order to fit strangers.

"Oh, yes, we have to punish them," said the fat king of henequen. "We even are compelled to whip the house servants of the city. It is their nature; they demand it. A friend of mine, a very mild man, had a woman servant who was always wishing to serve somebody else. My friend finally sold the woman, and some months later he

met her on the street and asked her how she liked her new master.
'Finely,' she answered, 'finely. You see, my master is a very rough
man and he beats me nearly every day!' "

The philosophy of beating was made very clear to me by Don
Felipe G. Canton, secretary of the Camara.

"It is necessary to whip them—oh, yes, very necessary," he told
me, with a smile, "for there is no other way to make them do what
you wish. What other means is there of enforcing the discipline of
the farm? If we did not whip them they would do nothing."

I could make no reply. I could think of no ground upon which to
assail Don Felipe's logic. For what, pray, can be done to a chattel
slave to make him work but to beat him? With the wage worker you
have the fear of discharge or the reduction of wages to hold over his
head and make him toe the mark, but the chattel slave would welcome discharge, and as to reducing his food supply, you don't dare
to do that or you kill him outright. At least, that is the case in
Yucatan.

One of the first sights we saw on a henequen plantation was the
beating of a slave—a formal beating before the assembled toilers of
the ranch early in the morning just after the daily roll call. The
slave was taken on the back of a huge Chinaman and given fifteen
lashes across the bare back with a heavy, wet rope, lashes so lustily
delivered that the blood ran down the victim's body. This method
of beating is an ancient one in Yucatan and is the customary one
on all the plantations for boys and all except the heaviest men.
Women are required to kneel to be beaten, as sometimes are men of
great weight. Men and women are beaten in the fields as well as at
the morning roll call. Each foreman, or *capataz*, carries a heavy
cane with which he punches and prods and whacks the slaves at will.
I do not remember visiting a single field in which I did not see some
of this punching and prodding and whacking going on.

I saw no punishments worse than beating in Yucatan, but I heard
of them. I was told of men being strung up by their fingers or toes

to be beaten, of their being thrust into black dungeon-like holes, of water being dropped on the hand until the victim screamed, of the extremity of female punishment being found in some outrage to the sense of the modesty in the woman. I saw black holes and everywhere I saw the jail dormitories, armed guards and night guards who patrolled the outskirts of the farm settlements while the slaves slept. I heard also of planters who took special delight in personally superintending the beating of their chattels. For example, speaking of one of the richest planters in Yucatan, a professional man of Merida said to me:

"A favorite pastime of ———— was to sit on his horse and watch the 'cleaning up' (the punishment) of his slaves. He would strike a match to light his cigar. At the first puff of smoke the first stroke of the wet rope would fall on the bare back of the victim. He would smoke on, leisurely, contendedly, as the blows fell, one after another. When the entertainment finally palled on him he would throw away his cigar and the man with the rope would stop, for the end of the cigar was the signal for the end of the beating."

The great plantations of Yucatan are reached by private mule car lines built and operated specially for the business of the henequen kings. The first plantation that we visited was typical. Situated fifteen miles west of Merida, it contains thirty-six square miles of land, one-fourth of it in henequen, part of the rest in pasture and a part unreclaimed. In the center of the plantation is the farm settlement, consisting of a grass-grown *patio*, or yard, surrounding which are the main farm buildings, the store, the factory, the house of the *administrador*, or general manager; the house of the *mayordomo primero*, or superintendent; the houses of the *mayordomos secundos*, or overseers, and the little chapel. Behind these are the corrals, the drying yard, the stable, the jail dormitory. Finally, surrounding all are the rows of one-room huts set in little patches of ground, in which reside the married slaves and their families.

Here we found fifteen hundred slaves and about thirty bosses of

various degrees. Thirty of the slaves were Koreans, about two
hundred were Yaquis and the rest were Mayas. The Maya slaves,
to my eyes, differed from the free Mayas I had seen in the city
principally in their clothing and their general unkempt and overworked appearance. Certainly they were of the same clay. Their
clothing was poor and ragged, yet generally clean. The women wore
calico, the men the thin, unbleached cotton shirt and trousers of the
tropics, the trousers being often rolled to the knees. Their hats were
of coarse straw or grass, their feet always bare.

Seven hundred of the slaves are able-bodied men, the rest women
and children. Three hundred and eighty of the men are married and
live with their families in the one-room huts. These huts are set in
little patches of ground 144 feet square, which, rocky and barren
as they are, are cultivated to some small purpose by the women and
children. In addition to the product of their barren garden patch
each family receives daily credit at the plantation store for twenty-
five *centavos,* or twelve and one-half cents' worth of merchandise.
No money is paid; it is all in credit, and this same system prevails
on about one-half the plantations. The other half merely deal out
rations. It amounts to the same thing, but some of the planters
stick to the money credit system merely in order to keep up the
pretense of paying wages. I priced some of the goods at the store—
corn, beans, salt, peppers, clothing and blankets was about all there
was—and found that the prices were high. I could not understand
how a family could live on twelve and one-half cents' worth of it
each day, a hard-working family, especially.

The slaves rise from their beds when the big bell in the *patio*
rings at 3:45 o'clock in the morning, and their work begins as soon
thereafter as they can get to it. Their work in the fields ends when
it is too dark to see, and about the yards it sometimes extends until
long into the night.

The principal labor of the plantation is harvesting the henequen
leaves and cleaning the weeds from between the plants. Each slave

is given a certain number of leaves to cut or plants to clean, and it is the policy of the planter to make the stint so hard that the slave is compelled to call out his wife and children to help him. Thus nearly all the women and children of the plantation spend a part of the day in the field. The unmarried women spend all the day in the field, and when a boy reaches the age of twelve he is considered to be a man and is given a stint of his own to do. Sundays the slaves do not work for the master. They spend their time in their patches, rest or visit. Sunday is the day on which the youths and maidens meet and plan to marry. Sometimes they are even permitted to go off the farm and meet the slaves of their neighbor, but never are they permitted to marry the people of other plantations, for this would necessitate the purchase of either the wife or the husband by one or the other of the two owners, and that would involve too much trouble.

Such are the conditions in general that prevail on all the plantations of Yucatan.

We spent two days and two nights on the plantation called San Antonio Yaxche and became thoroughly acquainted with its system and its people.

Not only do not the owners of the great henequen farms of Yucatan live on their farms, but neither do the managers. Like the owners, the managers have their homes and their offices in Merida, and visit the plantations only from two to half a dozen times a month. The *mayordomo primero* is ordinarily the supreme ruler of the plantation, but when the manager, or *administrador*, heaves in sight, the *mayordomo primero* becomes a very insignificant personage indeed.

At least that was the case on San Antonio Yaxche. The big *mayordomo* was compelled to bow and scrape before the boss just as were the lesser foremen, and at meal time Manuel Rios, the *administrador*, I and my companion—the latter, much to the disgust of Rios, who looked upon him as an underling—dined alone in state while the *mayordomo* hovered in the background, ready to fly away instantly to do our bidding. At the first meal—and it was the best I had in all Mexico—I felt strongly impelled to invite Mister *Mayordomo* to sit down and have something. I did not do it, and afterwards I was glad that I did not, for before I left the ranch I realized what an awful breach of etiquette I would have been guilty of.

In the fields we found gangs of men and boys, some gangs hoeing the weeds from between the gigantic plants and some sawing off the big leaves with machetes. The harvest of the leaves goes on unceasing all the twelve months of the year, and during the cycle every plant on the farm is gone over four times. Twelve leaves are usually clipped, the twelve largest, the thirty smallest being left to mature for another three months. The workman chops off the leaf at its root, trims the sharp briars off the two edges, trims the spear-like tip, counts the leaves left on the plant, counts the leaves he is cutting, piles his leaves into bundles, and finally carries the bundles to the end of his row, where they are carted away on a movable-track mule-car line.

I found the ground uneven and rocky, a punishment for the feet, the henequen leaves thorny and treacherous and the air thick, hot and choking, though the season was considered a cool one. The ragged, bare-footed harvesters worked steadily, carefully and with the speed of better paid laborers who work "by the piece." They were working "by the piece," too, the reward being immunity from the lash. Here and there among them I saw tired-looking women and children, sometimes little girls as young as eight or ten. Two thousand leaves a day is the usual stint on San Antonio Yaxche. On other plantations I was told that it is sometimes as high as three thousand.

The henequen leaves, once cut, are carted to a large building in the midst of the farm settlement, where they are hoisted in an elevator and sent tumbling down a long chute and into the stripping machine. Here hungry steel teeth tear the tough, thick leaves to pieces, and the result is two products—a green powder, which is refuse, and long strands of greenish, hair-like fibre, which is henequen. The fibre is sent on a tramway to the drying yard, where it turns the color of the sun. Then it is trammed back, pressed into bales, and a few days or weeks later the observer will see it at Progreso, the port of Yucatan, twenty-five miles north of Merida, being loaded into a steamship flying the British flag. The United States buys nearly all the henequen of Yucatan, our cordage trust, an alleged concern of Standard Oil, absorbing more than half of the entire product.

Eight *centavos* per pound was the 1908 price received for sisal hemp in the bale. One slave dealer told me that the production cost no more than one.

About the machinery we found many small boys working. In the drying yard we found boys and men. All of the latter impressed me with their listless movements and their haggard, feverish faces. This was explained by the foreman in charge. "When the men are sick we let them work here," he said—"on half pay!"

Such was the men's hospital. The hospital for the women we discovered in a basement of one of the main buildings. It was simply a row of windowless, earthen-floor rooms, half-dungeons, in each of which lay one woman on a bare board, without a blanket to soften it.

More than three hundred of the able-bodied slaves spend the nights in a large structure of stone and mortar, surrounded by a solid wall twelve feet high, which is topped with the sharp edges of thousands of broken glass bottles. To this inclosure there is but one door, and at it stands a guard armed with a club, a sword and a pistol. These are the quarters of the unmarried men of the plantation, Mayas, Yaquis and Chinese; also of the "half-timers," slaves whom the plantation uses only about half of the year, married men, some of them, whose families live in little settlements bordering on the farm.

These "half-timers" are found on only about one-third of the
plantations, and they are a class which has been created entirely
for the convenience of the masters. They become "full-timers" at
the option of the masters, and are then permitted to keep their
families on the plantations. They are compelled to work longer than
half the year if they are wanted, and during the time when they are
not working they are not permitted to go away on a hunt for other
work. Generally their year's labor is divided into two sections, three
months in the spring and three in the fall, and during that period
they cannot go to visit their families. They are always kept in jail
at night, they are fed by the farm, and their credit of twelve and
one-half cents per day is kept back and doled out to their families
a little at a time to prevent starvation.

A moment's figuring will show that the yearly credit for a half-
timer who works six months is $22.50, and this is all—absolutely
all—that the family of the half-time slave has to live on each year.

Inside the large, one-room building within the stone wall at San
Antonio Yaxche we found, swinging so close that they touched one
another, more than three hundred rope hammocks. This was the
sleeping place of the half-timers and the unmarried full-timers. We
entered the enclosure just at dusk, as the toilers, wiping the sweat
from their foreheads, came filing in. Behind the dormitory we found
half a dozen women working over some crude, open-air stoves. Like
half-starved wolves the ragged workers ringed about the simple
kitchen, grimy hands went out to receive their meed of supper, and
standing there the miserable creatures ate.

I sampled the supper of the slaves. That is, I sampled a part of it
with my tongue, and the rest, which my nostrils warned me not to
sample with my tongue, I sampled with my nostrils. The meal consisted of two large corn *tortillas*, the bread of the poor of Mexico, a
cup of boiled beans, unflavored, and a bowl of fish— putrid, stinking
fish, fish that reeked with an odor that stuck in my system for days.

How could they ever eat it? Ah, well, to vary a weary, unending row of meals consisting of only beans and *tortillas* a time must come when the most refined palate will water to the touch of something different, though that something is fish which offends the heavens with its rottenness.

"Beans, *tortillas*, fish! I suppose that they can at least keep alive on it," I told myself, "provided they do no worse at the other two meals." "By the way," I turned to the *administrador*, who was showing us about, "what do they get at the other two meals?"

"The other two meals?" The *administrador* was puzzled. "The other two meals? Why, there aren't any others. This is the only meal they have!"

Beans, *tortillas*, fish, once a day, and a dozen hours under the hottest sun that ever shone!

"But, no," the *administrador* corrected himself. "They do get something else, something very fine, too, something that they can carry to the field with them and eat when they wish. Here is one now."

At this he picked up from one of the tables of the women a something about the size of his two small fists, and handed it to me, triumphantly. I took the round, soggy mass in my fingers, pinched, smelled and tasted it. It proved to be corn dough, half fermented and patted into a ball. This, then, was the other two meals, the rest of the substance besides beans, *tortillas* and decayed fish which sustained the toilers throughout the long day. I turned to a young Maya who was carefully picking a fish bone.

"Which would you rather be," I asked of him, "a half-timer or a full-timer?"

"A full-timer," he replied, promptly, and then in a lower tone: "They work us until we are ready to fall, then they throw us away to get strong again. If they worked the full-timers like they work us they would die."

"We come to work gladly," said another young Maya, "because we're starved to it. But before the end of the first week we want to run away. That is why they lock us up at night."

"Why don't you run away when you're free to do it?" I asked. "When they turn you out, I mean?"

The *administrador* had stepped away to scold a woman. "It's no use," answered the man earnestly. "They always get us. Everybody is against us and there is no place to hide."

"They keep our faces on photographs," said another. "They always get us and give us a cleaning-up (beating) besides. When we're here we want to run away, but when they turn us out we know that it's no use."

I was afterwards to learn how admirably the Yucatan country is adapted to preventing the escape of runaways. No fruits or eatable herbs grow wild in that rocky land. There are no springs and no place where a person can dig a well without a rock drill and dynamite. So every runaway in time finds his way to a plantation or to the city, and at either place he is caught and held for identification. A free laborer who does not carry papers to prove that he is free is always liable to be locked up and put to much trouble to prove that he is not a runaway slave.

Yucatan has been compared to Russia's Siberia. "Siberia," Mexican political refugees have told me, "is hell frozen over; Yucatan is hell aflame." But I did not see many points in common between the two countries. True, the Yaquis are exiles in a sense, and political exiles at that, but they are also slaves. The political exiles of Russia are not slaves. According to Kennan, they are permitted to take their families with them, to choose their own abode, to live their own life, and are often given a small monthly stipend on which to live. I could not imagine Siberia as being as bad as Yucatan.

The Yucatan slave gets no hour for lunch, as does the American ranch hand. He goes to the field in the morning twilight, eating his lump of sour dough on the way. He picks up his machete and attacks the first thorny leaf as soon as it is light enough to see the thorns and he never lays down that machete until the twilight of the evening. Two thousand of the big green leaves a day is his "stint," and besides cutting, trimming and piling them, he must count them, and he must count the number of leaves on each plant and be sure that he does not count too many nor too few. Each plant is supposed to grow just 36 new leaves a year. Twelve of these, the 12 largest, are cut every four months, but whatever the number cut just 30 leaves must be left after the clipping. If the slave leaves 31 or 29 he is beaten, if he fails to cut his 2,000 he is beaten, if he trims his leaves raggedly he is beaten, if he is late at roll-call he is beaten. And he is beaten for any other little shortcoming that any of the bosses may imagine that he detects in his character or in his make-up. Siberia? To my mind Siberia is a foundling asylum compared to Yucatan.

Over and over again I have compared in my mind the condition of the slaves of Yucatan with what I have read of the slaves of our southern states before the Civil War. And always the result has been in favor of the black man. Our slaves of the South were almost always well fed, as a rule they were not overworked, on many plantations they were rarely beaten, it was usual to give them a little spending money now and then and to allow them to leave the plantation at least once a week. Like the slaves of Yucatan they were cattle of the ranch, but, unlike the former, they were treated as well as cattle. In the South before the War there were not so many plantations where the negroes died faster than they were born. The lives of our black slaves were not so hard but that they could laugh, sometimes—and sing. But the slaves of Yucatan do not sing!

I shall never forget my last day in Merida. Merida is probably the cleanest and most beautiful little city in all Mexico. It might even challenge comparison in its white prettiness with any other in the world. The municipality has expended vast sums on paving, on parks and on public buildings, and over and above this the henequen

kings not long since made up a rich purse for improvements extraordinary. My last afternoon and evening in Yucatan I spent riding
and walking about the wealthy residence section of Merida. Americans might expect to find nothing of art and architecture down on
this rocky Central American peninsula, but Merida has its million
dollar palaces like New York, and it has miles of them set in miracu-
lous gardens.

Wonderful Mexican palaces! Wonderful Mexican gardens! A
wonderful fairyland conjured out of slavery—slavery of Mayas,
and of Yaquis. Among the Yucatan slaves there are ten Mayas to
one Yaqui, but of the two the story of the Yaquis appealed to me
the more. The Mayas are dying in their own land and with their
own people. The Yaquis are exiles. They are dying in a strange land,
they are dying faster, and they are dying alone, away from their
families, for every Yaqui family sent to Yucatan is broken up on
the way. Husbands and wives are torn apart and babes are taken
from their mothers' breasts.

The Extermination of the Yaquis

My real purpose in journeying to Yucatan was to find out what became of the Yaqui Indians of Sonora. In common with thousands of other Americans who have lived for years in our Southwest and near the border line of Mexico, I knew something of the sufferings of the Yaquis in their native state, of the means which had been taken to stir them to revolt, of the confiscation of their lands, of the methods of extermination employed by the army, of the indignation voiced by the decent element of Sonora, finally of President Diaz's sweeping order of deportation.

I knew that the order of deportation was being carried out, that hundreds of families were being gathered up monthly and sent away into exile. But what fate was awaiting them there at the end of that exile road? The answer was always vague, indefinite, unsatisfactory. Even well-informed Mexicans of their country's metropolis could not tell me. After the Yaqui exiles sailed from the port of Veracruz the curtain dropped upon them. I went to Yucatan in order to witness, if possible, the final act in the life drama of the Yaqui nation. And I witnessed it.

The Yaquis are being exterminated and exterminated fast. There is no room for controversy as to that; the only controversy relates to whether or not the Yaquis deserve to be exterminated. It is undoubtedly true that a portion of their number have persistently refused to accept the destiny that the government has marked out for them. On the other hand, there are those who assert that the Yaquis are as worthy as other Mexicans and deserve as much consideration at the hands of their rulers.

The extermination of the Yaquis began in war; its finish is being accomplished in deportation and slavery.

The Yaquis are called Indians. Like the Mayas of Yucatan, they are Indians and yet they are not Indians. In the United States we would not call them Indians, for they are workers. As far back as their history can be traced they have never been savages. They have been an agricultural people. They tilled the soil, discovered and developed mines, constructed systems of irrigation, built adobe towns, maintained public schools, had an organized government and their own mint. When the Spanish missionaries came among them they were in possession of practically the whole of that vast territory south of Arizona which today comprises the state of Sonora.

"They are the best workers in Sonora," Colonel Francisco B. Cruz, the very man who has charge of their deportation to Yucatan, and of whom I will have more to say later, told me. "One Yaqui laborer is worth two ordinary Americans and three ordinary Mexicans," E. F. Trout, a Sonora mine foreman told me. "They are the strongest, soberest and most reliable people in Mexico," another one told me. "The government is taking our best workmen away from us and destroying the prosperity of the state," said another. "The government says it wants to open up the Yaqui country for settlers," S. R. DeLong, secretary of the Arizona Historical Society and an old resident of Sonora, told me, "but it is my opinion that the Yaquis themselves are the best settlers that can possibly be found."

Such expressions are heard very frequently in Sonora, in the border states and in border publications. The Yaqui certainly has an admirable physical development. During my journeys in Mexico I learned to pick him out at a glance, by his broad shoulders, his deep chest, his sinewy legs, his rugged face. The typical Yaqui is almost a giant, the race a race of athletes. Perhaps that is just the reason why he has not bent his head in submission to the will of the masters of Mexico.

American mine-owners and railroad men of Sonora are repeatedly complaining against the deportation of the Yaquis, and it is because they are such good workmen. Another matter which I have heard much remarked about by border Americans is the regard of the so-called renegade, or fighting Yaquis, for the property of Americans and other foreigners. When the Yaquis first took up arms against the present government some twenty-five years ago they did so because of a definite grievance. Usually they fought on the defensive. Driven to the mountains, they have been compelled at times to sally forth and plunder for their stomachs' sake. But for many years it was known to all men that they seldom attacked Americans or any people but Mexicans. And for a long time they never committed any depredations on railroads or railroad property, which in Sonora has always been American.

The origin of the Yaqui troubles is generally attributed to a plot on the part of a number of politicians, the purpose being to get possession of the rich lands in Southern Sonora which the Yaquis had held for hundreds of years. For twenty-four years past the only governors Sonora has had have been Ramon Corral, now Diaz's vice-president, Rafael Yzabal and Luis Torres. These three have rotated in office, as it were, for more than a generation. As no popular elections were held at all, these three friends had absolutely no one to answer to except President Diaz, and their authority in Sonora has been practically absolute.

The Yaquis seem to have had a pretty good title to their lands when Corral, Yzabal and Torres came upon the scene. At the time

of the Spanish conquest they were a nation of from one to two
hundred thousand people, supposed by some authorities to have
been offshoots from the Aztecs. The Spanish were never able to
subdue them completely, and after two hundred and fifty troublous
years a peace was entered into whereby the Yaquis gave up a part
of their territory and, as acknowledgment of their rightful ownership of the rest of it, the King of Spain gave them a patent signed
by his own hand. This was nearly one hundred and fifty years ago,
but the royal patent was honored by every ruler and chief executive
of Mexico down to Diaz. During all that time the Yaquis were at
peace with the world. Their reputation as a naturally peaceful
nation was established. It remained for the government of Diaz to
stir them into war.

During these years of peace the Yaquis became part and parcel
of the Mexican nation. They lived like other Mexicans. They had
their own personal farms, their own homes, and they paid taxes on
their property like other Mexicans. During the war against Maximilian they sent soldiers to help Mexico, and many of them distinguished themselves by brilliant service.

But the Yaquis were goaded into war. The men at the head of
the government of Sonora wanted the Yaqui lands. Moreover, they
saw an opportunity for graft in bringing a large body of soldiers into
the state. So they harassed the Yaquis. They sent bogus surveyors
through the Yaqui valley to mark out the land and tell the people
that the government had decided to give it to foreigners. They confiscated $80,000 in a bank belonging to Chief Cajeme. Finally, they
sent armed men to arrest Cajeme, and when the latter could not find
him they set fire to his house and to those of his neighbors, and
assaulted the women of the village, even Cajeme's wife not being
respected. Finally, the victims were goaded into war.

Since that day twenty-five years ago the Mexican government
has maintained an army almost perpetually in the field against the
Yaquis, an army ranging in numbers from 2,000 to 6,000 men.

Thousands of soldiers and tens of thousands of Yaquis have been killed in battle and many hundreds of the latter have been executed after being taken prisoners. After a few years Chief Cajeme was captured and publicly executed in the presence of a large body of his people who had been taken prisoner with him. Tetabiate, another Yaqui, was promptly elected to Cajeme's place, and the fight went on. Finally, in 1894, at one fell swoop, as it were, the ground was literally taken from under the feet of the rebels. By act of the federal government the best of their lands were taken from them and handed over to one man, General Lorenzo Torres, who is at this writing chief of the army in Sonora, then second in command.

The government is credited with having been guilty of the most horrible atrocities. Two examples are cited by Santa de Cabora, a Mexican writer, as follows:

On May 17, 1892, General Otero, of the Mexican army, ordered the imprisonment of the Yaquis, men, women and children, in the town of Navajoa, and hung so many of these people that the supply of rope in the town was completely exhausted, it being necessary to use each rope five or six times.

A colonel in the army, Antonio Rincon, in July, of 1892, took two hundred Yaquis, men, women and children, prisoners, and carried them in the gunboat *El Democrata* and dropped them in the ocean between the mouth of the Yaqui river and the seaport of Guaymas, all of them perishing.

A report was circulated along our Mexican border that an incident similar to the last mentioned happened in February, 1908. Colonel Francisco B. Cruz, who was in charge of the exiles and who claims to have been on board of the gunboat and witnessed the incident, declared to me, however, that this report was not true. The Yaquis were drowned, he declared, but not by the authorities, and, since at that time the government was not killing any Yaquis whom it could catch and sell, I accept the version of Colonel Cruz as the correct one.

"Suicide—nothing but suicide," asseverated the Colonel. "Those Indians wanted to cheat me out of my commission money and so they threw their children into the sea and jumped in after them. I was on board myself and saw it all. I heard a loud cry, and looking, saw some of the crew running to the starboard side of the vessel. I saw the Yaquis in the water. Then there was a cry from the port side and I saw the Yaquis jumping overboard on that side. We lowered boats, but it was no use; they all went down before we got to them."

"Every soldier who kills a Yaqui," an army physician who served two years with the troops against the Yaquis and whom I met in Mexico City, told me, "is paid a reward of one hundred dollars. To prove his feat the soldier must show the ears of his victim. 'Bring in the ears,' is the standing order of the officers. Often I have seen a company of soldiers drawn up in a square and one of their number receiving one hundred dollars for a pair of ears.

"Sometimes small squads of the Indians are captured, and when I was with the army it was customary to offer the men freedom and money to lead the troops over the secret mountain trails to the fastnesses of their friends. The alternative was the rope, yet I never knew of one of these captives turning traitor. 'Give me the rope,' they would cry, and I have seen such a man run, put the rope round his own neck and demand that it be tightened quickly, that he might not again be subjected to so base an insult."

I have before me a letter signed by G. G. Lelevier, a former member of the Mexican Liberal Party and editor of one of their papers in the United States. Lelevier is said to have afterwards gone over to the cause of the government. Commenting on a photograph showing a lot of Yaquis hanging from a tree in Sonora, the letter says:

"This picture resembles very much another one that was taken at the Yaqui river when General Angel Martinez was in command of the Mexican army of occupation. It was the custom of this general to hang men because they could not tell him where the insurrecto

Yaquis were at the time, and he went so far as to lasso the women of the Yaquis and to hang them also. It went on so until the chief of the geographical commission reported the facts to the City of Mexico and threatened to resign if the practice continued. Then this monster of a general was removed.

"But later on Governor Rafael Ysabel—it must have been in 1902 —made a raid on Tiburon Island where some peaceful Yaquis had taken refuge, and then and there ordered the Seri Indians to bring to him the right hand of every Yaqui there, with the alternative of the Seri themselves being exterminated. Doctor Boido took a snap-shot with a kodak, and you could see in it the governor laughing at the sight of a bunch of hands that had been brought to him and that were dangling from the end of a cane. This picture was even pub-lished in derision of the exploits of Governor Ysabal in the news-paper *El Imparcial*, of Mexico City."

In 1898 the government troops were armed for the first time with the improved Mauser rifle, and in that year they met and wiped out an army of Yaquis at Mazacoba, the killed numbering more than 1,000. This ended warfare on anything like an equal footing. There were no more large battles; the Yaqui warriors were merely hunted. Thousands of the Indians surrendered. Their leaders were executed, and they and their families were granted a new territory to the north, to which they journeyed as to a promised land. But it proved to be a barren desert, entirely waterless and one of the most unin-habitable spots in all America. Hence the peaceful Yaquis moved to other sections of the state, some of them becoming wage-workers in the mines, others finding employment on the railroads, and still others becoming peons on the farms. Then and there this portion of the Yaqui nation lost its identity and became merged with the peo-ples about it. But it is these Yaquis, the peaceful ones, who are sought out and deported to Yucatan.

A few Yaquis, perhaps four or five thousand, refused to give up the battle for their lands. They found inaccessible peaks and estab-

lished a stronghold high up in the Bacetete mountains, which border
upon their former home. Here flow never-ceasing springs of cold
water. Here, on the almost perpendicular cliffs, they built their little
homes; planted their corn, raised their families and sang, sometimes,
of the fertile valleys which once were theirs. The army of several
thousand soldiers still hunted them. The soldiers could not reach
those mountain heights, but they could wait for the Indians in the
gorges and shoot them as they came down in search of meat, of
clothes, and of other comforts which they yearned to add to their
existence.

Many small bands of these so-called renegades have been killed.
Others have been captured and executed. Rumors of peace have
traveled the rounds only to prove untrue a little later. Peace confer-
ences with the government have been held, but have failed because
the "renegades" could secure no guarantee that they would not be
either executed or deported after they laid down their arms. In
January, 1909, the report was officially sent out by Governor Torres
that Chief Bule and several hundred of his warriors had surrendered
on conditions. But later troubles showed this announcement to have
been premature. There are at least a few hundred Yaquis among
those Bacetete crags. They refuse to surrender. They are outlaws.
They are cut off from the world. They have no connection with the
peaceful element of their nation that is scattered all over the state
of Sonora. Yet the existence of this handful of "renegades" is the
only excuse the Mexican government has for gathering up peaceful
Mexican families and deporting them—at the rate of 500 per month!

Why should a lot of women and children and old men be made to
suffer because some of their fourth cousins are fighting away off
there in the hills? The army physician with whom I talked in Mexico City answered the question in very energetic terms.

"The reason?" he said. "There is no reason. It is only an excuse.
The excuse is that the workers contribute to the support of the fight-

ers. If it is true, it is true only in an infinitesimal minority of cases, for the vast majority of the Yaquis are entirely out of touch with the fighters. There may be a few guilty parties, but absolutely no attempt is made to find them out. For what a handful of patriotic Yaquis may possibly be doing tens of thousands are made to suffer and die. It is as if a whole town were put to the torch because one of its inhabitants had stolen a horse."

The deportation of Yaquis to Yucatan and other slave sections of Mexico began to assume noticeable proportions about 1905. It was carried out on a small scale at first, then on a larger one.

Finally, in the spring of 1908, a despatch was published in American and Mexican newspapers saying that President Diaz had issued a sweeping order decreeing that every Yaqui, wherever found, men, women and children, should be gathered up by the War Department and deported to Yucatan.

During my journeys in Mexico I inquired many times as to the authenticity of this despatch, and the story was confirmed. It was confirmed by men in the public departments of Mexico City. It was confirmed by Colonel Cruz, chief deporter of Yaquis. And it is certain that such an order, wherever it may have come from, was carried out. Yaqui workingmen were taken daily from mines, railroads and farms, old workingmen who never owned a rifle in their lives, women, children, babes, the old and the young, the weak and the strong. Guarded by soldiers and *rurales* they traveled together over the exile road. And there are others besides Yaquis who traveled over that road. Pimas and Opatas, other Indians, Mexicans, and any dark people found who were poor and unable to protect themselves were taken, tagged as Yaquis, and sent away to the land of henequen. What becomes of them there? That is what I went to Yucatan to find out.

The secret that lies at the roots of the whole Yaqui affair was revealed to me and the whole matter summed up in a few words by

Colonel Francisco B. Cruz of the Mexican army, in one of the most remarkable interviews which I obtained during my entire trip to Mexico.

For the past four years this officer has been in immediate charge of transporting all the Yaqui exiles to Yucatan. I was fortunate enough to take passage on the same steamer with him returning from Progreso to Veracruz. He is a stout, comfortable, talkative old campaigner of about sixty years. The steamship people put us in the same stateroom, and, as the colonel had some government passes which he hoped to sell me, we were soon on the most confidential terms.

"In the past three and one-half years," he told me, "I have delivered just fifteen thousand seven hundred Yaquis in Yucatan— delivered, mind you, for you must remember that the government never allows me enough expense money to feed them properly, and from ten to twenty per cent die on the journey.

"These Yaquis," he said, "sell in Yucatan for $65 apiece—men, women and children. Who gets the money? Well, $10 goes to me for my services. The rest is turned over to the Secretary of War. This, however, is only a drop in the bucket, for I know this to be a fact, that every foot of land, every building, every cow, every burro, everything left behind by the Yaquis when they are carried away by the soldiers, is appropriated for the private use of authorities of the state of Sonora."

So according to this man, who has himself made at least $157,000 out of the business, the Yaquis are deported for the money there is in it—first, the money from the appropriation of their property, second, the money from the sale of their bodies. He declared to me that the deportations would never stop until the last possible dollar had been squeezed out of the business. The company of officials who have rotated in office in Sonora for the past twenty-five years would see to that, he said.

These little confidences of the colonel were given me merely as bits of interesting gossip to a harmless foreigner. He had no notion of exposing the officials and citizens whose names he mentioned. He expressed no objection whatever to the system, rather gloried in it.

"In the past six months," the fat colonel told me, "I have handled three thousand Yaquis—five hundred a month. That's the capacity of the government boats between Guaymas and San Blas, but I hope to see it increased before the end of the year. I have just been given orders to hurry 1,500 more to Yucatan as quickly as I can get them there. Ah, yes, I ought to have a comfortable little fortune for myself before this thing is over, for there are at least 100,000 more Yaquis to come!

"One hundred thousand more to come!" he repeated at my exclamation. "Yes, one hundred thousand, if one. Of course, they're not all really Yaquis, but—"

And President Diaz's chief deporter of Sonora working-people lolling there upon the deck of the freight steamer passed me a smile which was illuminating, exceedingly illuminating—yes, terribly illuminating!

Over the Exile Road

Yaquis traveling to Yucatan, after arriving at the port of Guaymas, Sonora, embark on a government war vessel for the port of San Blas. After a journey of four or five days they are disembarked and are driven by foot over some of the roughest mountains in Mexico, from San Blas to Tepic and from Tepic to San Marcos. As the crow flies the distance is little more than one hundred miles; as the road winds it is twice as far, and requires from fifteen to twenty days to travel. "Bull pens," or concentration camps, are provided all along the route, and stops are made at the principal cities. All families are broken up on the way, the chief points at which this is done being Guaymas, San Marcos, Guadalajara and Mexico City. From San Marcos the unfortunates are carried by train over the Mexican Central Railway to Mexico City and from Mexico City over the International Railway to Veracruz. Here they are bundled into one of the freight steamers of the "National" company, and in from two to five days are disembarked at Progreso and turned over to the waiting consignees.

On the road to Yucatan the companion of my journeys, L. Gutierrez De Lara, and I, saw gangs of Yaqui exiles, saw them in the "bull
pen" in the midst of the army barracks in Mexico City; finally we
joined a party of them at Veracruz and traveled with them on ship
from Veracruz to Progreso.

There were 104 of them shoved into the unclean hole astern of the
freight steamer *Sinaloa*, on which we embarked. We thought it
might be difficult to obtain the opportunity to visit this unclean hole,
but, luckily, we were mistaken. The guard bent readily to friendly
words, and before the ship was well under way my companion and
I were seated on boxes in the hold with a group of exiles gathered
about us, some of them, tobacco-famished, pulling furiously at the
cigarettes which we had passed among them, others silently munch-
ing the bananas, apples and oranges which we had brought.

There were two old men past fifty, one of them small, active,
sharp-featured, talkative, dressed in American overalls, jumper,
shoes and slouch hat, with the face and manner of a man bred to
civilization; the other, tall, silent, impassive, wrapped to the chin
in a gay colored blanket, the one comfort he had snatched from his
few belongings as the soldiers were leading him away. There was
a magnificent specimen of an athlete under thirty, with a wizened
baby girl of two held in the crook of one arm, an aggressive-faced
woman of forty against whom was closely pressed a girl of ten
shivering and shaking in the grasp of a malarial attack, two over-
grown boys who squatted together in the background and grinned
half foolishly at our questions, bedraggled women, nearly half of
them with babies, and an astonishingly large number of little
chubby-faced, bare-legged boys and girls who played uncompre-
hendingly about the floor or stared at us from a distance out of their
big solemn black eyes.

"Revolutionists?" I asked of the man in overalls and jumper.

"No; workingmen."

"Yaquis?"

"Yes, one Yaqui," pointing to his friend in the blanket. "The rest are Pimas and Opatas."

"Then why are you here?"

"Ah, we are all Yaquis to General Torres. It makes no difference to him. You are dark. You dress in my clothes and you will be a Yaqui—to him. He makes no investigation, asks no questions—only takes you."

"Where are you from?" I asked of the old man.

"Most of us are from Ures. They took us in the night and carried us away without allowing us to make up bundles of our belongings."

"I am from Horcasitas," spoke up the young athlete with the babe on his arm. "I was plowing in the field when they came, and they did not give me time to unhitch my oxen."

"Where is the mother of your baby?" I inquired curiously of the young father.

"Dead in San Marcos," he replied, closing his teeth tight. "That three weeks' tramp over the mountains killed her. They have allowed me to keep the little one—so far."

"Did any of you make resistance when the soldiers came to take you?" I asked.

"No," answered the old man from Ures. "We went quietly; we did not try to run away." Then with a smile: "The officers found more trouble in looking after their men, their privates, to prevent them from running away, from deserting, than they did with us.

"We were one hundred and fifty-three at the start, we of Ures," went on the old man. "Farm laborers, all of us. We worked for small farmers, poor men, men with not more than half a dozen families in their employ. One day a government agent visited the neighborhood and ordered the bosses to give an account of all their laborers. The bosses obeyed, but they did not know what it meant until a few days later, when the soldiers came. Then they knew, and they saw ruin coming to them as well as to us. They begged the officers, saying 'This is my peon. He is a good man. He has been with me for twenty years. I need him for the harvest.'"

"It is true," broke in the woman with the ague-stricken child. "We were with Carlos Romo for twenty-two years. The night we were taken we were seven; now we are two."

"And we were with Eugenio Morales for sixteen years," spoke another woman.

"Yes," went on the spokesman, "our bosses followed us, begging, but it was no use. Some of them followed us all the way to Hermosillo. There was Manuel Gandara, and Jose Juan Lopez, and Franco Tallez, and Eugenio Morales and the Romo brothers, Jose and Carlos. You will find them there now and they will tell you that what we say is true. They followed us, but it was no use. They had to go back and call vainly at our empty houses for laborers. We were stolen—and they were robbed!

"They died on the way like starving cattle," went on the old man from Ures. "When one fell ill he never got well again. One woman was deathly sick at the start. She begged to be left behind, but they wouldn't leave her. She was the first to fall—it happened on the train between Hermosillo and Guaymas.

"But the cruelest part of the trail was between San Blas and San Marcos. Those women with babies! It was awful! They dropped down in the dust again and again. Two never got up again, and we buried them ourselves there beside the road."

"There were burros in San Blas," interrupted a woman, "and mules and horses. Oh, why didn't they let us ride? But our men were good. When the little legs of the *ninos* were weary our men carried them on their backs. And when the three women who were far gone in pregnancy could walk no more our men made stretchers of twigs and carried them, taking turns. Yes, our men were good, but now they are gone. We do not see them any more!"

"The soldiers had to tear me away from my husband," said another, "and when I cried out they only laughed. The next night a solider came and tried to take hold of me, but I pulled off my shoes and beat him with them. Yes, the soldiers bothered the women often, especially that week we starved in Mexico City, but always the women fought them back."

"I have a sister in Yucatan," said a young woman under twenty. "Two years ago they carried her away. As soon as we arrive I shall try to find her. We will keep each other company, now that they have taken my husband from me. Tell me, is it so terribly hot in Yucatan as they say it is? I do not like hot weather, yet if they will only let me live with my sister I will not mind."

"To whom do all these bright little tads, these *muchachos*, all of the same size belong?" I inquired.

"Quien sabe?" answered an old woman. "Their parents are gone, just as are our babes. They take our children from us and give us the children of strangers. And when we begin to love the new ones, they take them away, too. Do you see that woman huddled over there with her face in her hands? They took her four little boys at Guadalajara and left her nothing. Myself? Yes, they took my husband. For more than thirty years we had never been parted for a single night. But that made no difference; he is gone. Yet perhaps I am lucky; I still have my daughter. Do you think, though, that we may meet our husbands again in Yucatan?"

As we breasted the Veracruz lighthouse, the shoulder of a Norther heaved itself against the side of the vessel, the ocean streamed in at the lower portholes and the quarters of the unhappy exiles were flooded with water. They fled for the deck, but here were met by flying sheets of rain, which drove them back again. Between the flooded hold and the flooded poop the exiles spent the night, and when, early the next morning, as we drove into the Coatzacoalcos river, I strolled aft again, I saw them lying about the deck, all of them drenched and shivering, some of them writhing in the throes of acute seasickness.

We steamed thirty miles up the Coatzacoalcos river, then anchored to the shore and spent a day loading jungle bulls for the tough beef market of New Orleans. Two hundred ordinary cattle may be coaxed through a hole in the side of a ship in the space of two hours, but these bulls were as wild as wolves, and each had to be half butchered before he would consent to walk in the straight and narrow way. Once inside, and ranged along the two sides of the vessel, they fought, trampled each other, bawled as loud as steam whistles, and in a number of instances broke their head ropes and smashed through the flimsy railing which had been erected to prevent them from over-running other portions of the lower deck. In a bare space at the stern of the vessel, surrounded on three sides by plunging, bawling bulls, were the quarters of the "Yaquis." It was stay there and run the risk of being trampled, or choose the unsheltered deck. For the remaining four days of the journey, one of which we spent waiting for the Norther to pass, the "Yaquis" chose the deck.

At last we arrived at Progreso. As we entered the train for Merida we saw our friends being herded into the second class coaches. They left us at the little station of San Ignacio, on their way to a plantation belonging to Governor Olegario Molina, and we saw them no more.

In Yucatan I soon learned what becomes of the Yaqui exiles. They are sent to the henequen plantations as slaves, slaves on almost exactly the same basis as are the 100,000 Mayas whom I found on the plantations. They are held as chattels, they are bought and sold, they receive no wages, but are fed on beans, *tortillas* and putrid fish. They are beaten, sometimes beaten to death. They are worked from dawn until night in the hot sun beside the Mayas. The men are locked up at night. The women are required to marry Chinamen or Mayas. They are hunted when they run away, and are brought back by the police if they reach a settlement. Families, broken up in Sonora or on the way, are never permitted to reunite. After they

once pass into the hands of the planter the government cares no
more for them, takes no more account of them. The government has
received its money, and the fate of the Yaquis is in the hands of the
planter.

I saw many Yaquis in Yucatan. I talked with them. I saw them
beaten. One of the first things I saw on a Yucatan plantation was
the beating of a Yaqui. His name was Rosanta Bajeca.

The act, though not intentionally so, perhaps, was theatrically
staged. It was at 3:45 o'clock in the morning, just after roll-call of
the slaves. The slave gang was drawn up in front of the plantation
store, the fitful rays of the lanterns sputtering high on the store front
playing uncertainly over their dusky faces and dirty white forms.
There were seven hundred of them. Now and then a brighter lantern
beam shot all the way to the towering tropical trees, which, standing shoulder to shoulder, walled in the grass-grown *patio*. Under
the hanging lanterns and facing the ragged band stood the *administrador*, or general manager, the *mayordomo primero*, or superintendent, and the lesser bosses, the *mayordomos secundos*, the *majacol*
and the *capataces*.

"Rosanta Bajeca!"

The name, squeaked out by the voice of the *administrador*,
brought from the crowd a young Yaqui, medium-sized, sinewy-
bodied, clean-featured, with well-formed head erect on square
shoulders, bony jaw fixed, dark, deep set eyes darting rapidly from
one side to another of the circle which surrounded him, like a tiger
forced out of the jungle and into the midst of the huntsmen.

"Off with your shirt!" rasped the *administrador*, and at the words
superintendent and foremen ringed closer about him. One reached
for the garment, but the Yaqui fended the hand, then with the quick-
ness of a cat, dodged a cane which swished at his bare head from
the opposite direction. For one instant—no more—with the hate of
his eyes he held the circle at bay, then with a movement of consent
he waved them back, and with a single jerk drew the shirt over his

head and bared his muscular bronze body, scarred and discolored from previous beatings, for the whip. Submissive but dignified he stood there, for all the world like a captive Indian chief of a hundred years ago, contemptuously awaiting the torture of his enemies.

Listlessly the waiting slaves looked on. A regiment of toil, they stood half a dozen deep, with soiled calico trousers reaching half way to the ankles or rolled to the knees, shirts of the same material with many gaping mouths showing the bare bronze skin beneath, bare legs, bare feet, battered grass hats held deferentially in the hands— a tatterdemalion lot, shaking the sleep from their eyes, blinking at the flickering lanterns. Three races there were, the sharp-visaged, lofty-browed Maya, aborigine of Yucatan, the tall, arrow-backed Chinaman and the swarthy, broad-fisted Yaqui from Sonora.

At a third command of the *administrador* there stepped from the host of waiting slaves a giant Chinese. Crouching, he grasped the wrists of the silent Yaqui. The next moment he was standing straight with the Yaqui on his back in the manner of a tired child being carried by one of its elders.

Not one of that throng who did not know what was coming, yet not until a *capataz* reached for a bucket hanging high on the store front did there come a tension of nerves among those seven hundred men. The whipper extraordinary, known as a *majocol*, a deep-chested, hairy brute, bent over the bucket and soused his hands deep into the water within. Withdrawing them, he held high for inspection four dripping ropes, each three feet long. The thick writhing things in the dim lamplight seemed like four bloated snakes, and at sight of them the tired backs of the ragged seven hundred straightened with a jerk and an involuntary gasp rippled over the assemblage. Laggard slumber, though unsated, dropped from their eyes. At last all were awake, wide awake.

The ropes were of native henequen braided tight and thick and heavy for the particular purpose in hand. Water-soaked, to give them more weight and cutting power, they were admirably fitted for the work of "cleaning up," the term whereby corporal punishment is known on the plantations of Yucatan.

The hairy *majocol* selected one of the four, tossed back the remaining three, the pail was carried away and the giant Chinaman squared off with the naked body of the victim to the gaze of his fellow bondsmen. The drama was an old one to them, so old that their eyes must have ached many times at the sight, yet for them it could never lose its fascination. Each knew that his own time was coming, if it had not already come, and not one possessed the physical power to turn his back upon the spectacle.

Deliberately the *majocol* measured his distance, then as deliberately raised his arm high and brought it swiftly down again; the bloated snake swished through the air and fell with a spat across the glistening bronze shoulders of the Yaqui!

The *administrador*, a small, nervous man of many gestures, nodded his approval and glanced at his watch, the *mayordomo*, big, stolid, grinned slowly, the half dozen *capataces* leaned forward a little more obliquely in their eagerness, the regiment of slaves swayed bodily as by some invisible force, and a second gasp, painful and sharp like the bursting air from a severed windpipe, escaped them.

Every eye was riveted tight upon that scene in the uncertain dimness of the early morning—the giant Chinaman, bending slightly forward now, the naked body upon his shoulders, the long, uneven, livid welt that marked the visit of the wet rope, the deliberate, the agonizingly deliberate *majocol*, the *administrador*, watch in hand, nodding endorsement, the grinning *mayordomo*, the absorbed *capataces*.

All held their breath for the second blow. I held my breath with the rest, held it for ages, until I thought the rope would never fall. Not until I saw the finger signal of the *administrador* did I know that the blows were delivered by the watch and not until it was all over did I know that, in order to multiply the torture, six seconds were allowed to intervene between each stroke.

The second blow fell, and the third, and the fourth. I counted the blows as they fell, ages apart. At the fourth the strong brown skin broke and little pin-heads of crimson pushed themselves out, burst, and started downward in thin tricklets. At the sixth the glistening back lost its rigidity and fell to quivering like a jellyfish. At the ninth a low whine somewhere in the depths of that Yaqui, found its devious way outward and into the open. Oh, that whine! I hear it now, a hard, hard whine, as if indurated to diamond hardness by drilling its way to the air through a soul of adamant.

At last the spats ceased—there were fifteen—the *administrador,* with a final nod, put away his watch, the giant Chinaman released his grip on the brown wrists and the Yaqui tumbled in a limp heap to the ground. He lay there for a moment, his face in his arms, his quivering, bleeding flesh to the sky, then a foreman stepped forward and put a foot roughly against his hip.

The Yaqui lifted his head, disclosing to the light a pair of glazed eyes and a face twisted with pain. A moment later he rose to his feet and staggered forward to join his fellow bondsmen. In that moment the spell of breathless silence on the seven hundred snapped, the ranks moved in agitation and there rose a hum of low speech from every section of the crowd. The special "cleaning up" of the morning was over. Five minutes later the day's work on the farm had begun.

Naturally I made inquiries about Rosanta Bajeca to find out what crime he had committed to merit fifteen lashes of the wet rope. I ascertained that he had been only a month in Yucatan, and but three days before had been put in the field with a harvesting gang to cut and trim the great leaves of the henequen plant. Two thousand a day was the regular stint for each slave, and Bajeca had been given three days in which to acquire the dexterity necessary to harvest

the required number of leaves. He had failed. Hence the flogging.
There had been no other fault.

"It's a wonder," I remarked to a *capataz*, "that this Yaqui did not
tear himself from the back of the Chinaman. It's a wonder he did
not fight. He seems like a brave man; he has the look of a fighter."

The *capataz* chuckled.

"One month ago he was a fighter," was the reply, "but a Yaqui
learns many things in a month in Yucatan. Still, there was a time
when we thought this dog would never learn. Now and then they
come to us that way; they never learn; they're never worth the
money that's paid for them."

"Tell me about this one," I urged.

"He fought; that's all. The day he came he was put to work loading bundles of leaves onto the elevator which leads to the cleaning
machine. The *mayordomo*—yes, the *mayordomo primero*—happened along and punched the fellow in the stomach with his cane. A
half minute later a dozen of us were struggling to pull that Yaqui
wolf away from the throat of the *mayordomo*. We starved him for a
day and then dragged him out for a cleaning up. But he fought with
his fingers and with his teeth until a *capataz* laid him out with the
blunt edge of a machete. After that he tasted the rope daily for a
while, but every day for no less than a week the fool fought crazily
on until he kissed the earth under the weight of a club. But our
majocol never faltered. That *majocol* is a genius. He conquered the
wolf. He wielded the rope until the stubborn one surrendered, until
that same Yaqui came crawling, whimpering, on hands and knees
and licked with his naked tongue the hand of the man who had
beaten him!"

During my travels in Yucatan I was repeatedly struck with the
extremely human character of the people whom the Mexican government called Yaquis. The Yaquis are Indians, they are not white,
yet when one converses with them in a language mutually understood one is struck with the likenesses of the mental processes of

White and Brown. I was early convinced that the Yaqui and I were
more alike in mind than in color. I became convinced, too, that the
family attachments of the Yaqui mean quite as much to the Yaqui
as the family attachments of the American mean to the American.
Conjugal fidelity is the cardinal virtue of the Yaqui home and it
seems to be so not because of any tribal superstition of past times
or because of any teachings of priests, but because of a constitutional
tenderness sweetened more and more with the passing of the years,
for *the one* with whom he had shared the meat and the shelter and
the labor of life, the joys and sorrows of existence.

Over and over again I saw this exemplified on the exile road and
in Yucatan. The Yaqui woman feels as keenly the brutal snatching
away of her babe as would the cultivated American woman. The
heart-strings of the Yaqui wife are no more proof against a violent
and unwished-for separation from her husband than would be the
heart-strings of the refined mistress of a beautiful American home.

The Mexican government forbids divorce and remarriage within
its domain, but for the henequen planters of Yucatan all things are
possible. To a Yaqui woman a native of Asia is no less repugnant
than he is to an American woman, yet one of the first barbarities the
henequen planter imposes upon the Yaqui slave woman, freshly
robbed of the lawful husband of her bosom, is to compel her to
marry a Chinaman and live with him!

"We do that," explained one of the planters to me, "in order to
make the Chinamen better satisfied and less inclined to run away.
And besides we know that every new babe born on the place will
some day be *worth anywhere from $500 to $1,000 cash!*"

The cultivated white woman, you say, would die of the shame
and the horror of such conditions. But so does the brown woman of
Sonora. No less a personage than Don Enrique Camara Zavala, president of the "Camara de Agricola de Yucatan," and a millionaire
planter himself, told me:

"If the Yaquis last out the first year they generally get along all right and make good workers, but the trouble is, *at least two-thirds of them die off in the first twelve months!*"

On the ranch of one of the most famous henequen kings we found about two hundred Yaquis. One-third of these were men, who were quartered with a large body of Mayas and Chinamen. Entirely apart from these, and housed in a row of new one-room huts, each set in a tiny patch of uncultivated land, we discovered the Yaqui women and children.

We found them squatting around on their bare floors or nursing an open-air fire and a kettle just outside the back door. We found no men among them, Yaquis or Chinamen, for they had arrived only one month before—all of them—from Sonora.

In one house we found as many as fourteen inmates. There was a woman past fifty with the strength of an Indian chief in her face and with words which went to the mark like an arrow to a target. There was a comfortable, home-like woman with a broad, pock-marked face, pleasant words and eyes which kindled with friendliness despite her troubles. There were two women who watched their fire and listened only. There was a girl of fifteen, a bride of four months, but now alone, a wonderfully comely girl with big eyes and soft mouth, who sat with her back against the wall and smiled and smiled—until she cried. There was a sick woman who lay on the floor and groaned feebly but never looked up, and there were eight children.

"Last week we were fifteen," said the home-like woman, "but one has already gone. They never get well." She reached over and gently stroked the hair of the sister who lay on the floor.

"Were you all married?" I asked.

"All," nodded the old woman with the face of a chief.

"And where are they now?"

"*Quien sabe?*" And she searched our eyes deep for the motive of our questions.

"I am a Papago," reassured De Lara. "We are friends."

"You are not working," I remarked. "What are you doing?"

"Starving," said the old woman.

"We get that once a week—for all of us," explained the home-like one, nodding at three small chunks of raw beef—less than a five-cent stew in the United States—which had just been brought from the plantation store. "Besides that we get only corn and black beans and not half enough of either of them."

"We are like hogs; we are fed on corn," put in the old woman. "In Sonora we made our *tortillas* of wheat."

"How long will they starve you?" I asked.

"Until we marry Chinamen," flashed the old woman, unexpectedly.

"Yes," confirmed the home-like one. "Twice they have brought the Chinamen before us, lined them up, and said: 'Choose a man.' Twice."

"And why didn't you choose?"

This question several of the women answered in chorus. In words and wry faces they expressed their abhorrence of the Chinamen, and with tremulous earnestness assured us that they had not yet forgotten their own husbands.

"I begged them," said the old woman, "to let me off. I told them I was too old, that it was no use, that I was a woman no longer, but they said I must choose, too. They will not let me off; they say I will have to choose with the rest."

"Twice they have lined us up," reiterated the home-like one, "and said we must choose. But we wouldn't choose. One woman chose, but when she saw the rest hang back she pushed the man away from her. They threatened us with the rope, but still we hung back. They will give us but one more chance, they say. Then if we do not choose, they will choose for us. And if we do not consent we will be put in the field and worked and whipped like the men."

"And get twelve *centavos* a day (six cents American) to live on,"
said the old woman. "Twelve *centavos* a day with food at the store
twice as dear as in Sonora!"

"Next Sunday morning they will make us choose," repeated the
home-like woman. "And if we don't choose—"

"Last Sunday they beat that sister there," said the old woman.
"She swore she'd never choose, and they beat her just like they beat
the men. Come, Refugio, show them your back."

But the woman at the fire shrank away and hung her head in
mortification.

"No, no," she protested, then after a moment she muttered:
"When the Yaqui men are beaten they die of shame, but the women
can stand to be beaten; they cannot die."

"It's true," nodded the old woman, "the men die of shame sometimes—and sometimes they die of their own will."

When we turned the talk to Sonora and to the long journey the
voices of the women began to falter. They were from Pilares de
Teras, where are situated the mines of Colonel Garcia. The soldiers
had come in the daytime while the people were in the field picking
the ripe corn from the stalks. They had been taken from their harvest labor and compelled to walk all the way to Hermosillo, a three
weeks' tramp.

The Yaqui love for the one who suckled them is strong, and several of the younger women recounted the details of the parting from
the mother. Then we spoke of their husbands again, but they held
their tears until I asked the question: "How would you like to go
back with me to your homes in Sonora?"

That opened the flood-gates. The tears started first down the
plump cheeks of the cheery, home-like woman, then the others broke
in, one at a time, and at last the listening children on the floor were
blubbering dolefully with their elders. Weeping, the unhappy exiles
lost their last modicum of reserve. They begged us please to take

them back to Sonora or to find their husbands for them. The old woman implored us to get word to her boss, Leonardo Aguirre, and would not be content until I had penned his name in my note-book. The bashful woman at the fire, aching for some comforting, hopeful words, parted her dress at the top and gave us a glimpse of the red marks of the lash upon her back.

I looked into the face of my companion; the tears were trickling down his cheeks. As for me, I did not cry. I am ashamed now that I did not cry!

Such is the life of the Yaqui nation in its last chapter. When I looked upon those miserable creatures there I said: "There can be nothing worse than this." But when I saw Valle Nacional I said: "This is worse than Yucatan."

The Contract Slaves of Valle Nacional

Valle Nacional is undoubtedly the worst slave hole in Mexico. Probably it is the worst in the world. When I visited Valle Nacional I expected to find it milder than Yucatan. I found it more pitiless.

In Yucatan the Maya slaves die off faster than they are born and two-thirds of the Yaqui slaves are killed during the first year after their importation into the country. In Valle Nacional all of the slaves, all but a very few—perhaps five per cent—pass back to earth within a space of seven or eight months.

This statement is almost unbelievable. I would not have believed it; possibly not even after I had seen the whole process of working them and beating them and starving them to death, were it not the fact that the masters themselves told me that it was true. And there are fifteen thousand of these Valle Nacional slaves—fifteen thousand new ones every year!

"By the sixth or seventh month they begin to die off like flies at the first winter frost, and after that they're not worth keeping. The cheapest thing to do is to let them die; there are plenty more where they came from."

Word for word, this is a statement made to me by Antonio Pla, general manager of one-third the tobacco lands in Valle Nacional.

"I have been here for more than five years and every month I see hundreds and sometimes thousands of men, women and children start over the road to the valley, but I never see them come back. Of every hundred who go over the road not more than one ever sees this town again." This assertion was made to me by a station agent of the Veracruz al Pacifico railroad.

"There are no survivors of Valle Nacional—no real ones," a government engineer who has charge of the improvement of certain harbors told me. "Now and then one gets out of the valley and gets beyond El Hule. He staggers and begs his way along the weary road toward Cordoba, but he never gets back where he came from. Those people come out of the valley walking corpses, they travel on a little way and then they fall."

This man's work has carried him much into Valle Nacional and he knows more of the country, probably, than does any Mexican not directly interested in the slave trade.

"They die; they all die. The bosses never let them go until they're dying."

Thus declared one of the police officers of the town of Valle Nacional, which is situated in the center of the valley and is supported by it.

And everywhere over and over again I was told the same thing. Even Manuel Lagunas, *presidente* (mayor) of Valle Nacional, protector of the planters and a slave owner himself, said it. Miguel Vidal, secretary of the municipality, said it. The bosses themselves said it. The Indian dwellers of the mountain sides said it. The slaves said it. And when I had seen, as well as heard, I was convinced that it was the truth.

The slaves of Valle Nacional are not Indians, as are the slaves of Yucatan. They are Mexicans. Some are skilled artizans. Others are artists. The majority of them are common laborers. As a whole, ex-

cept for their rags, their bruises, their squalor and their despair, they
are a very fair representation of the Mexican people. They are not
criminals. Not more than ten per cent were even charged with any
crime. The rest of them are peaceful, law-abiding citizens. Yet not
one came to the valley of his own free will, not one would not leave
the valley on an instant's notice if he or she could get away.

Do not entertain the idea that Mexican slavery is confined to
Yucatan and Valle Nacional. Conditions similar to those of Valle
Nacional are the rule in many sections of Diaz-land, and especially
in the states south of the capital. I cite Valle Nacional because it is
most notorious as a region of slaves, and because, as I have already
suggested, it presents just a little bit the worst example of chattel
slavery that I know of.

The secret of the extreme conditions of Valle Nacional is mainly
geographical. Valle Nacional is a deep gorge from two to five miles
wide and twenty miles long tucked away among almost impassable
mountains in the extreme northwestern corner of the state of
Oaxaca. Its mouth is fifty miles up the Papaloapan river from El
Hule, the nearest railroad station, yet it is through El Hule that
every human being passes in going to or coming from the valley.
There is no other practical route in, no other one out. The magnificent tropical mountains which wall in the valley are covered
with an impenetrable jungle made still more impassable by jaguars,
pumas and gigantic snakes. Moreover, there is no wagon road to
Valle Nacional; only a river and a bridle path—a bridle path which
carries one now through the jungle, now along precipitous cliffs
where the rider must dismount and crawl, leading his horse behind
him, now across the deep, swirling current of the river. It takes a
strong swimmer to cross this river at high water, yet a pedestrian
must swim it more than once in order to get out of Valle Nacional.

The equestrian must cross it five times—four times in a canoe
alongside which his mount swims laboriously, once by fording, a

long and difficult route over which large rocks must be avoided and deep holes kept away from. The valley itself is as flat as a floor, clear of all rank growth, and down its gentle slope winds the Papaloapan river. The valley, the river and its rim form one of the most beautiful sights it has ever been my lot to look upon.

Valle Nacional is three days' journey from Cordoba, two from El Hule. Stray travelers sometimes get as far as Tuztepec, the chief city of the political district, but no one goes on to Valle Nacional who has not business there. It is a tobacco country, the most noted in Mexico, and the production is carried on by about thirty large plantations owned and operated almost exclusively by Spaniards. Between El Hule and the head of the valley are four towns, Tuztepec, Chiltepec, Jacatepec and Valle Nacional, all situated on the banks of the river, all provided with policemen to hunt runaway slaves, not one of whom can get out of the valley without passing the towns. Tuztepec, the largest, is provided with ten policemen and eleven *rurales* (mounted country police). Besides, every runaway slave brings a reward of $10 to the man or policeman who catches and returns him to his owner.

Thus it will be understood how much the geographical isolation of Valle Nacional accounts for its being just a little worse than most other slave districts of Mexico. Combined with this may be mentioned the complete understanding that is had with the government and the nearness to a practically inexhaustible labor market.

Just as in Yucatan, the slavery of Valle Nacional is merely peonage, or labor for debt, carried to the extreme, although outwardly it takes a slightly different form—that of contract labor.

The origin of the conditions of Valle Nacional was undoubtedly contract labor. The planters needed laborers. They went to the expense of importing laborers with the understanding that the laborers would stay with their jobs for a given time. Some laborers tried to jump their contracts and the planters used force to compel them to

stay. The advance money and the cost of transportation was looked
upon as a debt which the laborer could be compelled to work out.
From this it was only a step to so ordering the conditions of labor
that the laborer could under no circumstances ever hope to get free.
In time Valle Nacional became a word of horror with the working
people of all Mexico. They refused to go there for any price. So the
planters felt compelled to tell them they were going to take them
somewhere else. From this it was only a step to playing the workman
false all round, to formulating a contract not to be carried out, but
to help get the laborer into the toils. Finally, from this it was only
a step to forming a business partnership with the government,
whereby the police power should be put into the hands of the planters to help them carry on a traffic in slaves.

The planters do not call their slaves slaves. They call them contract laborers. I call them slaves because the moment they enter
Valle Nacional they become the personal property of the planter
and there is no law or government to protect them.

In the first place the planter buys his slave for a given sum. Then
he works him at will, feeds or starves him to suit himself, places
armed guards over him day and night, beats him, pays him no
money, kills him, and the laborer has no recourse. Call it by another
name if it pleases you. I call it slavery only because I do not know
of a name that will fit the conditions better.

I have said that no laborer sent to Valle Nacional to become a
slave travels the road of his own free will. There are just two ways
employed to get them there. They are sent over the road either by a
jefe politico or by a "labor agent" working in conjunction with a *jefe
politico* or other officials of the government.

A *jefe politico* is a civil officer who rules political districts corresponding to our counties. He is appointed by the president or by
the governor of his state and is also mayor, or *presidente*, of the principal town or city in his district. In turn he usually appoints the

mayors of the towns under him, as well as all other officers of importance. He has no one to answer to except his governor—unless the national president feels like interfering—and altogether is quite a little Czar in his domain.

The methods employed by the *jefe politico* working alone are very simple. Instead of sending petty prisoners to terms in jail he sells them into slavery in Valle Nacional. And as he pockets the money himself, he naturally arrests as many persons as he can. This method is followed more or less by the *jefes politicos* of all the leading cities of southern Mexico.

The *jefe politico* of each of the four largest cities in southern Mexico, so I was told by Manuel Lagunas, by "labor agents," as well as by others whose veracity in the matter I have no reason to question —pays an annual rental of $10,000 per year for his office. The office would be worth no such amount were it not for the spoils of the slave trade and other little grafts which are indulged in by the holder. Lesser *jefes* pay their governors lesser amounts. They send their victims over the road in gangs of from ten to one hundred or even more. They get a special government rate from the railroads, send along government-salaried *rurales* to guard them; hence the selling price of $45 to $50 per slave is nearly all clear profit.

But only ten per cent of the slaves are sent directly to Valle Nacional by the *jefes politicos*. There is no basis in law whatsoever for the proceeding, and the *jefes politicos* prefer to work in conjunction with "labor agents." There is also no basis in law for the methods employed by the "labor agents," but the partnership is profitable. The officials are enabled to hide behind the "labor agents" and the "labor agents" are enabled to work under the protection of the officials and absolutely without fear of criminal prosecution.

In this partnership of the government and the labor agent—popularly known as an *enganchador* (snarer)—the function of the labor agent is to snare the laborer, the function of the government to stand behind him, help him, protect him, give him low transportation rates and free guard service, and finally, to take a share of the profits.

The methods employed by the labor agent in snaring the laborer are many and various. One is to open an employment office and advertise for workers who are to be given high wages, a comfortable home and plenty of freedom somewhere in the south of Mexico. Free transportation is offered. These inducements always cause a certain number to take the bait, especially men with families who want to move with their families to a more prosperous clime. The husband and father is given an advance fee of $5 and the whole family is locked up in a room as securely barred as a jail.

After a day or two, as they are joined by others, they come to have misgivings. Perhaps they ask to be let out, and then they find that they are indeed prisoners. They are told that they are in debt and will be held until they work out their debt. A few days later the door opens and they file out. They find that *rurales* are all about them. They are marched through a back street to a railroad station, where they are put upon the train. They try to get away, but it is no use; they are prisoners. In a few days they are in Valle Nacional.

Usually the laborer caught in this way is taken through the formality of signing a contract. He is told that he is to get a good home, good food, and one, two or three dollars a day wages for a period of six months or a year. A printed paper is shoved under his nose and the *enganchandor* rapidly points out several alluring sentences written thereon. A pen is put quickly into his hand and he is told to sign in a hurry. The five dollars advance fee is given him to clinch the bargain and put him in debt to the agent. He is usually given a chance to spend this, or a part of it, usually for clothing or other necessaries in order that he may be unable to pay it back when he discovers that he has been trapped. The blanks on the printed contract—fixing the wages, etc.—are usually filled out afterwards by the labor agent or the consignee.

In Mexico City and other large centers of population there are permanently maintained places called *casas de los enganchadores* (houses of the snarers). They are regularly known to the police and to large slave buyers of the hot lands. Yet they are nothing more nor less than private jails into which are enticed laborers, who are held there against their will until such time as they are sent away in gangs guarded by the police powers of the government.

A third method employed by the labor agent is outright kidnapping. I have heard of many cases of the kidnapping of women and of men. Hundreds of half-drunken men are picked up about the *pulque* shops of Mexico City every season, put under lock and key, and later hurried off to Valle Nacional. Children, also, are regularly kidnapped for the Valle Nacional trade. The official records of Mexico City say that during the year ending September 1, 1908, 360 little boys between the ages of six and twelve disappeared on the streets. Some of these have later been located in Valle Nacional.

During my first Mexican trip *El Imparcial*, a leading daily newspaper of Mexico, printed a story of a boy of seven who had disappeared while his mother was looking into the windows of a pawn shop. A frantic search failed to locate him; he was an only child, and as a result of sorrow the father drank himself to death in a few days' time, while the mother went insane and also died. Three months later, the boy, ragged and footsore, struggled up the steps and knocked at the door that had been his parents'. He had been kidnapped and sold to a tobacco planter. But he had attained the well-nigh impossible. With a boy of nine, he had eluded the plantation guards, and, by reason of their small size, the two had escaped observation, and, by stealing a canoe, had reached El Hule. By slow stages, begging their food on the way, the baby tramps had reached home.

The typical life story of a labor agent I heard in Cordoba on my way to the valley. It was told me first by a negro contractor from New Orleans, who had been in the country for about fifteen years.

It was told me again by the landlord of my hotel. Later, it was confirmed by several tobacco planters in the valley. The story is this:

Four years ago Daniel T——, an unsuccessful Spanish adventurer, arrived, penniless, in Cordoba. In a few days he was having trouble with his landlord over the non-payment of rent. But he had learned a thing or two in those few days, and he set about to take advantage of his knowledge. He went for a stroll about the streets and, coming upon a farm laborer, thus addressed him:

"Would you care to earn *dos reales* (25 *centavos*) very easily, my man?"

Of course the man cared, and in a few minutes he was on his way to the Spaniard's room carrying a "message." The wily fellow took another route, arrived first, met the messenger at the door, took him by the neck, and, dragging him inside, gagged and bound him and left him on the floor while he went out to hunt up a labor agent. That night the adventurer sold his prisoner for $20, paid his rent, and immediately began laying plans for repeating the operation on a larger scale.

The incident marked the entrance of this man into the business of "labor contracting." In a few months he had made his bargain with the political powers of Mexico City, of Veracruz, of Oaxaca, of Tuztepec and other places. Today he is El Senor Daniel T——. I saw his home, a palatial mansion with the sign of three cocks above the door. He uses a private seal and is said to be worth $100,000, all acquired as a "labor agent."

The prevailing price in 1908 for men was $45 each, women and children half price. In 1907, before the panic, it was $60 per man. All slaves entering the valley must wait over at Tuztepec, where Rodolpho Pardo, the *jefe politico* of the district, counts them and exacts a toll of ten per cent of the purchase price, which he puts into his own pocket.

The open partnership of the government in the slave traffic must necessarily have some excuse. The excuse is the debt, the $5 advance fee usually paid by the labor agent to the laborer. It is unconstitutional, but it serves. The *presidente* of Valle Nacional told me, "There is not a police official in all southern Mexico who will not recognize that advance fee as a debt and acknowledge your right to take the body of the laborer where you will."

When the victim arrives in the valley of tobacco he learns that the promises of the labor agent were made merely to entrap him. Moreover, he learns also that the contract—if he has been lucky enough to get a peep at that instrument—was made exactly for the same purpose. As the promises of the labor agent belie the provisions of the contract, so the contract belies the actual facts. The contract usually states that the laborer agrees to sell himself for a period of six months, but no laborer with energy left in his body is by any chance set free in six months. The contract usually states that the employer is bound to furnish medical treatment for the laborers; the fact is that there is not a single physician for all the slaves of Valle Nacional. Finally, the contract usually binds the employer to pay the men fifty *centavos* (25 cents American) per day as wages, and the women three *pesos* a month ($1.50 American), but I was never able to find one who ever received one copper *centavo* from his master—never anything beyond the advance fee paid by the labor agent.

The bosses themselves boasted to me—several of them—that they never paid any money to their slaves. Yet they never called their system slavery. They claimed to "keep books" on their slaves and juggle the accounts in such a way as to keep them always in debt. "Yes, the wages are fifty *centavos* a day," they would say, "but they must pay us back what we give to bring them here. And they must give us interest on it, too. And they must pay for the clothing that we give them—and the tobacco, and anything else."

This is exactly the attitude of every one of the tobacco planters of Valle Nacional. For clothing, and tobacco, and "anything else," they charge ten prices. It is no exaggeration. Senor Rodriguez, pro-

prietor of the farm "Santa Fe," for example, showed me a pair of
unbleached cotton pajama-like things that the slaves use for pantaloons. His price, he said, was three dollars a pair. A few days later
I found the same thing in Veracruz at thirty cents.

Trousers at $3, shirts the same price—suits of clothes so flimsy
that they wear out and drop off in three weeks' time. Eight suits in
six months at $6 is $48. Add $45, the price of the slave; add $5, the
advance fee; add $2 for discounts, and there's the $90 wages of the
six months gone.

Such is keeping books to keep the slave a slave. On the other hand,
when you figure up the cost of the slave to yourself, it is quite different. "Purchase price, food, clothes, wages—everything," Senor
Rodriguez told me, "costs from $60 to $70 per man for the first six
months of service."

Add your purchase price, advance fee and suits at cost, 60 cents
each, and we discover that between $5 and $15 are left for both
food and wages for each six months. It all goes for food—beans and
tortillas.

Yes, there is another constant item of expense that the masters
must pay—the burial fee in the Valle Nacional cemetery. It is $1.50.
I say this is a constant item of expense because practically all the
slaves die and are supposed to be buried. The only exception to the
rule occurs when, in order to save the $1.50, the masters bury their
slaves themselves or throw them to the alligators of the neighboring
swamps.

Every slave is guarded night and day. At night he is locked up in
a dormitory resembling a jail. In addition to its slaves, each and
every plantation has its *mandador*, or superintendent, its *cabos*, who
combine the function of overseer and guard; and several free laborers to run the errands of the ranch and help round up the runaways
in case of a slave stampede.

The jails are large barn-like buildings, constructed strongly of
young trees set upright and wired together with many strands of

barbed wire fencing. The windows are iron barred, the floors dirt. There is no furniture except sometimes long, rude benches which serve as beds. The mattresses are thin grass mats. In such a hole sleep all the slaves, men, women and children, the number ranging, according to the size of the plantation, from seventy to four hundred.

They are packed in like sardines in a box, crowded together like cattle in a freight car. You can figure it out for yourself. On the ranch "Santa Fe" the dormitory measures 75 by 18 feet, and it accommodates 150. On the ranch "La Sepultura," the dormitory is 40 by 15 feet, and it accommodates 70. On the ranch "San Cristobal," the dormitory is 100 by 50 feet, and it accommodates 350. On the ranch "San Juan del Rio," the dormitory is 80 by 90, and it accommodates 400. From nine to eighteen square feet for each person to lie down in—so runs the space. And on not a single ranch did I find a separate dormitory for the women or the children. Women of modesty and virtue are sent to Valle Nacional every week and are shoved into a sleeping room with scores and even hundreds of others, most of them men, the door is locked on them and they are left to the mercy of the men.

Often honest, hard-working Mexicans are taken into Valle Nacional with their wives and children. If the wife is attractive in appearance she goes to the planter or to one or more of the bosses. The children see their mother being taken away and they know what is to become of her. The husband knows it, but if he makes objection he is answered with a club. Time and time again I have been told that this was so, by masters, by slaves, by officials. And the women who are thrust into the sardine box must take care of themselves.

One-fifth of the slaves of Valle Nacional are women; one-third are boys under fifteen. The boys work in the fields with the men. They cost less, they last well, and at some parts of the work, such as planting the tobacco, they are more active and hence more useful. Boys as young as six sometimes are seen in the field planting tobacco. Women are worked in the field, too, especially during the harvest time, but their chief work is as household drudges. They serve the master and the mistress, if there is a mistress, and they grind the corn and cook the food of the male slaves. In every slave house I visited I found from three to a dozen women grinding corn. It is all done by hand with two pieces of stone called a *metate*. The flat stone is placed on the floor, the woman kneels beside it, bends almost double and works the stone roller up and down. The movement is something like that of a woman washing clothes, but it is much harder. I asked the *presidente* of Valle Nacional why the planters did not purchase cheap mills for grinding the corn, or why they did not combine and buy a mill among them, instead of breaking several hundred backs yearly in the work. "Women are cheaper than machines," was the reply.

In Valle Nacional the slaves seemed to me to work all the time. I saw them working in the morning twilight. I saw them working far into the night. "If we could use the water power of the Papaloapan to light our farms we could work our farms all night," Manuel Lagunas told me, and I believe he would have done it. The rising hour on the farms is generally 4 o'clock in the morning. Sometimes it is earlier. On all but three or four of the thirty farms the slaves work every day in the year—until they fall. At San Juan del Rio, one of the largest, they have a half holiday every Sunday. I happened to be at San Juan del Rio on a Sunday afternoon. That half holiday! What a grim joke! The slaves spent it in jail, locked up to keep them from running away!

And they fall very fast. They are beaten, and that helps. They are starved, and that helps. They are given no hope, and that helps. They die in anywhere from one month to a year, the time of greatest mortality being between the sixth and eight month. Like the cotton planters of our South before the war, the tobacco planters seem to have their business figured down to a fine point. It was a well-established business maxim of our cotton planters that the greatest amount of profit could be wrung from the body of a negro slave by working him to death in seven years and then buying another one. The Valle Nacional slave holder has discovered that it is cheaper to buy a slave for $45 and work and starve him to death in seven *months,* and then spend $45 for a fresh slave, than it is to give the first slave better food, work him less sorely and stretch out his life and his toiling hours over a longer period of time.

In the Valley of Death

I visited Valle Nacional in the latter part of 1908, spending a week in the region and stopping at all the larger plantations. I passed three nights at various plantation houses and four more at one or another of the towns. As in Yucatan, I visited the country in the guise of a probable purchaser of plantations.

As in Yucatan, I succeeded in convincing authorities and planters that I had several million dollars behind me just aching to be invested. Consequently, I put them as completely off their guard as it would be possible to do. As in Yucatan, I was able to secure my information, not only from what I saw of and heard from the slaves, but from the mouths of the masters themselves. Indeed, I was more fortunate than I was in Yucatan. I chummed with bosses and police so successfully that they never once became suspicious, and for months some of them were doubtless looking for me to drop in any fine day with a few million in my pocket, prepared to buy them out at double the value of their property.

The nearer we approached Valle Nacional the greater horror of the place we found among the people. None had been there, but all had heard rumors, some had seen survivors, and the sight of those walking corpses had confirmed the rumors. As we got off the train at Cordoba, we saw crossing the platform a procession of fourteen men, two in front and two behind with rifles, ten with their arms bound behind them with ropes, their heads down. Some were ragged, some well dressed, and several had small bundles on their shoulders.

"On their way to the valley!" I whispered. My companion nodded, and the next moment the procession disappeared through a narrow gateway on the opposite side of the street, the entrance to a most conveniently situated "bull pen" for the accommodation over night of the exiles.

After supper I mingled with the crowds in the leading hotels of the town, and was aggressive enough in my role of investor to secure letters of introduction from a wealthy Spaniard to several slave holders of the valley.

"You'd better call on the *jefe politico* at Tuztepec as soon as you get there," advised the Spaniard. "He's a friend of mine. Just show him my signature and he'll pass you along, all right."

When I arrived at Tuztepec I took the advice of the Senor and to my good fortune, for the *jefe politico*, Rodolpho Pardo, not only passed me along, but gave me a personal letter to each of his subordinates along the road, the *presidentes* of Chiltepec, Jacatepec and Valle Nacional, instructing them to neglect their official business, if necessary, but to attend to my wants. Thus it was during my first days in the Valley of Death I was the guest of the *presidente*, and on the nights which I spent in the town a special police escort was appointed to see that I came to no harm.

In Cordoba, a negro building contractor, an intelligent fellow, who had sojourned in Mexico for fifteen years, said to me:

"The days of slavery ain't over yet. No sir, they ain't over. I've been here a long time and I've got a little property. I know I'm pretty safe, but sometimes I get scared myself—yes, sir, I get scared, you bet!"

Early next morning as I was dressing I glanced out of my window and saw a man walking down the middle of the street with one end of a riata around his neck and a horseman riding behind at the other end of the riata.

"Where's that man going?" I inquired of the servant. "Going to be hanged?"

"Oh, no, only going to jail," answered the servant. "It's the easiest way to take them, you know. In a day or two," he added, "that man will be on his way to Valle Nacional. Everybody arrested here goes to Valle Nacional—everybody except the rich."

"I wonder if that same gang we saw last night will be going down on the train today," my companion, De Lara, said, as we made for the depot.

He did not wonder long, for we had hardly found seats when we saw the ten slaves and their *rurale* guards filing into the second-class coach adjoining. Three of the prisoners were well dressed and had unusually intelligent faces; the others were of the ordinary type of city or farm laborers. Two of the former were bright boys under twenty, one of whom burst into tears as the train pulled slowly out of Cordoba toward the dreaded valley.

Down into the tropics we slid, into the jungle, into the dampness and perfume of the lowlands, known as the hot country. We flew down a mountain, then skirted the rim of a gash-like gorge, looking down upon coffee plantations, upon groves of bananas, rubber and sugar cane, then into a land where it rains every day except in mid-winter. It was not hot—not real hot, like Yuma—but the passengers perspired with the sky.

We watched the exiles curiously, and at the first opportunity we made advances to the chief of the *rurale* squad. At Tierra Blanca we stopped for dinner and, as the meal the *rurales* purchased for their charges consisted only of *tortillas* and *chili*, we bought a few extras for them, then sat and watched them eat. Gradually we drew the exiles into conversation, carefully nursing the good will of their guards at the same time, and presently we had the story of each.

The prisoners were all from Pachuca, capital of the state of Hidalgo, and, unlike the vast majority of Valle Nacional slaves, they were being sent over the road directly by the *jefe politico* of that district. The particular system of this particular *jefe* was explained to us two days later by Espiridion Sanchez, a corporal of *rurales*, as follows:

"The *jefe politico* of Pachuca has a contract with Candido Fernandez, owner of the tobacco plantation 'San Cristobal la Vega,' whereby he agrees to deliver 500 able-bodied laborers a year for fifty *pesos* each. The *jefe* gets special nominal government rates on the railroads, his guards are paid for by the government, so the four days' trip from Pachuca costs him only three *pesos* and a half per man. This leaves him forty-six and one-half *pesos*. Out of it he must pay something to his governor, Pedro L. Rodriguez, and something to the *jefe politico* at Tuztepec. But even then his profits are very large.

"How does he get his men? He picks them up on the street and puts them in jail. Sometimes he charges them with some crime, real or imaginary, but in either case the man is never tried. He is held in jail until there are enough others to make up a gang, and then all are sent here. Why, men who may be safely sent to Valle Nacional are getting so scarce in Pachuca that the *jefe* has even been known to take young boys out of school and send them here just for the sake of the fifty *pesos!*"

Of our ten friends from Pachuca, all had been arrested and put in jail, but not one had been taken before a judge. Two had been charged with owing money that they could not pay, one had been arrested when drunk, another had been drunk and had discharged a firearm into the air, the fifth had shouted too loudly on Independence Day, September 16th, another had attempted rape, the seventh had had a mild-mannered quarrel with another boy over the sale of a five-cent ring, two had been musicians in the army and had left one company and joined another without permission, and the tenth had been a clerk of *rurales* and had been sold for paying a friendly visit to the previous two while they were in jail serving out their sentence for desertion.

When we smiled our incredulity at the tale of the tenth prisoner and asked the chief *rurale* pointblank if it was true, he astonished us with his reply. Nodding his grizzled head he said in a low voice:

"It is true. Tomorrow may be my time. It is always the poor that suffer."

We would have looked upon the stories of these men as "fairy tales," but all of them were confirmed by one or the other of the guards. The case of the musicians interested us most. The older carried the forehead of a university professor. He was a cornet player and his name was Amado Godaniz. The younger was a boy of but eighteen, the boy who cried, a basso player named Felipe Gomez.

"They are sending us to our death—to our death," muttered Godaniz. "We will never get out of that hole alive." And all along the route, wherever we met him, he said the same thing, repeating over and over again: "They are sending us to our death—to our death!" And always at the words the soft-faced, cringing boy of eighteen at his side would cry silently.

At El Hule, The Gateway to the Mexican Hell, we parted from our unfortunate friends for a time. As we left the railroad depot to board our launch in the river, we saw the ten, strung out in single file, one mounted *rurale* in front and one behind, disappear in the jungle toward Tuztepec. Four hours later, as we approached the district metropolis in the thickening twilight, we saw them again. They had beaten the launch in the journey up the river, had crossed in a canoe, and now stood resting for a moment on a sandy bank, silhouetted against the sky.

Rodolpho Pardo, the *jefe politico*, whom we visited after supper, proved to be a slender, polished man of forty, smooth-shaven, with eyes which searched our bodies like steel probes at first. But the thoughts of fresh millions to be invested where he might levy his toll upon them sweetened him as we became acquainted, and when we shook his cold, moist hand good-bye, we had won all that we had asked for. Don Rodolpho even called in the chief of police and instructed him to find us good horses for our journey.

Early the following morning found us on the jungle trail. During the forenoon we encountered several other travelers, and we lost no opportunity to question them.

"Run away? Yes; they try to—sometimes," said one native, a Mexican cattleman. "But too many are against them. The only escape is down river. They must cross many times and they must pass Jacatepec, Chiltepec, Tuztepec and El Hule. And they must hide from every one on the road, for a reward of ten *pesos* is paid for every runaway captured. We don't love the system, but ten *pesos* is a lot of money, and no one would let it go by. Besides, if one doesn't get it another will, and even though the runaway should get out of the valley, when he reaches Cordoba he finds the *enganchador* Tresgallo, waiting there to send him back."

"One time," another native told us, "I saw a man leaning against a tree beside the trail. As I rode up I spoke to him, but he did not move. His arm was doubled against the tree trunk and his eyes seemed to be studying the ground. I touched his shoulder and found that he was stiff—dead. He had been turned out to die and had walked so far. How do I know he was not a runaway? Ah, *Senor*, I knew. You would have known, too, had you seen his swollen feet and the bones of his face—almost bare. No man who looks like that could run away!"

Just at nightfall we rode into Jacatepec, and there we found the slave gang ahead of us. They had started first and had kept ahead, walking the twenty-four miles of muddy trail, though some of them were soft from jail confinement. They were sprawled out on a patch of green beside the detention house.

The white linen collar of Amado Godaniz was gone now. The pair of fine shoes, nearly new, which he wore on the train, were on the ground beside him, heavy with mud and water. His bare feet were small, as white as a woman's and as tender, and both showed bruises and scratches. Since that evening at Jacatepec I have often thought of Amado Godaniz and have wondered—with a shiver—how those tender white feet fared among the tropical flies of Valle Nacional. "They are sending us to our death—to our death!" The news that Amado Godaniz were alive today would surprise me. That night he seemed to realize that he would never need those fine shoes again, and before I went to bed I heard him trying to sell them to a passer-by for twenty-five cents.

Wherever we stopped we induced people, by careless questions, to talk about the valley. I wanted to make no mistake. I wanted to hear the opinion of everybody. I did not know what might be denied us farther on. And always the story was the same—slavery and men and women beaten to death.

We arose at five the next morning and missed our breakfast in order to follow the slave gang over the road to Valle Nacional. At first the chief of the two *rurales*, a clean, handsome young Mexican, looked askance at our presence, but before we were half way there he was talking pleasantly. He was a Tuztepec *rurale* and was making his living out of the system, yet he was against it.

"It's the Spanish who beat our people to death," he said bitterly. "All the tobacco planters are Spanish, all but one or two."

The *rurale* chief gave us the names of two Spaniards, partners, Juan Pereda and Juan Robles, who had become rich on Valle Nacional tobacco and had sold out and gone back to spend the rest of their days in Spain. After they were gone, said he, the new owner, in looking over the place, ran upon a swamp in which he found hundreds of human skeletons. The toilers whom Pereda and Robles had starved and beaten to death they had been too miserly to bury.

Nobody ever thought of having a planter arrested for murdering his slaves, the *rurale* told us. To this rule he mentioned two exceptions; one, the case of a foreman who had shot three slaves; the other, a case in which an American figured and in which the American ambassador took action. In the first case the planter had disapproved the killing because he needed the slaves, so he himself had secured the arrest of the foreman. As to the other case:

"In past years they used to pick up a derelict American once in awhile and ship him down here," said my informant, "but the trouble this particular one kicked up has resulted in Americans being barred altogether. This American was sent to 'San Cristobal,' the farm of Candido Fernandez. At this plantation it was the custom to kill a steer every two weeks to provide meat for the family and the foremen; the only meat the slaves ever got was the head and entrails. One Sunday, while helping butcher a steer, the hunger of the American slave got the better of him, and he seized some of the entrails and ate them raw. The next day he died and a few weeks later an escaped slave called on the American ambassador in Mexico City, gave him the name and home address of the American, and told him the man had been beaten to death. The ambassador secured the arrest of the planter Fernandez and it cost him a lot of money to get out of jail."

Our trip was a very beautiful one, if very rough. At one point we climbed along the precipitous side of a magnificent mountain, allowing our horses to pick their way over the rocks behind us. At another we waited while the slaves took off their clothing, piled them in bundles on their heads and waded across a creek; then we followed on our horses. At many points I yearned mightily for a camera, yet I knew if I had it that it would get me into trouble.

Picture merely that procession as it wound in single file around
the side of a hill, the tropical green above broken now and then by
a ridge of gigantic grey rocks, below a level meadow and a little
farther on the curving, feminine lines of that lovely river, the Papaloapan. Picture those ten slaves, six with the regulation high straw
hat of the plebeian Mexican, four with felts, all barefooted now except the boy musician, who is sure to throw away his shoes before
the end of the journey, half of them bare-handed, imagining that
the masters will furnish them blankets or extra clothing, the other
half with small bundles of bright-colored blankets on their backs;
finally, the mounted and uniformed *rurales*, one in front and one
behind; and the American travelers at the extreme rear.

Soon we began to see gangs of men, from twenty to one hundred,
at work in the fields preparing the ground for tobacco planting. The
men were the color of the ground, and it struck me as strange that
they moved incessantly while the ground was still. Here and there
among the moving shapes stood others—these seemed different;
they really looked like men—with long, lithe canes in their hands
and sometimes swords and pistols in their belts. We knew then that
we had reached Valle Nacional.

The first farm at which we stopped was "San Juan del Rio."
Crouching beside the porch of the main building was a sick slave.
One foot was swollen to twice its natural size and a dirty bandage
was wrapped clumsily about it. "What's the matter with your foot?"
I asked. "Blood poisoning from insect bites," replied the slave. "He'll
have maggots in another day or two," a boss told us with a grin.

As we rode away we caught our first glimpse of a Valle Nacional
slave-house, a mere jail with barred windows, a group of women
bending over *metates*, and a guard at the door with a key.

I have said that our *rurale* corporal was opposed to the system,
yet how perfectly he was a part of it he soon showed. Rounding a
bluff suddenly we caught sight of a man crouching half hidden
behind a tree. Our *rurale* called him and he came, trembling, and

trying to hide the green oranges that he had been eating. The ensuing conversation went something like this:

Rurale—Where are you going?

Man—To Oaxaca.

Rurale—Where are you from?

Man—From the port of Manzanillo.

Rurale—You've come a hundred miles out of your way. Nobody
ever comes this way who doesn't have business here. What farm
did you run away from, anyhow?

Man—I didn't run away.

Rurale—Well, you fall in here.

So we took the man along. Later it was ascertained that he had
run away from "San Juan del Rio." The *rurale* got the ten *pesos*
reward.

At the plantation "San Cristobal" we left the slave gang behind,
first having the temerity to shake the hands of the two musicians,
whom we never saw again. Alone on the road we found that the
attitude of those we met was widely different from what it had been
when we were traveling in the company of the *rurales*, the agents
of the state. The Spanish horsemen whom we encountered did not
deign to speak to us, they stared at us suspiciously through half
closed eyes and one or two even spoke offensively of us in our hearing. Had it not been for the letter to the *presidente* in my pocket it
would doubtless have been a difficult matter to secure admission to
the tobacco plantations of Valle Nacional.

Everywhere we saw the same thing—gangs of emaciated men
and boys at work clearing the ground with *machetes* or ploughing
the broad fields with oxen. And everywhere we saw guards, armed
with long, lithe canes, with swords and pistols. Just before we
crossed the river for the last time to ride into the town of Valle
Nacional we spoke to an old man with a stump of a wrist who was
working alone near the fence.

"How did you lose your hand?" I asked.

"A *cabo* (foreman) cut it off with a sword," was the reply.

Manuel Lagunas, *presidente* of Valle Nacional, proved to be a very amiable fellow, and I almost liked him—until I saw his slaves. His secretary, Miguel Vidal, was even more amiable, and we four sat for two hours over our late dinner, thoroughly enjoying ourselves —and talking about the country. During the entire meal a little half-negro boy of perhaps eight years stood silent behind the door, emerging only when his master, needing to be waited upon, called "Negro!"

"I bought him cheap," said Vidal. "He cost me only twenty-five *pesos*."

Because of its great beauty Valle Nacional was originally called "Royal Valley" by the Spaniards, but after the Independence of Mexico it was rechristened Valle Nacional. Thirty-five years ago the land belonged to the Chinanteco Indians, a peaceable tribe among whom it was divided by President Juarez. When Diaz came into power he failed to make provision for protecting the Chinantecos against scheming Spaniards, so in a few years the Indians had drunk a few bottles of *mescal* and the Spaniards had gobbled up every foot of their land. The Valle Nacional Indians now secure their food from rented patches high up on the mountain sides which are unfit for tobacco cultivation.

Though the planters raise corn and beans, and sometimes bananas or other tropical fruits, tobacco is the only considerable product of the valley. The plantations are usually large, there being only about thirty in the entire district. Of this number twelve are owned by Balsa Hermanos (Brothers), who operate a large cigar factory in Veracruz and another in the city of Oaxaca.

After dinner we went for a stroll about town and for a bodyguard the *presidente* assigned us a policeman, Juan Hernandez. We proceeded to question the policeman.

"All the slaves are kept until they die—all," said Hernandez. "And when they are dead the bosses do not always take the trouble to bury them. They throw them in the swamps where the alligators eat them. On the plantation 'Hondura de Nanche' so many are given to the alligators that an expression has arisen among the slaves: 'Throw me to The Hungry!' There is a terrible fear among those slaves that they will be thrown to 'The Hungry' before they are dead and while they are yet conscious, as this has been done!"

Slaves who are worn out and good for nothing more, declared the policeman, and yet who are strong enough to cry out against being thrown to "The Hungry," are turned out on the road without a cent, and in their rags many of them crawl to town to die. The Indians give them some food and on the edge of town there is an old house in which the miserable creatures are permitted to pass their last hours. This place is known as "The House of Pity." We visited it with the policeman and found an old woman lying on her face on the bare floor. She did not move when we came in, nor when we spoke to each other and finally to her, and for some time we were not sure that she was alive. At last she groaned feebly. It can be imagined how we felt, but we could do nothing, so we tip-toed to the door and hurried away.

"You will find this a healthy country," the municipal secretary told us a little later in the evening. "Don't you notice how fat we all are? The laborers of the plantations? Ah, yes, they die—die of malaria and consumption—but it is only because they are under-fed. Tortillas and beans—sour beans at that, usually, is all they get, and besides they are beaten too much. Yes, they die, but nobody else here ever has any sickness."

Notwithstanding the accounts of Juan Hernandez, the policeman, the secretary assured us that most of the dead slaves were buried. The burying is done in the town and it costs the bosses one and one-half *pesos* for each burial. By charity the town puts a little bamboo cross over each grave. We strolled out in the moonlight and took a look at the graveyard. And we gasped at the acres and acres of crosses! Yes, the planters bury their dead. One would guess by those crosses that Valle Nacional were not a village of one thousand souls, but a city of one hundred thousand!

On our way to our beds in the house of the *Presidente* we hesitated at the sound of a weak voice hailing us. A fit of heart-breaking coughing followed and then we saw a human skeleton squatting beside the path. He wanted a penny. We gave him several, then questioned him and learned that he was one who had come to die in "The House of Pity." It was cruel to make him talk, but we did it, and in his ghastly whispering voice he managed to piece out his story between paroxysms of coughing.

His name was Angelo Echavarria, he was twenty years old and a native of Tampico. Six months previously he had been offered wages on a farm at two *pesos* a day, and had accepted, but only to be sold as a slave to Andres M. Rodriguez, proprietor of the plantation "Santa Fe." At the end of three months he began to break down under the inhuman treatment he received and at four months a foreman named Augustin broke a sword over his back. When he regained consciousness after the beating he had coughed up a part of a lung. After that he was beaten more frequently because he was unable to work as well, and several times he fell in a faint in the field. At last he was set free, but when he asked for the wages that he thought were his, he was told that he was $1.50 in debt to the ranch! He came to the town and complained to the *Presidente*, but was given no satisfaction. Now too weak to start to walk home, he was coughing his life away and begging for subsistence at the same time. In all my life I have never seen another living creature so emaciated as Angelo Echavarria, yet only three days previously he had been working all day in the hot sun!

We visited the plantation "Santa Fe" the following day, as well as a half dozen others. We found the system of housing, feeding, working and guarding the slaves alike on all.

The main dormitory at "Santa Fe" consisted of one windowless, dirt-floored room, built of upright poles set in the ground an inch apart and held firmly together by strands of barbed wire fencing. It was as impregnable as an American jail. The beds consisted of a single grass mat each laid crosswise on a wooden bench. There were four benches, two on each side, one above another, running length-wise of the room. The beds were laid so close together that they touched. The dimensions of the room were 75 by 18 feet and in these cramped quarters 150 men, women and children slept every night. The Valle Nacional tobacco planters have not the decency of slave-holders of fifty years ago, for on not one of the plantations did I find a separate dormitory for the women. And I was repeatedly told that the women who enter that foul hole all become common to the men, not because they wish to become so, but because the overseers do not protect them from the unwelcome advances of the men!

On the "Santa Fe" ranch the *mandador*, or superintendent, sleeps in a room at one end of the slave dormitory and the *cabos*, or over-seers, sleep in a room at the other end. The single door is padlocked, but a watchman paces all night up and down the passageway be-tween the rows of shelves. Every half hour he strikes a clamorous gong. In answer to a question Senor Rodriguez assured me that the gong did not disturb the sleeping slaves, but even if it had that the rule was necessary to prevent the watchman from going to sleep and permitting a jail-break.

Observing the field gangs at close range, I was astonished to see so many children among the laborers. At least half were under twenty and at least one-fourth under fourteen.

"The boys are just as good in the planting as the men," remarked the *Presidente*, who escorted us about. "They last longer, too, and they cost only half as much. Yes, all the planters prefer boys to men."

During my ride through fields and along the roads that day I often wondered why some of those bloodless, toiling creatures did not cry out to us and say: "Help us! For God's sake help us! We are being murdered!" Then I remembered that all men who pass this

way are like their own bosses, and in answer to a cry they could
expect nothing better than a mocking laugh, and perhaps a blow
besides.

Our second night in Valle Nacional we spent on the *Presidente's*
plantation. As we approached the place we lagged behind the *Presidente* to observe a gang of 150 men and boys planting tobacco on
the adjoining farm, "El Mirador." There were half a dozen overseers among them and as we came near we saw them jumping here
and there among the slaves, yelling, cursing and striking this way
and that with their long, lithe canes. Whack! Whack! went the sticks
on back, shoulders, legs and even heads. The slaves weren't being
beaten. They were only being urged a little, possibly for our benefit.

We stopped, and the head foreman, a big black Spaniard, stepped
over to the fence and greeted us.

"Do they ever fight back?" he repeated, at my question. "Not if
they're wise. They can get all the fight they want from me. The
men that fight me don't come to work next day. Yes, they need the
stick. Better to kill a lazy man than to feed him. Run away? Sometimes the new ones try it, but we soon tame it out of them. And when
we get 'em tamed we keep 'em here. There never was one of these
dogs who got out of here and didn't go telling lies about us."

Should I live a thousand years I would never forget the faces of
dull despair I saw everywhere; and I would never forget the first
night I spent on a Valle Nacional slave farm, the farm of the *Presidente*. The place was well named, "La Sepultura," though its name
was given by the Indians long before it became the sepulchre of
Mexican slaves.

"La Sepultura" is one of the smallest farms in the valley. The
dormitory is only 40 by 15 feet and it accommodates 70 men and
women nightly. Inside there are no benches—nothing but the bare
ground and a thin grass mat for each sleeper. In it we found an old
woman lying sick and shivering alone. Later that night we saw it

crammed full of the miserables shivering with the cold, for the wind was blowing a hurricane and the rain was coming down in torrents. In a few hours the temperature must have dropped forty degrees.

One-third of the laborers here were women, one of them a girl of twelve. That night the buildings rocked so fearfully that the horses were taken out of the barn. But, though a building had blown down a few weeks previously, the slaves were not taken out of their jail. Their jail was built just off the dining-room of the dwelling and that night my companion and I slept in the dining-room. I heard the jail door open and shut for a late worker to enter and then I heard the voice of the twelve-year-old girl pleading in terror: "Please don't lock the door tonight—only tonight! Please leave it so we can be saved if the house falls!" The answer that I heard was only a brutal laugh.

When I went to bed that night at 9:30 a gang of slaves was still working about the barn. When I awoke at four the slaves were receiving their beans and *tortillas* in the slave kitchen. When I went to bed two of the *Presidente's* kitchen drudges were hard at work. Through the chinks in the poles which divided the two rooms I watched them, for I could not sleep. At eleven o'clock by my watch one disappeared. It was 12:05 before the other was gone, but in less than four hours more I saw her again, working, working, working, working!

Yet perhaps she fared better than did the grinders of corn and the drawers of water, for when, with the son of the *Presidente*, I visited the slave kitchen at five and remarked on the exhausted faces of the women there, he informed me that their rising hour was two o'clock and that they never had time to rest during the day!

Oh, it was awful! This boy of sixteen, manager of the farm in his father's absence, told me with much gusto of how fiercely the women sometimes fought against the assaults of the men and how he had at times enjoyed peering through a crack and watching those

tragic encounters of the night! All night we were disturbed—mostly
by the hacking, tearing coughs that came to us through the chinks,
sometimes by heart-breaking sobs.

De Lara and I did not speak about these things until the morning,
when I remarked upon his haggard face.

"I heard the sobs and the coughs and the groans," said De Lara.
"I heard the women cry, and I cried, too—three times I cried. I do
not know how I can ever laugh and be happy again!"

While we waited for breakfast the *Presidente* told us many things
about the slavery and showed us a number of knives and files which
had been taken from the slaves at various times. Like penitentiary
convicts, the slaves had somehow got possession of the tools in the
hope of cutting a way out of their prison at night and escaping the
sentries.

The *Presidente* told us frankly that the authorities of Mexico City,
of Veracruz, of Oaxaca, of Pachuca and of Jalapa regularly engage
in the slave traffic, usually in combination with one or more "labor
agents." He especially named the mayor of a certain well known
seaport, who was mentioned in the American newspapers as an honored guest of President Roosevelt in 1908 and a prominent visitor to
the Republican convention at Chicago. This mayor, said our *Presidente*, regularly employed his city detective force as a dragnet for
slaves. He arrested all sorts of people on all sorts of pretexts merely
for the sake of the forty-five *pesos* apiece that they would bring from
the tobacco planters.

Our conversation that morning was interrupted by a Spanish foreman who rode up and had a talk with the *Presidente*. They spoke in
low tones, but we caught most of what they said. The foreman had
killed a woman the previous day and had come to make his peace
about it. After a consultation of ten minutes the *Presidente* shook the
hand of his visitor and we heard him tell the murderer to go home
and attend to his business and think no more about the matter.

It was Sunday and we spent the entire day in the company of

Antonio Pla, probably the most remarkable human monster in Valle
Nacional. Pla is general manager for Balsa Hermanos in Valle
Nacional and as such he oversees the business of twelve large plantations. He resides on the ranch "Hondura de Nanche," the one of
special alligator fame, where the term "Throw me to The Hungry"
originated. Pla calls his slaves "*Los Tigres*" (the tigers) and he
took the greatest of pleasure in showing us the "dens of the tigers,"
as well as in explaining his entire system of purchase, punishment
and burial.

Pla estimated that the annual movement of slaves to Valle Nacional is 15,000 and he assured me that if the planters killed every
last one of them the authorities would not interfere.

"Why should they?" he asked. "Don't we support them?"

Pla, like many of the other planters, raised tobacco in Cuba before
he came to Valle Nacional, and he declared that on account of the
slave system in the latter place the same quality of tobacco was
raised in Valle Nacional for half the price that it cost to raise it in
Cuba. It was not practical, said he, to keep the slaves more than
seven or eight months, as they became "all dried out." He explained
the various methods of whipping, the informal slugging in the field
with a cane of *bejuco* wood, and the lining-up of the gangs in the
morning and the administration of "a few stripes to the lazy ones as
medicine for the day."

"But after awhile," declared Pla, "even the cane doesn't do any
good. There comes a time when they just can't work any longer."

Pla told us that an agent of the government had three months before tried to sell him 500 Yaquis for twenty thousand *pesos*, but he
had rejected the offer, as, though the Yaquis last like iron, they *will*
persist in taking long chances in a break for liberty.

"I bought a bunch of Yaquis several years ago," he said, "but most
of them got away after a few months. No, Yucatan is the only place
for the Yaquis."

We found two Yaquis, however, on the farm, "Los Mangos."

They said they had been there for two years and were the only ones left out of an original lot of two hundred. One had been out of commission for a few days, one of his feet being half gone—eaten off by insects.

"I expect I'll have to kill that tiger," said Pla, in the man's hearing. "He'll never be worth anything to me any more."

The second Yaqui we found in the field working with a gang. I stepped up to him and felt of his arms. They were still muscular. He was really a magnificent specimen and reminded me of the story of Ben Hur. As I inspected him he stood erect, staring straight ahead but trembling slightly in every limb. The mere attitude of that Yaqui was to me the most conclusive evidence of the beastliness of the system under which he was enslaved.

At "Los Mangos" a foreman let us inspect his long, lithe cane, the beating cane, the cane of *bejuco* wood. It bent like a rawhide buggy whip, but it would not break.

"The *bejuco* tree grows on the mountain side," explained the foreman. "See! The wood is like leather. With this cane I can beat twenty men to death and yet it will be good for twenty more!"

In the slave kitchen of the same ranch we found two girls of seventeen, both with refined and really beautiful faces, grinding corn. Though their boss, Pla, stood menacingly by, each dared to tell her story briefly. One, from Leon, State of Guanajuato, declared that the "labor agent" had promised her fifty *pesos* per month and a good home as cook in a small family, and when she discovered that all was not right it was too late; the *rurales* compelled her to come along. The other girl was from San Luis Potosi. She had been promised a good home and forty *pesos* a month for taking care of two small children!

Wherever we went we found the houses full of fine furniture made by the slaves.

"Yes," explained Antonio Pla, "some of the best artisans in the country come right here—in one way or another. We get carpenters and cabinet-makers and upholsterers and everything. Why, on my ranches I've had teachers and actresses and artists and one time I even had an ex-priest. I had one of the most beautiful actresses in the country one time, right here on 'Hondura de Nanche.' She was noted, too. How did she get here? Simple enough. A son of a millionaire in Mexico City wanted to marry her and, to get her out of the way, the millionaire paid the authorities a good price to kidnap her and give her to a labor agent. Yes, sir, that woman was a beauty!"

"And what became of her?" I asked.

"Oh," was the evasive reply. "*That was two years ago!*"

Truly, two years is a long time in Valle Nacional, longer than a life-time, usually. The story of the actress reminded me of a story told me by a newly-married runaway Mexican couple in Los Angeles just before I started on my trip. The young husband was a member of the middle class of Mexico City and his wife was the daughter of a millionaire. Because the boy was considered to be "below" the girl, the girl's father went to extremes in his efforts to prevent the marriage.

"George went through many dangers for me," is the way the young bride told the story. "One time my father tried to shoot him and another time my father offered the authorities five thousand *pesos* to kidnap him and send him to Valle Nacional. But I warned George and he was able to save himself!"

Pla also told of eleven girls who had come to him in a single shipment from Oaxaca.

"They were at a public dance," said he. "Some men got into a fight and the police jailed everybody in the hall. Those girls didn't have anything to do with the trouble, but the *jefe politico* needed the money and so he sent them all here."

"Well," I asked, "what sort of women were they? Public women?"

Pla shot me a glance full of meaning.

"No, *Senor!*" he said, with contempt in his voice, "do you suppose that I need to have *that* kind of women sent in here to *me?*"

The close attendance of owners and superintendents as well as the ubiquity of overseers, prevented us from obtaining many long interviews with the slaves. One of the most notable of our slave talks occurred the day following our visit to the Balsa Hermanos farm. Returning from a long day's visit to numerous plantations, we hailed a ploughman working near the road on "Hondura de Nanche." The nearest overseer happened to be half way across the field and the slave, at our inquiry, willingly pointed out the slough of the alligators and confirmed the story of dying men being thrown to "The Hungry."

"I have been here for six years and I believe I hold the record for the valley," he told us. "Other strong men come and turn to skeletons in a single season, but it seems that I cannot die. They come and fall, and come and fall, yet I stay on and live. But you ought to have seen me when I came! I was a *man* then—a man! I had shoulders and arms—I was a giant then. But now—"

Tears gathered in the fellow's eyes and rolled down his cheeks, but he went on:

"I was a carpenter and a good one—six years ago. I lived with my brother and sister in Mexico City. My brother was a student— he was only in his teens—my sister tended the little house that I paid for out of my wages. We were not poor—no. We were happy. Then work in my trade fell slack and one evening I met a friend who told me of employment to be had in the State of Veracruz at three *pesos* a day—a long job. I jumped at the chance and we came together, came here—*here!* I told my brother and sister that I would send the money regularly, and when I learned that I could send them nothing and wrote to let them know, they would not let me send the letter! For months I kept that letter, watching, waiting, trying to get an opportunity to speak to the carrier as he rode along the highway. At last I saw him, but when I handed him the letter, he only laughed in my face and handed it back. Nobody is allowed to send a letter out of here.

"Escape?" went on the ploughman. "Yes, I tried it many times. Once, only eight months ago, I got as far as Tuztepec. I was writing a letter. I wanted to get word to my people, but they caught me before the letter was finished. They don't know where I am. They must think I am dead. My brother must have had to leave school. My—"

"Better stop," I said. "A *cabo* is coming!"

"No, not yet," he answered. "Quick! I will give you their address. Tell them that I never read the contract. Tell them that I never saw it until I came here. My brother's name is Juan ————"

"Look out!" I cried, but too late. "Whack!" The long cane struck the ploughman across the back. He winced, started to open his mouth again, but at a second whack he changed his mind and turned sullenly to his oxen.

The rains of our last two days in Valle Nacional made the trail to Tuztepec impassable, so we left our horses and traveled down river in a *balsa*, a raft of logs on which was erected a tiny shelter house roofed with banana leaves. Two Indians, one at each end, poled and paddled the strange craft down the rushing stream, and from them we learned that the Indians themselves have had their day as slaves in Valle Nacional. The Spaniards tried to enslave them, but they fought to the death. They employed their tribal solidarity and fought in droves like wolves and in that way they regained and kept their freedom. Such a common understanding and such mass movements cannot, of course, be developed by the heterogeneous elements that today are brought together on the slave plantations.

At Tuztepec on our way we met *Senor* P————, politician, "labor agent," and relative of Felix Diaz, nephew of President Diaz and Chief of Police of Mexico City. *Senor* P————, who dressed like a prince, made himself agreeable and answered our questions freely because he hoped to secure the contract for furnishing slaves for my company.

"You can't help but make money in Valle Nacional," said he. "They all do. Why, after every harvest there's an exodus of planters to Mexico City, where some of them stay for months, spending their money in the most riotous living!"

Senor P——— was kind enough to tell us what became of the fifty *pesos* he received for each of his slaves. Five *pesos*, he said went to Rodolpho Pardo, *jefe politico* of Tuztepec, ten to Felix Diaz for every slave taken out of Mexico City, and ten to the mayor of the city or *jefe politico* of the district from whence came the other slaves.

"The fact that I am a brother-in-law of Felix Diaz," said *Senor* P———, "as well as a personal friend of the governors of the states of Oaxaca and Veracruz, and of the mayors of the cities of the same name, puts me in a position to supply your wants better than anyone else. I am prepared to furnish you any number of laborers up to forty thousand a year, men, women and children, and my price is fifty *pesos* each. Children workers last better than adults and I advise you to use them in preference to others. *I can furnish you* 1,000 *children a month under fourteen years of age, and I am prepared to secure their legal adoption as sons and daughters of the company, so that they can be legally kept until they reach the age of twenty-two!*"

"But how," I gasped, "is my company going to adopt 12,000 children a year as sons and daughters? Do you mean to tell me that the government would permit such a thing?"

"Leave that to me," replied *Senor* P———, significantly. "I'm doing it every day. You don't pay your fifty *pesos* until you get the children and the adoption papers too!"

The Country Peons and the City Poor

A whole book, and a large one, could very profitably be written upon the slavery of Mexico. But important as the subject is, it is not important enough to fill a greater fraction of space in this work than I have allotted to it. Most necessary is it that I dig beneath the surface and reveal the hideous causes which have made and are perpetuating that barbarous institution.

I trust that my exposition of the previous chapters has been lucid enough to leave no question as to the complete partnership of the government in the slavery.

In some quarters this slavery has been admitted, but the guilt of the government has been denied. But it is absurd to suppose that the government could be kept in ignorance of a situation in which one-third the entire population of a great state are held as chattels. Moreover, it is well known that hundreds of state and national officials are constantly engaged in rounding up, transporting, selling, guarding and hunting slaves. As I previously pointed out, every gang of *enganchados* leaving Mexico City or any other city for Valle Nacional or any other slave district are guarded by government *rurales*, or rural guards, in uniform. These *rurales* do not act on their own initiative; they are as completely under orders as are the soldiers of the regular army. Without the coercion of their guns and their authority the *enganchados* would refuse to travel a mile of the journey. A moment's thought is sufficient to convince any unprejudiced mind that without the partnership of the government the whole system of slavery would be an impossibility.

Slavery similar to that of Yucatan and Valle Nacional is to be found in nearly every state of Mexico, but especially in the coast states south of the great plateau. The labor on the henequen plantations of Campeche, in the lumber and fruit industries of Chiapas and Tabasco, on the rubber, coffee, sugar-cane, tobacco and fruit plantations of Veracruz, Oaxaca and Morelos, is all done by slaves. In at least ten of the thirty-two states and territories of Mexico the proportion of labor is overwhelmingly of slaves.

While the minor conditions vary somewhat in different places, the general system is everywhere the same—service against the will of the laborer, no pay, semi-starvation, and the whip. Into this arrangement of things are impressed not only the natives of the various slave states, but others—100,000 others every year, to speak in round numbers—who, either enticed by the false promises of labor agents, kidnapped by labor agents or shipped by political authorities in partnership with labor agents, leave their homes in other parts of the country to journey to their death in the hot lands.

Debt and contract slavery is the prevailing system of production all over the south of Mexico. Probably three-quarters of a million souls may properly be classed as human chattels. In all the rest of Mexico a system of peonage, differing from slavery principally in degree, and similar in many respects to the serfdom of Europe in the Middle Ages, prevails in the rural districts. Under this system the laborer is compelled to give service to the farmer, or *hacendado*, to accept what he wishes to pay, and even to receive such beatings as he cares to deliver. Debt, real or imaginary, is the nexus that binds the peon to his master. Debts are handed from father to son and on down through the generations. Though the constitution does not recognize the right of the creditor to take and hold the body of the debtor, the rural authorities everywhere recognize such a right and the result is that probably 5,000,000 people, or one-third of the entire population, are today living in a state of helpless peonage.

Farm peons are often credited with receiving wages, which nominally range from twelve and one-half cents a day to twenty-five cents a day, American money—seldom higher. Often they never receive a cent of this, but are paid only in credit checks at the *hacienda* store, at which they are compelled to trade in spite of the exorbitant prices. As a result their food consists solely of corn and beans, they live in hovels often made of no more substantial material than corn-stalks, and they wear their pitiful clothing, not merely until the garments are all rags and patches and ready to drop off, but until they actually do attain the vanishing act.

Probably not fewer than eighty per cent of all the farm and plantation laborers in Mexico are either slaves or are bound to the land as peons. The other twenty per cent are denominated as free laborers and live a precarious existence trying to dodge the net of those who would drag them down. I remember particularly a family of such whom I met in the State of Chihuahua. They were typical, though my memory of them is most vivid because I saw them on the first night I ever spent in Mexico. It was in a second-class car on the Mexican Central, traveling south.

They were six, that family, and of three generations. From the callow, raven-haired boy to the white-chinned grandfather, all six seemed to have the last ray of mirth ground out of their systems. We were a lively crowd sitting there near them—four were happy Mexicans returning home for a vacation after a season at wage labor in the United States. We sang a little and we made some music on a violin and a harmonica. But not one of that family of six behind us ever smiled or showed the slightest interest. They reminded me of a herd of cattle standing in a blizzard, their heads between their front legs, their backs to the storm.

The face of the old patriarch told a story of burdens and of a patient, ox-like bearing of them such as no words could possibly suggest. He had a ragged, grizzled beard and moustache, but his head was still covered with dark brown hair. He was probably seventy, but was evidently still an active worker. His clothing consisted of American jumper and overalls of ordinary denim washed and patched and washed and patched—a one-dollar suit patched until it was nothing but patches!

Beside the patriarch sat the old lady, his wife, with head bowed and a facial expression so like that of her husband that it might have been a copy by a great painter. Yes, the expression differed in one detail. The old woman's upper lip was compressed tight against her teeth, giving her an effect of perpetually biting her lip to keep back the tears. Perhaps her original stock of courage had not been equal to that of the man and it had been necessary to fortify it by an everlasting compression of the mouth.

Then there was a young couple half the age of the two. The man sat with head nodding and granulated lids blinking slowly, now and then turning his eyes to stare with far distant interest upon the merrymakers around him. His wife, a flat-breasted drooping woman, sat always in one position with her head bent forward and her right hand fingering her face about the bridge of the nose.

Finally, there were two boys, one of eighteen, second son of the old man, and one of sixteen, son of the second couple. In all that night's journey the only smile I saw from any of the six was a smile of the youngest boy. A passing news-agent offered the boy a book for seventy-five *centavos*. With slightly widening eyes of momentary interest the boy looked upon the gaily decorated paper cover, then turned toward his uncle and smiled a half startled smile. To think that anyone might imagine that *he* could afford to purchase one of those magical things, a book!

"We are from Chihuahua," the old man told us, when we had gained his confidence. "We work in the fields—all of us. All our lives we have been farm laborers in the corn and the beans and the melons of Chihuahua. But now we are running away from it. If the bosses would pay us the money they agree to pay, we could get along, but they never pay all—never. This time the boss paid us only two-thirds the agreed price, yet I am very thankful for that much, for he might have given us only one-third, as others have done in the past. What can I do? Nothing. I cannot hire a lawyer, for the lawyer would steal the other two-thirds, and the boss would put me in jail besides. Many times I and my sons have gone to jail for asking the boss to pay us the full amount of our agreement. My sons become angry more and more and sometimes I fear one may strike the boss or kill him. That would be the end of us.

"No, the best thing to do, I decided at last, was to get away. So we put our wages together and used our last dollar to pay for tickets to Torreon, where we hope to find work in the cotton fields. I hear we can get one *peso* a day in busy times. Is it so? Or will it be the same story over again there? Perhaps it will. But what else can I do but try? Work! work! work! That's all there is for us—and nothing in return for the work! We do not drink; we are not lazy; every day we pray to God. Yet debt is always following us, begging to be taken in. Many times I have wanted to borrow just a little from my boss, but my wife has always pleaded with me. 'No,' she would say, 'better die than to owe, for owing once means owing forever—and slavery.'

"But sometimes," continued the old man, "I think it might be better to owe, better to fall in debt, better to give up our liberty than to go on like this to the end. True, I am getting old and I would love to die free, but it is hard—too hard!"

The three-quarters of a million of chattel slaves and the five million peons do not monopolize the economic misery of Mexico. It extends to every class of men that toils. There are 150,000 mine and smelter workers who receive less money for a week's labor than an American miner of the same class gets for a day's wages. There are 30,000 cotton mill operatives whose wages average less than thirty cents a day in American money. There are a quarter of a million domestic servants whose wages range from one to five dollars a month. There are 40,000 impressed soldiers who get less than two dollars a month above the scantiest rations. The common policemen of Mexico City, 2,000 of them, are paid but fifty cents a day in our money. Fifty cents a day is a high average for street-car conductors in the metropolis, where wages are higher than in any other section of the country except close to the American border. And this proportion is constant throughout the industries. An offer of fifty cents a day without food, would, without the slightest doubt, bring in Mexico City an army of 50,000 able-bodied laborers inside of twenty-four hours.

From such miserable wages it must not be guessed that the cost of the necessities of life are less than they are here, as in the case of other low wage countries, such as India and China. On the contrary, the cost of corn and beans, upon which the mass of the Mexican people eke out their existence, is actually higher, as a rule, than it is in the United States. At this writing it costs nearly twice as much money to buy a hundred pounds of corn in Mexico City as it does in Chicago, and that in the same money, American gold or Mexican silver, take it as you like it. And this is the cheapest staple that the poverty-stricken Mexican is able to lay his hands upon.

As to clothing and shelter, the common Mexican has about as little of either as can be imagined. The tenements of New York City are palatial homes compared to the tenements of Mexico City. A quarter of a mile in almost any direction off Diaz's grand Paseo de la Reforma, the magnificent driveway over which tourists are always taken and by which they usually judge Mexico, will carry the investigator into conditions that are not seen in any city worthy the name of civilized. If in all Mexico there exists a city with a really modern sewer system I am ignorant of its name.

Travelers who have stopped at the best hotels of the metropolis may raise their eyebrows at this last statement, but a little investigation will show that not more than one-fifth of the houses within the limits of that metropolis are regularly supplied with water with which to flush the sewers, while there are many densely populated blocks which have no public water whatsoever, neither for sewer flushing nor for drinking.

It will take a few minutes' reflection to realize what this really means. As a result of such unsanitary conditions the death rate in that city ranges always between 5 and 6 per cent, usually nearer the latter figure, which places that percentage at more than double the death rate of well-regulated cities of Europe, the United States and even of South America. Which proves that half the people who die in Diaz's metropolis die of causes which modern cities have abolished.

A life-long resident once estimated to me that 200,000 people of the country's metropolis, or two-fifths the entire population, spend every night on the stones. "On the stones" means not on the streets, for sleeping is not permitted on the streets or in the parks, but on the floors of cheap tenements or lodging houses.

Possibly this is an exaggeration. From my own observations, however, I know that 100,000 would be a very conservative estimate. And at least 25,000 pass the nights in *mesones*—the name commonly applied to the cheapest class of transient lodging houses.

A *meson* is a pit of such misery as is surpassed only by the *galeras*, the sleeping jails, of the contract slaves of the hot lands—and the dormitories of the Mexican prisons. The chief difference between the *mesones* and the *galeras* is that into the latter the slaves are driven, tottering from overwork, semi-starvation and fever—driven with whips and locked in when they are there; while to the *mesones* the ragged, ill-nourished wretches from the city's streets come to buy with three precious copper *centavos* a brief and scanty shelter— a bare spot to lie down in, a grass mat, company with the vermin that squalor breeds, rest in a sickening room with hundreds of others —snoring, tossing, groaning brothers and sisters in woe.

During my most recent visit to Mexico—in the winter and spring of 1909—I visited many of these *mesones* and took a number of flashlight photos of the inmates. The conditions in all I found to be the same. The buildings are ancient ones—often hundreds of years old—which have been abandoned as unfit for any other purposes than as sleeping places for the country's poor. For three *centavos* the pilgrim gets a grass mat and the privilege of hunting for a bare spot large enough to lie down in. On cold nights the floor and yards are so thick with bodies that it is very difficult to find footing between the sleepers. In one room I have counted as high as two hundred.

Poor women and girls must sleep, as well as poor men and boys, and if they cannot afford more than three cents for a bed they must go to the *mesones* with the men. In not one of the *mesones* that I visited was there a separate room for the women and girls, though there were many women and girls among the inmates. Like a man, a girl pays her three cents and gets a grass mat. She may come early and find a comparatively secluded nook in which to rest her weary body. But there is nothing to prevent a man from coming along, lying down beside her and annoying her throughout the night.

And this thing is done. More than once, in my visits to *mesones*, I saw a young and unprotected girl awakened from her sleep and solicited by a strange man whose roving eye had lighted upon her as he came into the place. The *mesones* breed immorality as appallingly as they breed vermin. Homeless girls do not go to *mesones* because they are bad, but because they are poor. These places are licensed by the authorities and it would be a simple matter to require the proprietors to set apart a portion of the space exclusively for women. But this the authorities have not the decency to do.

Miserable as are the *mesones*, the 25,000 homeless Mexicans who spend their nights there are fortunate compared to the thousands of others who, when the shadows fall upon them, find that they cannot produce the three *centavos* to pay for a grass mat and a spot on a bare floor. Every night there is a hegira of these thousands from the city's streets. Carrying what pitiful belongings they have, if they have any belongings, moving along hand in hand, if they are a family together, husband and wife, or merely friends drawn closer together by their poverty; they travel for miles, out of the city to the open roads and fields, the great stock farms belonging to men high up in the councils of the government. Here they huddle about on the ground, shivering in the cold, for few nights in that altitude are not so cold that covering is not sorely needed. In the morning they travel back to the heart of the city, there to pit their feeble strength against the Powers that are conspiring to prevent them from earning a living; there, after vain and discouraging struggles, at last to fall into the net of the "labor agent," who is on the lookout for slaves for his wealthy clients, the planters of the lowland states.

Mexico contains 767,000 square miles. Acre for acre, it is as rich as, if not richer than the United States. It has fine harbors on both coasts. It is approximately as near the world's markets as are we. There is no natural or geographical reason why its people should not be as prosperous and happy as any in the world. In point of years it is an older country than ours. It is not over-populated. With a population of 15,000,000, it has eighteen souls to the square mile, which is slightly less than we have here. Yet, seeing the heart of Mexico, it is inconceivable that there could be more extreme poverty in all the world. India or China could not be worse off, for if they were, acute starvation would depopulate them. Mexico is a people starved —a nation prostrate. What is the reason? Who is to blame?

The Diaz System

The slavery and peonage of Mexico, the poverty and illiteracy, the general prostration of the people, are due, in my humble judgment, to the financial and political organization that at present rules that country—in a word, to what I shall call the "system" of General Porfirio Diaz.

That these conditions can be traced in a measure to the history of Mexico during past generations, is true. I do not wish to be unfair to General Diaz in the least degree. The Spanish Dons made slaves and peons of the Mexican people. Yet never did they grind the people as they are ground today. In Spanish times the peon at least had his own little patch of ground, his own humble shelter; today he has nothing. Moreover, the Declaration of Independence, proclaimed just one hundred years ago, in 1810, proclaimed also the abolition of chattel slavery. Slavery was abolished, though not entirely. Succeeding Mexican governments of class and of church and of the individual held the people in bondage little less severe. But fiinally came a democratic movement which broke the back of the church, which overthrew the rule of caste, which adopted a form of government as modern as our own, which freed the slave in fact as well as in name, which gave the lands of the people back to the people, which wiped the slate clean of the blood of the past.

It was at this juncture that General Porfirio Diaz, without any valid excuse and apparently for no other reason than personal ambition, stirred up a series of revolutions which finally ended in his capture of the governmental powers of the land. While professing to respect the progressive institutions which Juarez and Lerdo had established before him, he built up a system all his own, a system in which he personally was the central and all-controlling figure, in which his individual caprice was the constitution and the law, in which all circumstances and all men, big and little, were bent or broken at his will. Like Louis *XIV*, The State—Porfirio Diaz was The State!

It was under Porfirio Diaz that slavery and peonage were reestablished in Mexico, and on a more merciless basis than they had existed even under the Spanish Dons. Therefore, I can see no injustice in charging at least a preponderance of the blame for these conditions upon the system of Diaz.

I say the "system of Diaz" rather than Diaz personally because, though he is the keystone of the arch, though he is the government of Mexico more completely than is any other individual the government of any large country on the planet, yet no one man can stand alone in his iniquity. Diaz is the central prop of the slavery, but there are other props without which the system could not continue upright for a single day. For example, there is the collection of commercial interests which profits by the Diaz system of slavery and autocracy, and which puts no insignificant part of its tremendous powers to holding the central prop upright in exchange for the special privileges that it receives. Not the least among these commercial interests are American, which, I blush to say, are quite as aggressive defenders of the Diaz citadel as any. Indeed, as I shall show in future chapters, these American interests undoubtedly form the de-

termining force in the continuation of Mexican slavery. Thus does
Mexican slavery come home to us in the full sense of the term. For
the horrors of Yucatan and Valle Nacional, Diaz is to blame, but
so are we; we are to blame insofar as governmental powers over
which we are conceded to have some control are employed under
our very eyes for the perpetuation of a regime of which slavery and
peonage are an integral part.

In order that the reader may understand the Diaz system and its
responsibility in the degradation of the Mexican people, it will be
well to go back and trace briefly the beginnings of that system.
Mexico is spoken of throughout the world as a Republic. That is because it was once a Republic and still pretends to be one. Mexico has
a constitution which has never been repealed, a constitution said to
be modeled after our own, and one which is, indeed, like ours in the
main. Like ours, it provides for a national congress, state legislatures
and municipal aldermen to make the laws, federal, state and local
judges to interpret them, and a president, governors and local executives to administer them. Like ours, it provides for manhood suffrage, freedom of the press and of speech, equality before the law,
and the other guarantees of life, liberty and the pursuit of happiness
which we ourselves enjoy, in a degree, as a matter of course.

Such was Mexico forty years ago. Forty years ago Mexico was at
peace with the world. She had just overthrown, after a heroic war,
the foreign prince, Maximilian, who had been seated as emperor
by the armies of Napoleon Third of France. Her president, Benito
Juarez, is today recognized in Mexico and out of Mexico as one of
the most able as well as unselfish patriots of Mexican history. Never
since Cortez fired his ships there on the gulf coast had Mexico enjoyed such prospects of political freedom, industrial prosperity and
general advancement.

But in spite of these facts and the additional fact that he was
deeply indebted to Juarez, all his military promotions having been
received at the hands of the latter, General Porfirio Diaz stirred up

a series of rebellions for the purpose of securing for himself the supreme power of the land. Diaz not only led one armed rebellion against a peaceable, constitutional and popularly approved government, but he led three of them. For nine years he plotted as a common rebel. The support that he received came chiefly from bandits, criminals and professional soldiers who were disgruntled at the anti-militarist policy which Juarez had inaugurated and which, if he could have carried it out a little farther, would have been effective in preventing military revolutions in the future—and from the Catholic church.

Repeatedly it was proved that the people did not want Diaz at the head of their government. Three times during his first five years of plotting he was an unsuccessful candidate at the polls. In 1867 he received a little more than one-third the votes counted for Juarez. In 1871 he received about three-fifths as many votes as Juarez. In 1872, after the death of Juarez, he ran against Lerdo de Tejada and received only one-fifteenth as many votes as his opponent. While in arms he was looked upon as a common rebel at home and abroad and when he marched into the national capital at the head of a victorious army and proclaimed himself president hardly a European nation would at first recognize the upstart government, while the United States for a time threatened complications.

In defiance of the will of the majority of the people of Mexico, General Diaz, thirty-four years ago, came to the head of government. In defiance of the will of the majority of the people he has remained there ever since—except for four years, from 1880 to 1884, when he turned the palace over to an intimate friend, Manuel Gonzalez, on the distinct understanding that at the end of the four years Gonzalez would turn it back to him again.

Since no man can rule an unwilling people without taking away the liberties of that people, it can be very easily understood what sort of regime General Diaz found it necessary to establish in order to make his power secure. By the use of the army and the police powers generally, he controlled elections, the press and public speech and made of popular government a farce. By distributing the public offices among his generals and granting them free rein to plunder at will, he assured himself of the continued use of the army. By making political combinations with men high in the esteem of the Catholic church and permitting it to be whispered about that the church was to regain some of its former powers, he gained the silent support of the priests and the Pope. By promising full payment of all foreign debts and launching at once upon a policy of distributing favors among citizens of other countries, he made his peace with the world at large.

In other words, General Diaz, with a skill that none can deny, annexed to himself all the elements of power in the country except the nation at large. On the one hand, he had a military dictatorship. On the other, he had a financial camarilla. Himself was the center of the arch and he was compelled to pay the price. The price was the nation at large. He created a machine and oiled the machine with the flesh and blood of a people. He rewarded all except the people; the people were the sacrifice. Inevitable as the blackness of night, in contrast to the sun-glory of the dictator, came the degradation of the people—the slavery, the peonage and every misery that walks with poverty, the abolition of democracy and the personal security that breeds providence, self-respect and worthy ambition; in a word, general demoralization, depravity.

Take, for example, Diaz's method of rewarding his military chiefs, the men who helped him overthrow the government of Lerdo. As quickly as possible after assuming the power, he installed his generals as governors of the various states and organized them and other influential figures in the nation into a national plunderbund. Thus he assured himself of the continued loyalty of the generals, on the one hand, and put them where he could most effectively use them for keeping down the people, on the other. One variety of rich plum which he handed out in those early days to his governors came in the form of charters giving his governors the right, as individuals, to organize companies and build railroads, each charter carrying with it a huge sum as a railroad subsidy.

The national government paid for the road and then the governor and his most influential friends owned it. Usually the railroads were ridiculous affairs, were of narrow-gauge and of the very cheapest materials, but the subsidy was very large, sufficient to build the road and probably equip it besides. During his first term of four years in office Diaz passed sixty-one railroad subsidy acts containing appropriations aggregating $40,000,000, and all but two or three of these acts were in favor of governors of states. In a number of cases not a mile of railroad was actually built, but the subsidies are supposed to have been paid, anyhow. In nearly every case the subsidy was the same, $12,880 per mile in Mexican silver, and in those days Mexican silver was nearly on a par with gold.

This huge sum was taken out of the national treasury and was supposedly paid to the governors, although Mexican politicians of the old times have assured me that it was divided, a part going out as actual subsidies and a part going directly into the hands of Diaz to be used in building up his machine in other quarters.

Certainly something more than mere loyalty, however invaluable it was, was required of the governors in exchange for such rich financial plums. It is a well authenticated fact that governors were required to pay a fixed sum annually for the privilege of exploiting to the limit the graft possibilities of their offices. For a long time Manuel Romero Rubio, father-in-law of Diaz, was the collector of these perquisites, the offices bringing in anywhere from $10,000 to $50,000 per year.

The largest single perquisite whereby Diaz enriched himself, the members of his immediate family, his friends, his governors, his financial ring and his foreign favorites, was found for a long time in the confiscation of the lands of the common people—a confiscation, in fact, which is going on to this day. Note that this land robbery

was the first direct step in the path of the Mexican people back to
their bondage as slaves and peons.

In a previous chapter I showed how the lands of the Yaquis of
Sonora were taken from them and given to political favorites of the
ruler. The lands of the Mayas of Yucatan, now enslaved by the
henequen planters, were taken from them in almost the same manner. The final act in this confiscation was accomplished in the year
1904, when the national government set aside the last of their lands
into a territory called Quintana Roo. This territory contains 43,000
square kilometers or 27,000 square miles. It is larger than the
present state of Yucatan by 8,000 square kilometers, and moreover
is the most promising land of the entire peninsula. Separated from
the island of Cuba by a narrow strait, its soil and climate are strik-
ingly similar to those of Cuba and experts have declared that there
is no reason why Quintana Roo should not one day become as great
a tobacco-growing country as Cuba. Further than that, its hillsides
are thickly covered with the most valuable cabinet and dyewoods
in the world. It is this magnificent country which, as the last chapter
in the life of the Mayas as a nation, the Diaz government took and
handed over to eight Mexican politicians.

In like manner have the Mayos of Sonora, the Papagos, the
Tomosachics—in fact, practically all the native peoples of Mexico
—been reduced to peonage, if not to slavery. Small holders of every
tribe and nation have gradually been expropriated until today their
number as property holders is almost down to zero. Their lands are
in the hands of members of the governmental machine, or persons
to whom the members of the machine have sold for profit—or in
the hands of foreigners.

This is why the typical Mexican farm is the million-acre farm,
why it has been so easy for such Americans as William Randolph
Hearst, Harrison Gray Otis, E. H. Harriman, the Rockefellers, the
Guggenheims and numerous others each to have obtained possession
of millions of Mexican acres. This is why Secretary of Fomento

Molina holds more than 15,000,000 acres of the soil of Mexico, why ex-Governor Terrazas, of Chihuahua, owns 15,000,000 acres of the soil of that state, why Finance Minister Limantour, Mrs. Porfirio Diaz, Vice-President Corral, Governor Pimentel, of Chiapas, Governor Landa y Escandon of the Federal District, Governor Pablo Escandon of Morelos, Governor Ahumada of Jalisco, Governor Cosio of Queretaro, Governor Mercado of Michoacan, Governor Canedo of Sinaloa, Governor Cahuantzi of Tlaxcala, and many other members of the Diaz machine are not only millionaires, but they are millionaires in Mexican real estate.

Chief among the methods used in getting the lands away from the people in general was through a land registration law which Diaz fathered. This law permitted any person to go out and claim any lands to which the possessor could not prove a recorded title. Since up to the time the law was enacted it was not the custom to record titles, this meant all the lands in Mexico. When a man possessed a home which his father had possessed before him, and which his grandfather had possessed, which his great-grandfather had possessed, and which had been in the family as far back as history knew, then he considered that he owned that home, all of his neighbors considered that he owned it, and all governments up to that of Diaz recognized his right to that home.

Supposing that a strict registration law became necessary in the course of evolution, had this law been enacted for the purpose of protecting the land owners instead of plundering them the government would, naturally, have sent agents through the country to appraise the people of the new law and to help them register their property and keep their homes. But this was not done and the conclusion is inevitable that the law was passed for the purpose of plundering.

At all events, the result of the law was a plundering. No sooner had it been passed than the aforesaid members of the government machine, headed by the father-in-law of Diaz, and Diaz himself,

formed land companies and sent out agents, not to help the people
keep their lands, but to select the most desirable lands in the country,
register them, and evict the owners. This they did on a most tremendous scale. Thus hundreds of thousands of small farmers lost
their property. Thus small farmers are still losing their property. In
order to cite an example, I reprint a dispatch dated Merida, Yucatan,
April 11, 1909, and published April 12 in the Mexican Herald, an
American daily newspaper printed in Mexico City:

Merida, April 11.—Minister Olegario Molina, of the Department of
Fomento, Colonization and Industry, has made a denouncement before
the agency here of extensive territory lying adjacent to his lands in
Tizimin *partido*. The denouncement was made through Esteban Rejon
Garcia, his *administrador* at that place.

The section was taken on the ground that those now occupying them
have no documents or titles of ownership.

They measure 2,700 hectares (about 6,000 acres, or over nine square
miles), and *include perfectly organized towns,* some fine ranches, including those of Laureano Breseno and Rafael Aguilar, and other properties. The *jefe politico* of Tizimin has notified the population of the
town, the owners and laborers on the ranches, and others on the lands,
that they will be obliged to vacate within two months *or become subject
to the new owner.*

The present occupants have lived for years upon the land and have
cultivated and improved much of it. Some have lived there from generation to generation, and have thought themselves the rightful owners,
having inherited it from the original 'squatters.'

*Mr. Rejon Garcia has also denounced other similar public lands in
the Espita partido.*

Another favorite means of confiscating the homes of small owners
is found in the juggling of state taxes. State taxes in Mexico are
fearfully and wonderfully made. Especially in the less populous
districts owners are taxed inversely as they stand in favor with the
personality who represents the government in their particular dis-

trict. No court, board or other responsible body sits to review unjust assessments. The *jefe politico* may charge one farmer five times as much per acre as he charges the farmer across the fence, and yet Farmer No. 1 has no redress unless he is rich and powerful. He must pay, and if he cannot, the farm is a little later listed among the properties of the *jefe politico*, or one of the members of his family, or among the properties of the governor of the state or one of the members of his family. But if he is rich and powerful he is often not taxed at all. American promoters in Mexico escape taxation so nearly invariably that the impression has got abroad in this country that land pays no taxes in Mexico. Even Frederick Palmer made a statement to this effect in his recent writings about that country.

Of course such bandit methods as were employed and are still employed were certain to meet with resistance, and so we find numerous instances of regiments of soldiers being called out to enforce collection of taxes or the eviction of time-honored land-holders. Mexican history of the past generation is blotched with stories of massacres having their cause in this thing. Among the most noted of these massacres are those of Papantla and Tomosachic. Manuel Romero Rubio, the late father-in-law of General Diaz, denounced the lands of several thousand farmers in the vicinity of Papantla, Veracruz. Diaz backed him up with several regiments of regulars and before the farmers were all evicted four hundred, or some such number, were killed. In the year 1892, General Lauro Carrillo, who was then governor of Chihuahua, laid a tax on the town of Tomosachic, center of the Tomosachic settlement, which it was impossible for the people to pay. The immediate cause of the exorbitant tax, so the story goes, was that the authorities of the town had refused Carrillo some paintings which adorned the walls of their church and which he desired for his own home. Carrillo carried away some leading men of the town as hostages, and when the people still refused to pay, he sent soldiers for more hostages. The soldiers were driven away, after which Carrillo laid siege to the town with eight regiments. In the end the town was burned and a churchful of women and children were burned, too. Accounts of the Tomosachic massacre place the number of killed variously at from 800 to 2,000.

Cases of more recent blood spillings in the same cause are numerous. Hardly a month passes today without there being one or more reports in Mexican papers of disturbances, the result of confiscation of homes, either through the denunciation method or the excuse of nonpayment of taxes. Notable among these was the case of San Andreas, State of Chihuahua, which was exploited in the Mexican press in April, 1909. According to those press reports, the state authorities confiscated lands of several score of farmers, the excuse being that the owners were delinquent in their taxes. The farmers resisted eviction in a body and two carloads of troops, hurried to the scene from the capital of the state, promptly cleaned them out, shooting some and chasing half a hundred of them into the mountains. Here they stayed until starved out, when they straggled back, begging for mercy. As they came they were thrown into jail, men, women and children. The government carefully concealed the truth as to the number killed in the skirmish with the troops, but reports place it at from five to twenty-five.

An incident of the same class was that of San Carlos, also in the State of Chihuahua, which occurred in August, 1909. At San Carlos, center of a farming district, the misuse of the taxing power became so unbearable that four hundred small farmers banded together, defied a force of fifty *rurales*, forcibly deposed the *jefe politico*, and elected another in his place, then went back to their plows. It was a little revolution which the newspaper reports of the time declared was the first of its kind to which the present government of Mexico ever yielded. Whether the popularly constituted local government was permitted to remain or whether it was later overthrown by a regiment of soldiers is not recorded, though the latter seems most likely.

Graft is an established institution in the public offices of Mexico.

It is a right vested in the office itself, is recognized as such, and is respectable. There are two main functions attached to each public office, one a privilege, the other a duty. The privilege is that of using the special powers of the office for the amassing of a personal fortune; the duty is that of preventing the people from entering into any activities that may endanger the stability of the existing regime. Theoretically, the fulfillment of the duty is judged as balancing the harvest of the privilege, but with all offices and all places this is not so, and so we find offices of particularly rosy possibilities selling for a fixed price. Examples are those of the *jefes politicos* in districts where the slave trade is peculiarly remunerative, as at Pachuca, Oaxaca, Veracruz, Orizaba, Cordoba and Rio Blanco; of the districts in which the drafting of soldiers for the army is especially let to the *jefes politicos*; of the towns in which the gambling privileges are let as a monopoly to the mayors thereof; of the states in which there exist opportunities extraordinary for governors to graft off the army supply contracts.

Monopolies called "concessions," which are nothing more nor less than trusts created by governmental decree, are dealt in openly by the Mexican government. Some of these concessions are sold for cash, but the rule is to give them away gratis or for a nominal price, the real price being collected in political support. The public domain is sold in huge tracts for a nominal price or for nothing at all, the money price, when paid at all, averaging about fifty Mexican *centavos* an acre. But never does the government sell to any individual or company not of its own special choice; that is, the public domain is by no means open to all comers on equal terms. Public concessions worth millions of dollars—to use the water of a river for irrigation purposes, or for power, to engage in this or that monopoly, have been given away, but not indiscriminately. These things are the coin with which political support is bought and as such are grafts, pure and simple.

Public action of any sort is never taken for the sake of improving the condition of the common people. It is taken with a view to making the government more secure in its position. Mexico is a land of special privileges extraordinary, though frequently special privileges are provided for in the name of the common people. An instance is that of the "Agricultural Bank," which was created in 1908. To read the press reports concerning the purpose of this bank one would imagine that the government had launched into a gigantic and benevolent scheme to re-establish its expropriated people in agriculture. The purpose, it was said, was to loan money to needy farmers. But nothing could be farther from the truth, for the purpose is to help out the rich farmer, and only the richest in the land. The bank has now been loaning money for two years, but so far not a single case has been recorded in which aid was given to help a farm that comprised less than thousands of acres. Millions have been loaned on private irrigation projects, but never in lumps of less than several tens of thousands. In the United States the farmer class is an humble class indeed; in Mexico the typical farmer is the king of millionaires, a little potentate. In Mexico, because of the special privileges given by the government, medievalism still prevails outside the cities. The barons are richer and more powerful than were the landed aristocrats before the French Revolution, and the canaille poorer, more miserable.

And the special financial privileges centering in the cities are no less remarkable than the special privileges given to the exploiters of the *hacienda* slave. There is a financial ring consisting of members of the Diaz machine and their close associates, who pluck all the financial plums of the "republic," who get the contracts, the franchises and the concessions, and whom the large aggregations of foreign capital which secure a footing in the country find it necessary to take as coupon-clipping partners. The "Banco Nacional," an institution having some fifty-four branches and which has been compared flatteringly to the Bank of England, is the special financial vehicle of the government camarilla. It monopolizes the major portion of the banking business of the country and is a convenient cloak for the larger grafts, such as the railway merger, the true significance of which I shall present in a future chapter.

Diaz encourages foreign capital, for foreign capital means the support of foreign governments. American capital has a smoother time with Diaz than it has even with its own government, which is very fine from the point of view of American capital, but not so good from the point of view of the Mexican people. Diaz has even entered into direct partnership with certain aggregations of foreign capital, granting these aggregations special privileges in some lines which he has refused to his own millionaires. These foreign partnerships which Diaz has formed have made his government international insofar as the props which support his system are concerned. The certainty of foreign intervention in his favor has been one of the powerful forces which have prevented the Mexican people from using arms to remove a ruler who imposed himself upon them by the use of arms.

When I come to deal with the American partners of Diaz I mention those of no other nationality in the same breath, but it will be well to bear in mind that England, especially, is nearly as heavily as interested in Mexico as is the United States. While this country has $900,000,000 (these are the figures given by Consul General Shanklin about the first of the year 1910) invested in Mexico, England (according to the South American Journal) has $750,000,000. However, these figures by no means represent the ratio between the degree of political influence exerted by the two countries. There the United States bests all the other countries combined.

Yet there are two English corporations so closely identified with the Mexican financial ring as to deserve special mention. They are the combination represented by Dr. F. S. Pearson, of Canada and London, and the other corporation distinct from the first, S. Pearson & Son, Limited. Of Dr. F. S. Pearson it is boasted that he can get any concession that he wants in Mexico, barring alone such a one as would antagonize other foreign interests equally powerful. Dr. Pearson owns the electric railway system of the Federal District and furnishes the vast quantity of electric light and power used in that political division of Mexico. Among other things, he is also a strong power along the American border, where he and his associates own the Mexico Northwestern Railway and several smaller lines, as well as vast tracts of lands and huge lumber interests. In Chihuahua he is establishing a large steel plant and in El Paso, just across the line, he is building a half million dollar sawmill as a part of his Mexican projects.

S. Pearson & Son have been given so many valuable concessions in Mexico that they were responsible for the invention of the term, "the partners of Diaz." Through concessions given them by the government they are in possession of vast oil lands, most of which are unexploited, yet so many of which are producing that the company recently gave out a statement that it would hereafter be in a position to supply its entire trade with Mexican oil. Its distributing company, "El Aguila," contains on its directorate a number of Diaz's closest friends. Pearson & Son, also, have monopolized the contracts for deepening and improving the harbors of Mexico. Since their advent into the country some fourteen years ago the government treasury has paid to this concern $200,000,000 for work on the harbors of Salina Cruz and Coatzacoalcos, and the Isthmus railroad. This amount, a government engineer told me personally, is an even double the price that should have been paid for the work. In 1908 Diaz's congress appropriated $50,000,000 to install an extensive irrigation project on the Rio Nasus, for the benefit of the cotton barons of the Laguna district in the State of Durango. Immediately afterwards the Pearson company organized a subsidiary irrigation concern with a capital of one million. The new company drew up plans for a dam, whereupon the Diaz congress promptly voted $10,000,000 out of the $50,000,000 to be paid to the Pearsons for their dam.

In this chapter I have attempted to give the reader an idea of the means which General Diaz employed to attract support to his government. To sum up, by means of a careful placing of public offices, public contracts and special privileges of multitudinous sorts, Diaz absorbed all of the more powerful men and interests within his sphere and made them a part of his machine. Gradually the country passed into the hands of his officeholders, their friends, and foreigners. And for this the people paid, not only with their lands, but with their flesh and blood. They paid in peonage and slavery. For this they forfeited liberty, democracy and the blessings of progress. And because human beings do not forfeit these things without a struggle, there was necessarily another function of the Diaz machine than that of distributing gifts, another material that went into the structure of his government than favors. Privilege—repression; they go hand in hand. In this chapter I have attempted to sketch a picture of the privilege attached to the Diaz system; in the succeeding chapter I shall attempt to define its elements of repression.

Repressive Elements of the Diaz Machine

Americans launching upon business in Mexico are usually given about the same treatment at the hands of local authorities as they have been used to at home. The readier hand for graft is more than overbalanced by the easier plucking of the special privilege plum. Sometimes an American falls into disfavor and is cautiously persecuted, but it is seldom. And if he is there to get rich quickly, as is usual, he judges the Mexican government by the aid it gives to his ambition. To him the system of Diaz is the wisest, most modern and most beneficent on the face of the earth.

To be wholly fair to Diaz and his system, I must confess that I am not judging Mexico from the viewpoint of the American investor. I am estimating it from its effects upon the mass of Mexicans generally, who, in the end, must surely determine the destiny of Mexico. From the viewpoint of the common Mexican the government is wholly the opposite of beneficent; it is a slave-driver, a thief, a murderer; it has neither justice nor mercy—nothing but exploitation.

In order to impose his rule upon an unwilling people General Diaz found it necessary not only to reward the powerful of his country and to be free and easy with the foreigner, but also to strip the people of their liberties to the point of nakedness. He took away from them all governmental powers, rights and securities, and all powers to demand the return of these things. Why do nations universally demand a popular form of government? Never until I saw Mexico did I appreciate to its full the reason why. The answer is that life under any other system is intolerable. The common interests can be conserved only by the common voice. Governments by individuals not responsible to the mass invariably result in robbery of the mass and debasement of the nation. The upbuilding of any people requires certain social guarantees which are not possible except under a government in which considerable numbers take part.

When General Diaz led his army into the Mexican capital back in 1876 he declared himself provisional president. Shortly afterwards he held a pretended election and declared himself constitutional president. By a "pretended election" I mean that he put his soldiers in possession of the polls and prevented, by intimidation, anyone from appearing as a candidate against him. Thus was he "elected" unanimously. And, except for one term, when he voluntarily relinquished the office, he has continued to elect himself unanimously in much the same way.

I do not need to dwell on the election farces of Mexico, since the warmest flatterers of Diaz admit that Mexico has not had one real election during the past thirty-four years. But to those who desire some statement of the matter it will only be necessary to point out the results of the Mexican "elections." Can anyone imagine a nation of some 15,000,000 with, say 3,000,000 persons of voting age, all preferring the same man for their chief executive, not only once, but year after year and decade after decade? Just picture such a condition obtaining in the United States, for example. Could anyone imagine Mr. Taft being re-elected by a unanimous vote? Mr. Roosevelt was undoubtedly the most popular president this country

ever had. Could anybody imagine Mr. Roosevelt being re-elected by
a unanimous vote? Moreover, could anyone imagine a country of
15,000,000 souls in which ambition never stirred the heart of more
than one individual with the desire to stand before the people as a
candidate for the highest office in the nation?

And yet this is exactly the condition we find in Mexico. Eight
times Don Porfirio has been seated as "president." Eight times he
has been elected "unanimously." Never has an opponent stood
against him at the polls.

And the story of the presidential succession is repeated in the
states. Re-election without contest is a rule which has seen exceedingly few exceptions. The governor of the state holds office for life,
unless for some reason he loses favor with Don Porfirio, which is
seldom. A member of the Mexican upper class once put the situation to me quite aptly. Said he: "Death is the only anti-re-electionist
in Mexico." The chief reason why the states are not governed by
men who have been in office for thirty-four years is because those
who were first put in have died and it has become necessary to fill
their places with others. As it is, Colonel Prospero Cahuantzi has
ruled the State of Tlaxcala for the whole Porfirian period. General
Aristeo Mercado has ruled the State of Michoacan for over twenty-
five years. Teodoro Dehesa has governed the State of Veracruz for
twenty-five years. When deposed in 1909, General Bernardo Reyes
had governed the State of Nuevo Leon for nearly twenty-five years.
General Francisco Canedo, General Abraham Bandala and Pedro
Rodriguez ruled the States of Sinaloa, Tabasco and Hidalgo, respectively, for over twenty years. General Luis Terrazas was governor
of Chihuahua for over twenty years, while Governors Martinez,
Cardenas and Obregon Gonzalez ruled the States of Puebla, Coahuila and Guanajuato, respectively, for about fifteen years.

Diaz's system of government is very simple, once it is explained.
The president, the governor, the *jefe politico*—these three names
represent all the power in the country. In Mexico there is but one

governmental power—the executive. The other two departments exist in name only. Not one elective office remains in the country. All are appointive. And through the appointive power the three executives mentioned control the entire situation. The word of these three officials in his particular sphere—the president in the twenty-seven states and two territories, the governor in his state, the *jefe politico* in his district—is the law of the land. Not one of the three is required to answer to the people for his acts. The governor must answer to the president and the *jefe politico* to the governor and the president. It is the most perfect one-man system on earth.

Of course such conditions were not established without a struggle. Neither can they be maintained without continued struggle. Autocracy cannot be created by fiat. Slavery cannot exist merely by decree of a ruler. There must be an organization and a policy to compel such things. There must be a military organization armed to the teeth. There must be police and police spies. There must be expropriations and imprisonments for political purposes. And there must be murder—murder all the time. No autocracy can exist without murder. Autocracy feeds upon murder. It has never been otherwise, and, thanks to human nature as we find it, never can be.

The succeeding two chapters are to be devoted to sketching the extirpation of political movements having for their purpose the reestablishment of republican institutions in Mexico. But first it seems well to define the public powers and institutions which are employed in this unholy work. These consist of:

The army.

The *rurale* forces.

The police.

The *acordada*.

The *Ley Fuga*.

Quintana Roo, the "Mexican Siberia."

The prisons.

The *jefes politicos*.

In a published interview issued during the Liberal rebellion in 1908, Vice-President Corral announced that the government had more than 50,000 soldiers who were ready to take the field at an hour's notice. In these figures he must have included the *rurale* forces, for employes of the War Department have since assured me that the regular army numbered less, almost an exact 40,000, in fact. On paper the Mexican army is, then, smaller than ours, but, according to estimates of the actual size of our army published by American experts during the past three years, it is larger, and in proportion to the population it is at least five times larger. General Diaz's excuse for the maintenance of such a large army has always been a hint that the country might at any time find itself in danger of invasion by the United States. That his purpose was not so much to prepare against invasion as against internal revolution is evidenced by the fact that, instead of fortifying the border, he fortified inland cities. Moreover, he keeps the bulk of the army concentrated near the large centers of population and his best and most extensive equipment consists of mountain batteries, recognized as specially well adapted to internal warfare.

Mexico is actually policed by the army and to this end the country is divided into ten military zones, three commanderies and fourteen *jefaturas*. One sees soldiers everywhere. There is not an important city in the country that has not its army barracks, and the barracks are situated in the heart of the city, where they are always ready. The discipline of war is maintained at all times, the presence of the soldiers and their constant drilling are a perpetual threat to the people. And they are used upon the people often enough to keep always fresh in the memories of the people the fact that the threat is not an empty one. Such readiness for war as is maintained on the part of the Mexican troops is not known in this country. There is no red tape when it comes to fighting and troops arrive at a scene of trouble in an incredibly short time. As one example, at the time of the Liberal rebellion in the fall of 1906 the Liberals attacked the city of Acayucan, Veracruz. Despite the fact that the city is situated in a comparatively isolated part of the tropics, the government concentrated 4,000 soldiers on the town within twenty-four hours after the first alarm.

As an instrument of repression, the Mexican army is employed effectively in two separate and distinct ways. It is an engine of massacre and it is an exile institution, a jail-house, a concentration camp for the politically undesirable.

This second function of the army abides in the fact that more than 95 per cent of the enlisted men are drafted, and drafted for the particular reason that they are politically undesirable citizens, or that they are good subjects for graft on the part of the drafter. The drafter is usually the *jefe politico*. A judge—at the instance of the executive authority—sometimes sentences a culprit to the army instead of to jail, and a governor—as at Cananea—sometimes personally superintends the placing of considerable bodies of men in the army, but as a rule the *jefe politico* is the drafting officer and upon him there is no check. He has no system other than to follow his own sweet will. He drafts laborers who dare to strike, editors who criticize the government, farmers who resist exorbitant taxation, and any other ordinary citizens who may present opportunities for graft.

As a dumping ground for the politically undesirable, the conditions within the army are ideal, from the point of view of the government. The men are prisoners rather than soldiers and they are treated as such. For this reason the Mexican army has gained the title of "The National Chain-gang." While in Diaz-land I visited a number of army barracks. The barracks at Rio Blanco are typical. Here, ever since the Rio Blanco strike, 600 soldiers and 200 *rurales* have been quartered within the shadow of the great mill, in barracks and upon ground furnished by the company, an hourly menace to the miserably exploited workers there.

At Rio Blanco a little captain showed us about—De Lara and I— at the behest of an officer of the manufacturing company. *El Senor*

Capitan informed us that the pay of the Mexican soldier, with rations, is $1.90 per month in American money and that the soldier is always expected to spend the major portion of this for extra food, as the food furnished is of too small a variety and too scarce a quantity to satisfy any human being. The captain confirmed the reports that I had often heard to the effect that the soldier, in all his five years service, never has an hour to himself away from the eye of an officer, that he is as much a prisoner in his barracks as is the life-termer in a penitentiary.

The proportion of involuntary soldiers the captain estimated at 98 per cent. Often, said he, the soldiers, crazy for freedom, break and run like escaping convicts. And they are hunted down like convicts.

But the thing that struck me most forcibly during my visit was that the little captain, in the hearing of half a company of men, told us that the soldiers were of the lowest class of Mexicans, were good for nothing, a bad lot, etc., apologizing thus in order to make us understand that in time of war the quality of the army would be much improved. The soldiers heard and failed to look pleasant and I decided right there that the loyalty of the Mexican army stands upon a very flimsy basis—merely fear of death—and that in case of any future rebellion against the dictatorship the army can be counted upon to revolt in a body as soon as the rebellion develops any appreciable strength—that is, enough strength to afford the deserters a fair chance for their lives.

The territory of Quintana Roo has been characterized as one of the "Siberias of Mexico," from the fact that to it, as convict-soldiers, are consigned thousands of political suspects and labor agitators. Sent there ostensibly to fight the Maya Indians, they are treated so harshly that probably not one per cent of them ever see their homes again. I did not succeed in penetrating personally to Quintana Roo, but I have heard accounts of it from so many authentic sources that I have no doubt whatever that my estimate of it is correct. One of these sources of information I shall quote at some length, a distinguished government physician who for three years was Chief of Sanitary Service with the army in the territory.

"For thirty years," said this man, "there has been an army of from 2,000 to 3,000 men constantly in the field against the Maya Indians. These soldiers are made up almost entirely of political suspects and even many of the officers are men who have been detailed to duty in the territory only because the government has some reason for wanting to get rid of them. Quintana Roo is the most unhealthy part of Mexico, but the soldiers die from five to ten times as fast as necessary because of the grafting of their chief, General Bravo. During the first two years I was there the death rate was 100 per cent a year, for in that period more than 4,000 soldiers died of starvation and sickness induced by starvation!

"For month after month," said this physician, "I have known the deaths to average thirty a day. For every soldier killed by a Maya at least one hundred die of starvation or sickness. General Bravo steals the commissary money and starves the soldiers with the connivance of the federal government. More than 2,000 have died of acute starvation alone during the past seven years, since General Bravo took command. Not only that, but Bravo steals the cremation money. The soil of the peninsula, you must know, is rocky, the hardpan is close to the surface and it is not practical to bury the dead. The government appropriates money to buy oil for cremation, but Bravo steals this money and leaves the bodies to lie in the sun and rot away!"

Because it would result in his imprisonment I cannot publish the name of this authority. I feel perfectly free, however, to name Colonel Francisco B. Cruz, chief deporter of Yaquis. Colonel Cruz told me that in three years General Bravo had saved $10,000,000 from money grafted off the army in Quintana Roo. The fact that nearly all the deaths of soldiers was the result of starvation was proven in the year 1902 to 1903, when General Bravo took a vacation and General Vega had command. General Vega stole no food or medicine or oil money and as a result he reduced the number of deaths from thirty a day to an average of three a day.

"In its campaign against the Mayas," the former Sanitary Chief told me, "the government built a railroad sixty kilometres long. This railroad is known among the soldiers as 'The Alley of Death,' for it is said that every tie cost five lives in the building. When this road was built many prisoners were taken from the military prison of San Juan de Ulua to do the work. To encourage them to toil all were promised that their sentences would be cut in half, but after a few weeks in the hands of Bravo the majority begged—but in vain—to be returned to Ulua, which is the most dreaded of all houses of incarceration in Mexico. These unfortunate prisoners were starved and when they staggered from weakness they were beaten, some being beaten to death. Some of them committed suicide at the first opportunity, as did many of the soldiers—fifty of them, while I was there."

Fancy a soldier committing suicide! Fancy the cruel conditions that would lead fifty soldiers among 2,000 to commit suicide in the space of three years!

As to the graft features of the army drafting system, as I have suggested, the *jefe politico* selects the names in his own way in the privacy of his own office and no one may question his methods. Wherefore he waxes rich. Since—allowing for a high death rate— some 10,000 men are drafted every year, it will be seen that the graft possibilities of the system are enormous. The horror of the army is used by the *jefe* to squeeze money out of wage-workers and small property-holders. Unless the victim is drafted for political reasons, the system permits the drafted person to buy another to take his place—provided the drafting officer is willing. This option on the part of the *jefe* is used as a great money-getter, since the *jefe* is never willing unless the victim buys the *jefe* as well as the substitute. Usually it is not necessary to buy the substitute, but only the *jefe politico*. In some districts it is said to be a regular practice to keep tab on the higher-paid class of wage-laborers and when they are paid after a long job, to drag them to jail and tell them that they have been drafted, then, a day or two later, to send word that $100, more or less, has been fixed as the price of their liberty. I was told of an instance in which a carpenter was drafted in this way five times in the space of three years. Four times he parted with his money, sums ranging from $50 to $100, but the fifth time he lost courage and permitted himself to be led away to the barracks.

The *rurales* are mounted police usually selected from the criminal classes, well equipped and comparatively well paid, whose energies have been turned to robbing and killing for the government. There are federal *rurales* and state *rurales*, the total of the two running somewhere between 7,000 and 9,000. They are divided among the various states in about an equal proportion to the population, but are utilized most in the rural districts. The *rurales* are the special rough riders of the *jefe politicos* and they are given almost unlimited powers to kill at their own discretion. Investigation of wanton killings by *rurales* working singly or in squads is almost never made and the victim must stand well indeed with the government before punishment is meted out to the murderer.

In Mexico it is a small town that has no soldiers or *rurales* and a smaller town that has no regular *gendarmes*. The City of Mexico has over 2,000, or twice as many as New York in comparison to its size, and the other municipalities are equipped in proportion. At night the *gendarmes* have little red lanterns which they set in the middle of the streets and hover near. One sees these lanterns, one at each corner, twinkling down the entire length of the principal streets. There is a system of lantern signals and when one lamp begins to swing the signal is carried along and in a trice every *gendarme* on the street knows what has happened.

While the "plain clothes" department of the Mexican police is a comparatively insignificant affair, there exists, outside of and beyond it, a system of secret police on a very extensive scale. An

American newspaperman employed on an English daily of the
capital once told me: "There are twice as many secret police as regular police. You see a uniformed policeman standing in the middle
of the street. That is all you see, or at least all you notice. But leaning against the wall of that alley entrance is a man whom you take
to be a loafer; over on the other side lounges a man whom you think
is a peon. Just start something and then try to get away. Both of
those men will be after you. There is no getting away in Mexico;
every alley is guarded as well as every street!

"Why," said he, "they know your business as well as you do yourself. They talk with you and you never suspect. When you cross
the border they take your name and business and address, and before
you've reached the capital they know whether you've told the truth
or not. They know what you're here for and have decided what
they're going to do about it."

Perhaps this man overstated the case—the exact truth of these
matters is hard to get at—but I know that it is impossible to convince
the average Mexican that the secret police system of his country is
not a colossal institution.

The *acordada* is an organization of secret assassins, a sort of secret
police, attached to the government of each of the Mexican states. It
consists of a *jefe de acordada* and anywhere from a half dozen to a
half hundred subordinates. Personal enemies of the governor or of
the *jefes politicos*, political suspects and highwaymen or others suspected of crime but against whom there is no evidence, are frequently put out of the way by the *acordada*. The names of the
marked men are furnished by the officials and the members of the
society are sent about the state with orders to kill quietly and without noise. Two notable cases where the *acordada* are reported as
having killed extensively are those of the days following the strikes
at Cananea and Rio Blanco. Personally I am acquainted with a Mexican whose brother was killed by the *acordada* for doing no more
than shouting "Viva Ricardo Flores Magon." I know also of a son of

a general high up in the councils of the Mexican government who became a *sub-jefe de acordada* in the state of Coahuila. He was a wild young fellow who had been put out of the army for acts of insubordination toward a superior officer. But his father was a friend of Diaz and Diaz himself appointed the youth to the *acordada* job, which paid a salary of three hundred *pesos* a month. This man was given two assistants and was sent out with orders to "kill quietly along the border" any and all persons whom he might suspect of connection with the Liberal Party. No check whatever was placed upon him. He was to kill at his own discretion.

The *acordada* at times work extensively even in the Mexican capital, which more nearly approaches the modern in its police methods than probably any other city in the country. Before the Liberal rebellion of 1906 the government, through spies, secured the detailed plans of the rebels, as well as the names of hundreds of the participants, and a large number of these were killed. What was done by the *acordada* in Mexico City at that time may be guessed by a statement made to me by a well known newspaperman of Mexico City. Said he: "I have it from the most reliable source that during the week preceding September 16 not less than 2,000 suspects were made away with quietly by the secret police and special deputies—the *acordada*—so quietly that not a line in regard to it has ever been published to this day!"

I hesitate to print this statement because it is too colossal for me to believe, and I do not expect the reader to believe it. But I have no doubt whatever that it was partially true; that, say, several score were killed at this time and in this way. Liberals whom I have met have often spoken to me of friends who had suddenly disappeared and never been heard of again and many of these were supposed to have been done away with by the *acordada*.

The *Ley Fuga*, or law of flight, is a method of killing resorted to by all branches of the Mexican police power. It was originated by order of General Diaz, who decreed that his police might shoot any

prisoners who should try to escape while under guard. While it may
not have originated for that purpose, this rule came to be used as
one of the means of putting to death persons against whom the government had not the shadow of another excuse for killing. The
marked man is simply arrested, taken to a lonely spot and there shot.
The matter is kept quiet, if possible, but if a situation should arise
that demands an explanation, the report is given out that the victim
had attempted to escape and had brought his fate upon himself.
Thus it is freely asserted that thousands of lives have been taken
during the past thirty-four years. Today instances of the *Ley Fuga*
are frequently reported in the Mexican press.

Many political outlaws end their days in prison. Among the Mexican prisons there are two whose horrors stand out far above the
others—San Juan de Ulua and Belem.

During both of my trips to Mexico made during 1908 and 1909
I put forth desperate efforts to secure admission as a visitor to Belem.
I saw the governor of the Federal District; I saw the American ambassador; I tried to enter with a prison physician. But I was never
able to travel farther than the inner door.

Through that door I could see into the central court, where ranged
hundreds of human beings made wild beasts by the treatment they
received, ragged, filthy, starving, wolfish wrecks of men—a sight
calculated to provoke a raucous laugh at the solemn declarations of
certain individuals that Mexico has a civilized government.

But farther than that inner court I could not go. I was permitted
to visit other prisons in Mexico, but not Belem. When I pressed
His Excellency, the Governor, he admitted that it was not safe. "On
account of the *malas condiciones*, the vile conditions," he said, "it
would not do. Why," he told me, "only a short time ago the vice-
president, Senor Corral, dared to make a hurried visit to Belem. He
contracted typhus and nearly died. You cannot go."

I told him that I had heard of Americans being permitted to visit
Belem. But he was unable to remember. Doubtless those other

Porfirio Díaz was the strong man of Mexico for thirty-odd years.

He was still active as he approached eighty.

His strength lay in a large army . . .

. . . and in the famed *rurales*.

Under Díaz, Mexico was called "the mother of foreigners and the stepmother of Mexicans." United States Ambassador Powell Clayton was a favorite son.

But in reality Mexico was a good mother to the rich of all nationalities, including Mexicans; they held charity affairs, . . .

. . . attended the races, . . .

. . . and went shopping.

The great mass of people, on the other hand, were indescribably poor.

There were the urban poor . . .

. . . and the rural poor, . . .

. . . who were mercilessly driven by brutal overseers.

A few were able to make a career in the lower ranks of the army.

Those at the bottom were forced to scavenge in the city dumps.

Their worldly goods were so few that a family could move its belongings in a barrow.

Life was dreary, but some found consolation in a glass of pulque.

From time to time the pot boiled over: the Río Blanco textile workers went on strike.

After a general massacre they were defeated and their pitiful belongings were confiscated.

The railroad workers went on strike, but they, too, were defeated.

The Cananea miners struck but were shot down by gunmen brought in from the United States.

The Yaqui Indians were always in a state of revolt against Díaz.

But Díaz always won.

In time, Mexican intellectuals became concerned about the plight of Mexico, and short-lived radical newspapers were founded.

The Mexican Liberal Party came into being; its most noted leader was Ricardo Flores Magón.

Díaz feared the Liberal Party and very soon he had driven Ricardo and his brother Enrique, . . .

... along with Antonio I. Villarreal ...

... and Librado Rivera, from Mexican soil and into the United States.

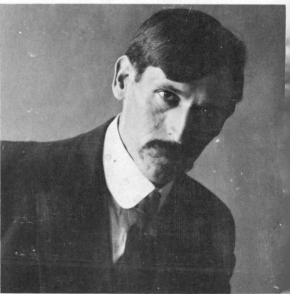

Job Harriman defended them when they were arrested for alleged violation of the neutrality laws.

While Ricardo and his colleagues were in jail in Los Angeles they were interviewed by John Kenneth Turner.

Turner and his wife Ethel soon became associated with the Los Angeles junta of the Mexican Liberal Party.

John Murray, a member of the Turner group, was sent to Mexico to get first-hand information.

After Murray's return, Turner and Lázaro Gutiérrez de Lara made an extensive trip in Mexico.

These expeditions were financed by Elizabeth Darling Trowbridge.

President Francisco I. Madero told Turner in an interview in early 1913 that *Barbarous Mexico* had contributed greatly to the success of the Revolution.

Americans were too well known—they were too much involved in Mexican affairs—to leave any danger of their coming out and telling the truth of what they saw. My credentials were not satisfactory enough to permit me to see Belem.

But I know Belem fairly well, I think, for I have talked with persons who have seen Belem as prisoners and come out of its horrors alive. Editors, many of them were; and I have talked with others—officials, prison physicians, and I have read the newspapers of Mexico.

Suffice it, however, to put down some bare and naked facts. Belem is the general prison for the Federal District, which comprises the Mexican capital and some surrounding suburbs, approximating, in all, a population of 600,000 people. It is alike city jail, county jail and penitentiary, except that there is also in the district another penitentiary, which is distinguished from Belem by confining within its walls only criminals who have been sentenced to more than eight years confinement. The penitentiary—which is so designated—is a modern institution, decently built and sewered. The prisoners are few and they are fairly well fed. Visitors are always welcome at the penitentiary, for it is principally for show. When you hear a traveler extolling the prison system of Mexico put it down that he was conducted through the Federal District penitentiary only—that he does not know of Belem.

Belem is a musty old convent which was turned into a prison by the simple act of herding some thousands of persons within its walls. It is not large enough decently to house five hundred inmates, but frequently it houses more than five thousand. These five thousand are given a daily ration of biscuit and beans insufficient in quantity to keep an ordinary person alive for many weeks. The insufficiency of this ration is so well realized by the prison officials that a regular system of feeding from the outside has grown up. Daily the friends and relatives of prisoners bring them baskets of food, in order that they may live through their term of confinement. Of course it is a terrible drain on the poor, but the system serves its purpose—except for those hundreds of unfortunates who have no friends on the outside. These starve to death without a finger being raised to help them.

"Within three days after entering Belem," a Mexican prison physician informed me, "every inmate contracts a skin disease, a terrible itch which sets the body on fire. This disease is entirely the result of the filthy conditions of the place. Every year," he continued, "the prison goes through an epidemic of typhus, which kills an average of at least ten per cent of the inmates. Within Belem there is no system of order among the prisoners. The weak are at the mercy of the strong. Immediately you enter as a prisoner you are set upon by a horde of half-crazed men who tear the clothes from your back, take away your valuables, if you have any, and usually commit nameless crimes upon your person, while officials of the prison stand grinning by. The only way to save yourself in Belem is to turn wild beast like the rest, and even then you must be strong —very strong."

Should I give the name of this physician every official at the national capital would instantly recognize him as a man of high standing with the government. I shall not name him only because if I did he also would go to Belem as a prisoner. Such stories as his I heard from too many widely different sources to be able to doubt them. The stories of the Belem epidemics always get more or less into the Mexican papers. I remember that during my first visit to Mexico, in the fall of 1908, the papers reported an epidemic of typhus. For the first three days the number of new cases were daily recorded, but after that the news was suppressed. The condition threatened to become too great a scandal, for on the third day there were 176 new cases!

According to an old prison director whom I interviewed, at least twenty per cent of the prisoners at Belem contract tuberculosis. This prison director spent many years in the prison at Puebla. There, he says, seventy-five per cent of the men who go into the place come out, if they ever come out, with tuberculosis.

Torture such as was employed in the Middle Ages is used in Belem to secure confessions. When a man is taken to the police station, if he is suspected of a felony he is strung up by the thumbs until he tells. Another method used is that of refusing the prisoner drink. He is given food but no water until he chokes. Often prisoners declare before the judge that they have been tortured into confession, but no investigation is made. There are—inevitably—records of innocent men who have confessed to murder in order to escape the torture of the thumbs or of the thirst. While I was in Mexico two Americans suspected of robbery were reported in the newspapers as having been arrested, their wrists strapped to the bars of their cells, and their finger nails jerked out with steel pincers. This incident was reported to our State Department, but no action was taken.

San Juan de Ulua is an old military fortress situated in the harbor of Veracruz—a fortress which has been turned into a prison. Officially San Juan de Ulua is known as a military prison, but in fact it is a political prison, a prison for political suspects, and so choice is the company that resides therein—resides, but is ever changing, for the members die fast—and so personal is the attention given to this place by President Diaz, that throughout Mexico San Juan de Ulua is popularly known as the "private prison of Diaz."

San Juan de Ulua is built of cement, the prison cells are under the sea and the salt water seeps through upon the prisoners, some of whom lie, half-naked and half-starved, in dark dungeons too small to permit of a full grown man lying down in comfort. To San Juan de Ulua was sent Juan Sarabia, vice-president of the Liberal Party, Margarita Martinez, a leader of the strike at Rio Blanco, Lazaro Puente, Carlos Humbert, Abraham Salcido, Leonardo Villarreal, Bruno Trevino and Gabriel Rubio, a sextet of gentlemen handed over to Mexico by the United States government at the request of the former as "undesirable immigrants"; Caesar Canales,

Juan de la Torre, Serrano, Ugalde, Marquez, and scores of other
leaders of the Liberal movement. Since entering those grey walls few
of these men or women have ever been heard of again. It is not
known whether they are dead or alive, whether they were shot
beyond the walls, whether they died of disease and starvation or
whether they are still eking out a miserable existence there, hoping
against hope that a freer government will come and set them free.
They have never been heard of because no political prisoner in San
Juan de Ulua is ever permitted to communicate in any way with his
friends or with the outside world. They cross the harbor in a little
boat, they disappear within the grey walls and that is all. Their
friends never learn how they get on, nor when they die or how.

Of the official assassins of Mexico the *jefe politico* is the arch fiend.
The *jefe politico* commands the local police and *rurales*, directs the
acordada and frequently gives orders to the regular troops. While,
because of government control of the press, comparatively few
crimes of the *jefes politicos* become public, yet during my most recent visit to Mexico—during the winter and spring of 1909—two
wholesale killings which were prompted by *jefes politicos* were
widely reported in the newspapers of that country. One was that of
Tehuitzingo, where sixteen citizens were executed without trial, and
the other was that of Velardena, where, for holding a street parade
in defiance of the *jefe politico*, several were shot down in the streets
and a number variously estimated as from twelve to thirty-two were
arrested, lined up and shot, and buried in trenches which they had
been compelled to dig previously with their own hands.

A comment of El Pais, a conservative Catholic daily of the capital
on the Tehuitzingo affair, published in April, was as follows:

> Terrible accounts have reached this capital as to what is taking place
> at Tehuitzingo, District of Acatlan, State of Puebla. It is insistently
> reported that sixteen citizens have been executed without trial and that
> many others will be condemned to twenty years' confinement in the
> fortress of San Juan de Ulua.

What are the causes that have given rise to this barbarous persecution, which has dyed our soil anew with the people's blood?

It is the fierce, infamous *caciquismo* which oppresses the people with a heavy yoke and which has deprived them of all the benefits of peace.

We ask, in the name of law and of humanity that this hecatomb cease; we ask that the guilty parties be tried fairly and calmly according to the law. But among those guilty parties should be included those who provoked the disturbance, those who drove the people to frenzy by trampling their rights. If the *jefe politico* sought to defy the law by dictating an election, he is guilty or more guilty than the rioters and ought to be made to appear with them before the authorities to answer for his acts.

This is about as violent an outburst as is ever permitted to appear in a Mexican publication, and there are few papers that would dare go this far. Had El Pais wished to charge the guilt to General Diaz as the founder and perpetuator of the little czardom of the *jefe politicos*, it would not have dared to do so, for in Mexico the king can do no wrong; there is no publication in the country so strong that it would not be suppressed *at once* did it directly criticize the head of the government. The comment of El Tiempo, another leading conservative daily of the capital, on the Velardena massacre, which appeared also in April, was:

These irregular executions are a cause of profound dissatisfaction and ought to be put a stop to at once for the sake of the prestige of the authorities; and in order to attain that end it is necessary that the authors of such outrages should be severely chastised, as we hope that those who are responsible for the sanguinary scenes that have been witnessed at Velardena, and which have occasioned so much horror and indignation throughout the republic, will be.

Let it not be said that Velardena is an isolated case without precedents. Only to mention a few of the cases that are fresh in the public memory, there is the Papantla affair, the affair at Acayucan, the shootings at Orizaba at the time of the strike, the shootings at Colima, of which the press has been talking just of late, and the frequent applica-

tion of the *ley fuga*, of which the most recent instance occurred at Cali-
maya, Tenango, State of Mexico.

In closing this chapter perhaps I can do no better than to quote an
item which appeared in The Mexican Herald, the leading daily published in English, February 15, 1910. Though the facts were perfectly well authenticated, the Herald dared to print the story only
on the authority of another paper, and it presented the matter in
such mild and cautious terms that it will require a careful reading
to bring out the full horror of the deed. Here is the item:

The Pais gives the following story, the details of which it qualifies as
too monstrous for even Zelaya to attribute to Estrada Cabrera:

Luis Villasenor, prefect of Cualcoman, Michoacan, recently shot without trial an old man because his son committed a murder. The victim
in this case was Ignacio Chavez Guizar, one of the principal merchants
of the place.

Some days ago a member of the rural police (a *rurale*) arrived at the
house of the deceased in a state of intoxication and began to insult and
abuse the family. A quarrel succeeded, in which the policeman was shot
by Jose Chavez.

The prefect of police arrived on the scene of the trouble and arrested
the father and another son, Benjamin, the slayer having made his escape, and took them to the police station. That was the last seen of them.
Soon the people of the town began to inquire what had happened to
them. The story was spread that they had escaped from prison. But a
relative, a nephew of the deceased father, having a certain suspicion
that this story was not true, opened what appeared to him a recently
made grave, near the police station, and there found the corpses of the
two men who had been recently arrested. The prefect, not having been
able to capture Jose or to learn where he was, had made the father and
brother suffer for his crime.

Commenting on this story, the Pais calls for the punishment of the
author and the guarantee of the carrying out of the laws of the country.

The Crushing of Opposition Parties

Men and women on our continent are daily suffering death, imprisonment or exile for contending for those political rights which we have considered as ours since the birth of our country, rights of free speech, of free press, the right of assembly, the right to vote to decide who shall hold the political offices and govern the land, the right to be secure in person and property. For these things hundreds of men and women have died within the past twelve months, tens of thousands within the past thirty years, in a country divided from ours only by a shallow river and an imaginary geographical line.

In Mexico today are being lived life stories such as carry one's imagination back to the days of the French Revolution and the times when constitutional government, that giant which was destined to complete the change from the Middle Ages to Modernity, was being born. In those days men yielded up their lives for republicanism. Men are doing the same today in Mexico. The repressive part of the Diaz governmental machine which I described in the last previous chapter—the army, the *rurales*, the ordinary police, the secret police, the *acordada*—are perhaps one-fifth for protection against common criminals and four-fifths for the suppression of democratic movements among the people. The deadly certainty of this repressive machine of Diaz is probably not equaled anywhere in the world, not even in Russia. I remember a trusted Mexican official once summing up to me the feeling of the Mexican people, taught them by experience, on this thing. Said he: "It is possible that a murderer may escape the police here, that a highwayman may get away, but a political offender never—it is not possible for one to escape!"

I myself have observed numerous instances of the deadly fear in which the secret police and the government assassin are held even by those who would seem to have no cause for fear. Notable among these is the panic which overtook the family of a friend with whom I was staying—his brother, sister, sister-in-law and nephew and niece—when the secret police surrounded their house in the capital and waited for my friend to come out. They were middle-class Mexicans of the most intelligent sort, this family, very well known and highly respected, and yet their fright was pitiful. Now they dashed this way and that, now to a window and now to a door, wringing their hands. Now they huddled together, verbally painting the dire calamities that were sure to descend not only upon the hunted one, but upon their own heads because he had been found with them. My friend had committed no crime. He had not been identified with the revolutionists, he had merely expressed sympathy for them, and yet his family could see nothing but death for him. And after the fugitive had escaped by jumping through a window and climbing over house-tops, the head of the family, speaking of his own danger, said to me: "I myself may go to jail for a time while they try to compel me to tell where my brother is hiding. If I do not go it will be only because the government has decided to respect me for my position and my influential friends, yet hourly I am expecting the tap on the arm that will tell me to go."

The case of most extreme fear which I observed was that of a wealthy and beautiful woman, wife of an official of the Rio Blanco mills, with whom De Lara and I took dinner one day. The official drank deeply of wine, and as the meal was near an end his tongue loosened and he spoke of matters which, for the sake of his own safety, he should have guarded. The wife sat opposite him, and as he spoke of government murders of which he knew her face blanched and with her eyes she tried to warn him to be more careful. Finally I turned my face away, and, glancing sidewise, saw her take the opportunity to bend forward over the table and shake a trembling, jeweled finger in his face. Again and again she tried skillfully to turn the conversation, but without success, until finally, unable to control herself longer, she sprang forward, and, clapping a hand over her husband's lips, tried to dam back the fearsome words he was saying. The animal terror on that woman's face I can never forget.

Fear so widespread and so extreme as I met with cannot be the result of imagined dangers. There must be something behind it, and there is. Secret killing is constantly going on in Mexico, but to what extent no one will ever know. It is asserted in some quarters that there are more political executions going on right now than ever before, but that they are more cleverly and secretly done than ever before. Whether that is true or not I do not know. Certainly the press is better controlled than ever before. The apparent quiescence of Mexico is entirely forced by means of club, pistol and knife.

Mexico has never really enjoyed political freedom. The country has merely had the promise of it. However, the promise has undoubtedly helped to keep patriotic Mexicans fighting for a fulfillment, however great the odds against them. When Porfirio Diaz captured the Mexican government in 1876 the Mexican battle for political freedom seemed won. The last foreign soldier had been driven out of the country, the throttling grip of the church on the state had been broken, the country had inaugurated a system of universal suffrage, it had adopted a constitution much like that of the United States, and finally, its president, one of the authors of the constitution, Lerdo de Tejada, was in the act of putting that consti-

tution in operation. The personal revolution of General Porfirio
Diaz, made successful by force of arms only after it had failed twice,
put a sudden stop to the progressive movement, and ever since that
time the country has gone back politically, year by year. If it were
humanly possibly to put a stop to the movement for democracy in a
country by killing the leaders and persecuting all connected with it,
democracy would long ago have been killed in Mexico, for the leaders of every political movement in opposition to President Diaz,
however peaceful their methods, however worthy their cause, have
either been put to death, imprisoned or hunted out of the country.
And as I shall show in the next chapter, this statement is literally
true down to the present day.

Briefly I will sketch some of the more important of these opposition movements. The first occurred toward the close of President
Diaz's first term in office and was a movement having for its purpose the re-election of Lerdo, who, upon Diaz's capture of the power,
had fled to the United States. The movement had not time to gain
any headway and come out in the open before it was crushed in the
most summary manner. The leaders were considered as conspirators
and were treated as if they were guilty of treasonable acts—worse,
in fact, for they were not even given a semblance of a trial. On a
night in June, 1879, nine men, prominent citizens of Veracruz, were
dragged from their beds, and on an order telegraphed from General
Diaz, *"Matalos en caliente,"* "Kill them in haste," Governor Mier y
Teran had them lined up against a wall and shot to death.

While this incident happened thirty years ago, it is perfectly authenticated, and the widow of General Teran exhibits to this day the
yellow paper upon which are inscribed the fatal words. The killing
is now known as the Massacre of Veracruz and is noted because of
the prominence of the victims rather than for the number of those
who lost their lives.

During the ten years following the Massacre of Veracruz two
Mexicans aspired at different times to oppose Diaz for the presi-

dency. One of these was General Ramon Corona, governor of Jalisco, and the other was General Garcia de la Cadena, ex-governor of Zacatecas. Neither lived to see "election day." While on his way home from a theatre one night Corona was stabbed to death by an assassin, who was in turn stabbed to death by a company of police which, by a strange coincidence, was waiting for him around a near corner. Cadena heard that assassins were on his trail and took flight. He tried to reach the United States, but was caught at Zacatecas and shot to death, being pierced by many bullets from the pistols of thugs, all of whom escaped. No one can prove who ordered the killing of Corona and Cadena, but it is easy to draw conclusions.

In 1891 Mexico was thrown into a ferment by the announcement of Diaz that he had decided to continue in power for still another term, a fourth one. An attempt was made to organize a movement in opposition, but it was beaten down by clubs and guns. Ricardo Flores Magon, the political refugee, took a student's part in this movement and was one of the many who suffered imprisonment for it. The choice of the opposition for presidency was Dr. Ignacio Martinez. Dr. Martinez was compelled to flee the country, and after a period spent in Europe he settled in Laredo, Texas, where he edited a newspaper in opposition to President Diaz. One evening Dr. Martinez was waylaid and shot down by a horseman who immediately afterwards crossed into Mexico and was seen to enter army barracks on the other side. It is a pretty well authenticated fact that on the night of the assassination the governor of the state of Nuevo Leon, who was at that time recognized as Diaz's right-hand man in the border states, received a telegram saying: "Your order obeyed."

The only movement which Diaz ever permitted to gain much headway in the matter of organization was the Liberal Party. The Liberal Party sprang into birth in the fall of 1900, after all danger of effective opposition against the dictator's entering upon a sixth term had been obviated. A speech delivered in Paris by the Bishop of San Luis Potosi, in which the priest declared that, in spite of the constitution and the laws of Mexico, the church in that country was in a most flourishing and satisfactory condition, was the immediate cause of the organization. Mexicans of all classes saw greater danger to the national welfare in the renascence of a church hierarchy than they did even in a dictatorship by a single individual, for death must some day end the rule of the man, while the life of the church is endless. They therefore once more took their lives in their hands and attempted to launch still another movement for the restoration of the republic.

In less than five months after the bishop's speech 125 Liberal clubs had arisen in all parts of the country, a half hundred newspapers were started, and a call was issued for a convention to be held in the city of San Luis Potosi on January 5, 1901.

The congress was held in the famous *Teatro de la Paz*. It was jammed with delegates and spectators, among the latter being many soldiers and *gendarmes*, while in the street below a battalion of soldiers was drawn up, ready to deal with the assembly should its voice be raised against the dictator.

Anything so radical as an armed rebellion was not spoken of, however, and the various speakers steered carefully away from any direct criticism of President Diaz. On the other hand, resolutions were adopted pledging the Liberals to pursue the campaign of reform only by peaceful means.

Nevertheless, as soon as it became evident that the Liberals were planning to nominate a candidate for the presidency, three years later, the government began operations. By Russian police methods, the clubs all over the country were broken up and the leading members were arrested on fictitious charges, imprisoned or forced into the army. A typical case was that of the club "Ponciano Arriaga," of San Luis Potosi, which formed the national center of the federation. On January 24, 1902, although other clubs had been violently broken up for doing so "Ponciano Arriaga" made bold to hold a public meeting. Here and there among the people were distributed soldiers and *gendarmes* in citizens' clothing, under the command of a prominent lawyer and congressman, an agent provocateur, who had been commissioned by the government to destroy the organization.

At a given moment, according to Librado Rivera, who was vice-secretary of the club, the agent provocateur jumped to his feet to protest against the work of the club, and at the signal the disguised soldiers and *gendarmes* feigned to join in the protest, smashing the chairs to pieces against the floor. Their leader fired some shots into the air, but the genuine audience and the members of the club did not make the least move lest they give some pretext for an attack, for they knew that the agent provocateur and his assistants were but staging a comedy in order to invite violence to themselves from some members of the club. Nevertheless, hardly were the shots fired when a crowd of policemen invaded the hall, striking right and left with their clubs. Camilo Arriaga, president of the club; Juan Sarabia, secretary; Professor Librado Rivera, vice-secretary, as well as twenty-five other members, were arrested and accused of fictitious crimes, such as resisting the police, sedition, and so on. The result was that they were all imprisoned for nearly a year and the club was dissolved.

Thus were dissolved the majority of the other clubs in the Liberal federation. The Liberal newspapers, public spokesmen of the clubs, were put out of business by the imprisonment of their editors and the destruction or confiscation of the printing plants. How many men and women lost their lives in the hunt of the Liberals which extended over the succeeding years will never be known. The jails, penitentiaries and military prisons were filled with them, thousands were impressed into the army and sent away to death in far Quintana Roo, while the *ley fuga* was called into requisition to get rid of men whom the government did not dare to execute openly and without excuse. In the prisons tortures such as would almost shame the Spanish Inquisition were resorted to.

Upon the organization of the Liberal Party some fifty newspapers sprang up to support it in different parts of the country. Every one of them was suppressed by the police. Ricardo Flores Magon once showed me a list of more than fifty newspapers that were suppressed and a list of more than a hundred editors that were jailed during the time he was struggling to publish a paper in Mexico. In his book Fornaro gives a list of thirty-nine newspapers that were persecuted or subjected to trial on trivial excuses in the year 1902 for the purpose of providing against any public agitation against a seventh term for President Diaz. During 1908 there were at least six outright suppressions, the newspapers to be put out of business being "El Piloto," a daily of Monterey; "La Humanidad" and "La Tierra," two weeklies of Yucatan; "El Tecolote," of Aguascalientes, and two of Guanajuato, "El Barretero" and "El Hijo del Pueblo." During the period while I was in Mexico at least two foreign newspaper men were deported for criticizing the government, two Spaniards, Ross y Planas and Antonio Duch, editors of the paper "La Tierra," in Merida. Finally, in 1909 and 1910 the story of the suppression of the Liberal Party and its press was repeated in the suppression of the Democratic Party and its press—but I must reserve that for another chapter.

During the Liberal agitation many of the best-known writers of Mexico fell by the assassin's hand. Among them were Jesus Valades of Mazatlan, Sinaloa. Having written articles against the despotism, while walking home from the theatre one night with his newly wedded wife he was set upon by several men, who killed him with daggers. In Tampico in 1902 Vincente Rivero Echeagarey, a newspaper man, dared to criticize the acts of the president. He was shot down at night while in the act of opening his own door. Jesus Olmos y Contreras, a newspaper man of the state of Puebla, about the same time published articles exposing an alleged licentious act of Governor Martinez. Two friends of the governor invited Contreras to supper. In the street the three walked arm in arm, the writer in the middle. Suddenly thugs fell upon him from behind. The false friends held Contreras tight until he had been struck down, when a heavy rock was used to beat the head of the victim into a pulp so that his identification might be impossible.

In Merida, Yucatan, in December, 1905, the writer, Abelardo Ancona, protested against the "re-election" of Governor Olegario Molina. Ancona was thrown into jail, where he was shot and stabbed to death.

In 1907 the writer, Augustin y Tovao, died of poison administered in Belem prison. Jesus Martinez Carrion, a noted newspaper artist, and Alberto Arans, a writer, left Belem to die in a hospital. Dr. Juan de la Pena, editor of a Liberal newspaper, died in the military prison of San Juan de Ulua. Juan Sarabia, another well-known editor, was also imprisoned there and for a long time was supposed to be dead, until recently, when his friends got word of him. Daniel Cabrera, one of the oldest Liberal editors, was a cripple, and many times he was carried to jail on a stretcher.

Professor Luis Toro, an editor of San Luis Potosi, was imprisoned and beaten in prison so severely that he died. In the same prison Primo Feliciano Velasquez, a lawyer and publisher of "El Estandarte," was beaten so severely that he became a life-long cripple. Another attorney and editor, Francisco de P. Morelos, was beaten in the city of Monterey for writing against the government in his paper, "La Defensa." In Guanajuato, Jose R. Granados, editor of "El Barretero," was beaten for writing against the government. In Napimi, a lawyer, Francisco A. Luna, was beaten and wounded with knives for writing against the government.

And so a list could be given pages long. Ricardo Flores Magon, Jesus Magon, Enrique Magon, Antonio J. Villarreal, Librado Rivera, Manuel Sarabia and many others spent months in prison for publishing opposition papers. Others were assassinated. As I said before, autocracy feeds on murder, and the rule of Porfirio Diaz has been one long story of murder. When assassination, imprisonment and countless forms of persecution had destroyed their organization in Mexico, the leaders who still retained their lives and liberty fled to the United States and established their headquarters here. They organized the Junta, or governing board of the Party, established newspapers, and it was only after the agents of the home government had followed them here and succeeded in so harassing them with false charges which resulted in their imprisonment that they abandoned all hope of doing anything peaceful for the regeneration of their country and decided to organize an armed force for the purpose of overthrowing the Mexican dictator.

The story of the persecutions visited upon the Mexican refugees in the United States I will detail in another chapter. It is sufficient here to pass over them and point merely to the result of their attempts to bring about a change in their government by revolution.

Briefly, the Liberal Party has launched two armed revolutions against Diaz. Both of these have come to grief at an early stage; first, because of the efficiency of the government in putting spies in the midst of the revolutionists and thus being able to anticipate them; second, because of the severe methods used in repression; and, third, because of the effective co-operation of the United States government, since the uprisings were necessarily directed from this side of the line.

The first Liberal attempt at revolution was to have been launched in September, 1906. The rebels claim to have had thirty-six military groups partially armed within Mexico and ready to rise at one signal. They expected that at the first show of strength on their part the army would desert to their standard and that the civilians would receive them with open arms.

Whether they judged the army and the people correctly will never be known, for they never succeeded in making any great show of strength. Government spies betrayed the various groups, and when the appointed hour struck the majority of the leaders were already dead or domiciled in San Juan de Ulua. The revolution was to begin on the national independence day, September 16, and the way the government prepared for it generally may be imagined from the report which I previously quoted of the large number of secret killings in Diaz's capital.

Liberal groups in two cities succeeded in making a start. One group captured the town of Jimenez, Coahuila, and another laid siege to the army barracks at Acayucan, state of Veracruz. Civilians joined them in these two cities, and for a day they enjoyed partial success. Then trainloads of troops got into each town, and in a few days what was left of the rebel force was on its way to prison. The concentration of troops into those towns was nothing short of wonderful. As before stated, though Acayucan is comparatively isolated, 4,000 regular soldiers reached the scene within twenty-four hours after hostilities began.

The second rebellion was scheduled to come off in July, 1908. This time the Liberals claimed to have forty-six military groups ready to rise in Mexico. But, as it turned out, nearly all the fighting was done by Mexican refugees, who recrossed from the United States at Del Rio, Texas, and other border centers, armed with guns purchased here. The Liberal leaders here claim that every military group in Mexico was anticipated by the government and the members arrested before the appointed hour. This certainly occurred at Casas Grandes, Chihuahua, and the affair, being given much publicity, caused the groups from the United States to act prematurely. It is also claimed that some of the strongest groups were betrayed by a criminal who, because of his facial resemblance to Antonio J. Villarreal, secretary of the Liberal Junta, was freed from the Torreon jail and pardoned by the authorities on condition that he go among the revolutionists, pass himself off as Villarreal and betray them. I personally know of two cases in which emissaries who left the Liberal headquarters in the United States carrying orders for the rising of certain groups fell into the clutches of the government soon after they crossed the line.

Nevertheless, the rebellion of June, 1908, profoundly shook Mexico for a time. The fighting in Coahuila furnished the American press with a week's sensation, and it was a month before the last of the rebels had been hunted down and shot by the superior forces of soldiers and *rurales*.

Such was the "Rebellion of Las Vacas," as it has come to be known both in the United States and Mexico. As a result of this rebellion and the previous one, the Mexican agents in the United States at last succeeded in breaking up the Liberal organization here almost as effectively as it was broken up in Mexico. Up to the time of the Congressional hearing on the persecutions in June, 1910, all the Liberal leaders in the United States were either in prison or in hiding, and no Mexican dared openly espouse the cause of the Liberal Party for fear that he, too, might be thrown behind the bars on a charge of having been in some way connected with one of those rebellions.

The Eighth Unanimous Election of Diaz

In order that the reader may entirely appreciate the fact that the political reign of terror established by Diaz thirty-four years ago continues in full bloom to the present day I shall devote this chapter to a record of the presidential campaign, so called, which ended June 26, 1910, with the eighth "unanimous election" of President Diaz.

To the end that the authenticity of this record may be beyond question, I have excluded from it all information that has come to me by means of rumor, gossip, letters and personal reports—everything except what has already been printed in newspapers as common news. In hardly an instance, moreover, was one of these newspapers opposed to the regime of General Diaz; nearly all were favorable to him. Therefore, if there are any errors in these reports, it is safe to assume that the truth has been minimized rather than overstated. It is safe to assume, also, that since the newspapers from which the reports were taken are published in Mexico where they are under the censorship of the police, that numerous other incidents of a similar, as well as of a worse, character, occurred which were never permitted to appear in print.

Before proceeding to these records I may be pardoned for restating the fact that President Diaz has held his position at the head of the Mexican government for more than a generation. In the latter part of 1876, nearly thirty-four years ago, heading a personal revolution, he led an army into the Mexican capital and proclaimed himself provisional president. Soon afterwards, he held what is called an election, and announced that the people had chosen him constitutional president—unanimously. In 1880 he turned the government over to a friend, Manuel Gonzalez, who was also elected unanimously. In 1884 Gonzalez reinstalled Diaz after a third unanimous election. Following 1884 Diaz was re-elected unanimously every four years for twenty years, until 1904, when the presidential term was lengthened to six years, and for the seventh time he was elected unanimously. Finally, July 10, 1910, Diaz was unanimously elected president of Mexico for the eighth time.

The Mexican presidential campaign just closed, if I may so denominate it, properly dates from the month of March, 1908. At that time, through James Creelman and Pearson's Magazine, President Diaz announced to the world, first, that under no circumstances would he consent to enter upon an eighth term, and, second, that he would be glad to assist in the transference of the governmental power from himself personally to a democratic organization of citizens. According to Mr. Creelman, his words were:

No matter what my friends and supporters say, I retire when my present term of office ends, and I shall not serve again. I shall be eighty years old then.

I have waited patiently for the day when the people of the Mexican Republic would be prepared to choose and change their government at every election without danger of armed revolutions and without injury to the national credit or interference with national progress. I believe that day has come.

I welcome an opposition party in the Mexican Republic. If it appears, I will regard it as a blessing, not an evil. And if it can develop power, not to exploit but to govern, I will stand by it, support it, advise it and forget myself in the successful inauguration of complete democratic government in the country.

The interview was reprinted by nearly every periodical in Mexico, and it produced a profound sensation. It is not exaggerating to say that the entire nation, outside of official circles, was overjoyed by the news. The nation took General Diaz at his word, and immediately there arose a lively but temperate discussion not only of the various possible candidates for the presidency, but also of innumerable questions relating to popular government. Books and pamphlets were written urging Diaz to immortalize himself as a second Washington by giving over the government to his people when he might very easily retain the supreme power until his death.

But at the height of this discussion the word was passed quietly about that the president's promise to retire at the end of the term was not final. To show how thoroughly the government had public speech and the press under control at this time it is only necessary to say that at once, upon the foregoing announcement being made, the discussion of presidential candidates for 1910 stopped.

Diaz was so thoroughly entrenched in power that there seemed little use of opposing him directly, but the people remembered the other statement that he had made and that he had not yet retracted —that he would welcome an opposition movement in Mexico. The declaration that he would support an opposition movement seemed paradoxical, and so the bright heads of the progressive element were laid together to devise a movement that, while not being in direct opposition to Diaz, would at the same time be able to work an opening wedge into the log of democracy.

The plan hit upon was to urge President Diaz to retain his seat and in the same voice ask that the country be permitted freely to choose a vice-president, so that in case Diaz should die during his next term his successor might be more or less in line with the desires and ambitions of the people.

The silence with which President Diaz received the publication of this plan was taken for consent, whereupon there began a widespread agitation, an organization of clubs, the holding of public discussions, newspaper debates, all of which might very well be taken as proof that President Diaz was right when he declared the Mexican people fit at last to enjoy the blessings of a real republic.

According to Mr. Barron, in an interview published in the New York World, within a short time no fewer than five hundred clubs were organized in Mexico. In January, 1909, these clubs held a convention in the capital, formed a central organization known as the Central Democratic Club, elected officers and adopted a platform, the main points of which were as follows:

Abolition of the *jefes politicos* and the transference of their power to municipal boards of aldermen.

The extension of primary education.

Suffrage laws to be enacted and enforced placing the franchise on a mixed educational and property basis.

Greater freedom for the press.

Stricter enforcement of the laws of reform (against monastic orders, etc.).

Greater respect for human life and liberty and a more effective administration of justice.

Legislation making it possible for workingmen to secure financial indemnity from their employers in case of accidents and to enable the public to sue transportation companies and other like corporations on the same ground.

Agrarian laws for the encouragement of agriculture.

The officers elected to head the new party were four bright young congressmen: Benito Juarez, Jr., president; Manuel Calero, vice-president; Diodoro Batalla, secretary; Jesus Urueta, treasurer.

April 2nd the Re-electionist Club, an organization consisting wholly of office-holders, appointees of Diaz, met and duly nominated General Diaz and his vice-president, Ramon Corral, for re-election. Shortly afterwards, in accordance with its original plan, the Democratic Party also named President Diaz for re-election. For vice-president it named General Bernardo Reyes, governor of Nuevo Leon.

Take a look at the general situation for a moment. Here was a party of men, consisting of the best educated, most intelligent and most progressive element in the country. Their platform shows their demands to have been excessively moderate. The party had sprung into existence through the published promise of General Diaz to permit it to function. In order to assure itself of safety at his hands, the party had placed General Diaz at the head of its ticket. Finally, the campaign which it launched was marvelously temperate and self-restrained. There was no call to arms. There was no hint of rebellion or revolution in any form. What criticism as was offered of existing institutions was offered with studious calmness and care. General Diaz was even praised. The people were asked to vote for him, but—to vote for Reyes for vice-president.

It required only a few days to develop the fact that in the event of an election Reyes would triumph over Corral by a large majority. Former enemies of Reyes were for him, not because they loved him, but because the movement behind him held out a promise of a little self-government for Mexico. As soon as the popularity of the Democratic Party became evident, despite the order that prevailed at its meetings, despite the temperance of its press, despite the fact that the laws were studiously observed, instead of supporting and advising, as he had promised to do, General Diaz moved to destroy it.

Diaz's first open move against the Democratic Party was to nip the propaganda for Reyes that was beginning in the army. This he did by banishing to remote parts of the country a dozen army officers who had subscribed themselves as favorable to the candidacy of Reyes.

This action of Diaz has been defended on the ground that he had a perfect right to prohibit members of the army from exercising political functions. But inasmuch as the president of the Re-electionist Club was an officer in the army, inasmuch as numerous army

officers engaged openly and actively in the Corral campaign, it
would seem that these men were proceeded against rather because
they were for Reyes than because they were members of the army.

Captain Reuben Morales, one of the punished officers, had accepted the vice-presidency of a Reyist club. He was ordered to resign
from the club or to resign from the army. He resigned from the
army, or attempted to do so, but his resignation was not accepted
and he was sent away to the territory of Quintana Roo. Eight of the
offending officers were sent to Sonora to be placed in the field against
the Yaqui Indians.

The banishment of the army officers took place at the end of May.
Following close upon the incident came action against some Democratic leaders who occupied positions in the government. Congressmen Urueta and Lerdo de Tejada, Jr., and Senator Jose Lopez
Portillo were among the first to be deposed from their positions.

Some students of the national schools of jurisprudence, mines,
medicine and the preparatory school of Mexico City, were encouraged in forming a club to further the candidacy of Corral. But
when the students of the Jalisco state schools of law and medicine
formed a club to further the candidacy of Reyes the government
ordered them either to abandon their political activity or to leave
school. They sent a committee to Diaz to appeal for fair play. But he
gave them no satisfaction, the threat of expulsion was renewed with
the result that so many students were expelled from the Jalisco
schools that the schools actually closed for lack of pupils.

In July, a committee of re-electionists from Mexico City held a
public meeting in favor of Corral in the Delgado theatre, Guadalajara, capital of Jalisco. The audience, composed largely of democratic students, hissed one of the speakers. Whereupon companies
of police, which had been held in readiness, were ordered to clear
the building and square.

This the police did after the manner of Mexico—with sabre,
club and pistol. The figures on the killed, wounded and imprisoned

were suppressed by the authorities, but all newspaper reports at the time agree that there were persons killed and wounded, as well as imprisoned. The highest estimate that I have seen placed the killed at twelve, the seriously wounded at thirty-five and the arrested at one thousand. Following the occurrence, Guadalajara was filled with state and national troops. General Ignacio Bravo, notorious as the most ruthless officer in the Mexican army, was hurried from Quintana Roo temporarily to replace the existing head of the military zone; and, finally, all political expression of the Democrats was put down with an iron hand.

Among the prominent leaders of the Democratic movement in Guadalajara who were made to suffer at this time was Ambrosio Ulloa, an engineer and lawyer, founder of a school for engineers, and head of the Corona Flour Milling Company. Ulloa happened to be president of the Reyes club of Guadalajara, and, on the theory that the club was in some way responsible for the so-called student riot, Ulloa, a week after the occurrence, was taken to jail and imprisoned under a charge of "sedition."

During the putting down of the student movement in Guadalajara at least one case of the *ley fuga* was reported from that city. The victim was William de la Pena, a former student of Christian Brothers' College, St. Louis, Mo., also of the Ohio State University. The case was reported in the St. Louis papers, from which place a dispatch was sent out through the Associated Press. Relating the occurrence, the press dispatch said:

He (Pena) was at his country home, when an officer of the Rurales invited him to go with him. He mounted his horse and went. Next day servants found his body, riddled with bullets.

September 7th Congressman Heriberto Barron, who had mildly criticized Diaz in an open letter, fled from the country and took up his residence in New York. One Mexican paper has it that agents of the Diaz secret police forced Barron upon a Ward liner at Veracruz

and compelled him to leave the country. In New York newspapers
Barron declared that he had fled to escape imprisonment. A few
months later he begged to be allowed to return home, but was told
that he must remain an exile until the death of the president of
Mexico. The heinousness of Barron's crime may be gathered from
the following paragraphs, the most uncomplimentary in his open
letter to Diaz:

"At the *velada* to which I have alluded, when your name was pronounced by the orators, it was received with unanimous hisses and
marks of disapproval.

"On the night of the performance given at the Principal theatre in
aid of the Guerrero victims, the entire audience maintained a sinister
silence on your arrival. The same silence prevailed when you departed.

"If you had occasion, as I have, to mingle with the gatherings and
groups of people of different classes, not all Reyists, you would hear, Mr.
President, expressions of indignation against you spoken openly on all
sides."

Within ten days after the banishment of Barron, a foreign resident, Frederick Palmer by name, an Englishman, was lodged in
Belem prison, denied bail, held *incommunicado* for some days, and
finally was sentenced to one month's imprisonment—for doing
nothing worse than remarking that he thought Diaz had been
president of Mexico long enough.

July 28th Celso Cortez, vice-president of the Central Club Reyista
of Mexico City, was lodged in Belem prison for making a speech at
the club rooms criticizing members of the Diaz cabinet.

Following came a long list of arrests of members of the Democratic movement throughout the country. Usually the charge was
"sedition," but never was any evidence produced to prove sedition
as Americans understand that term. In this movement there was
never any hint of armed rebellion or any concerted violation of
existing laws. In all of these cases I have yet to learn of any in
which reasonable ground for the arrest existed. In many cases the

victims were kept in jail for months, and in some cases they were sentenced to long terms in prison. The number persecuted in this way is problematical, as reports of only the more prominent cases got into the Mexican press. The following are a few of those recorded:

In August Jose Ignacio Rebollar, secretary of the Club Reyista of Torreon, with several others, was arrested for appearing at a serenade given to the governor of the state and attempting to proselyte for Reyes.

On August 1, 1909, a company of *rurales* broke up a meeting of Reyistas in Silao and placed a number of them in jail.

In November, 1909, Manuel Martinez de Arredondo, a wealthy planter; his nephew, Francisco de Arredondo; four attorneys, Pedro Reguera, Antonio Juarez, Enrique Recio and Juan Barrera, also Marcos Valencia, Amado Cardenas, Francisco Vidal and others were sent to jail for attempting to hold a Reyist meeting in Merida, Yucatan. Several of the number were kept in jail for more than six months.

In January, 1910, Attorney Francisco Perera Escobar, a member of the legislature in the state of Campeche, was arrested for distributing bills announcing a meeting of Reyists.

December 7, 1909, Jose Lopez Portillo y Rojas, a prominent Reyist of the capital, was imprisoned in Belem on a trumped up charge. Some months later it was reported that he was still there and that he was to be sentenced to nine years' imprisonment.

January 26, 1910, some Democrats held a public meeting in the Alameda, Mexico City. Dr. Manuel Espinosa de Los Monteros, president of the Central Club Reyista, presided, and Don Enrique Garcia de la Cadena y Ancona delivered a patriotic address. The police broke up the meeting and arrested Cadena and Monteros, charging them with sedition. At this writing it is reported that both of them will be sent for long terms to the penal colony on the Tres Marias Islands in the Pacific.

During the months following the attempt to place a candidate in the field against Vice-President Corral the Democrats tried to strengthen their position by contesting some state and local "elections." As a result there were many arrests and several massacres by troops or local authorities.

At Petape, Oaxaca, the Twenty-fifth battalion of regulars fired on a crowd of the opposition, killing several. Seventy were jailed.

At Tepames, Colima, there were many shootings. After the jail was full, the authorities are reported as having taken out some of the prisoners, compelled them to dig their own graves, then shot them so that they fell into the trenches.

At Tehuitzingo, Puebla, in April, it was reported that sixteen citizens were executed without trial, and that many others had been condemned to twenty years' confinement in the fortress of San Juan de Ulua.

In Merida, Yucatan, federal troops were placed in the polling booths and large numbers of Democrats were arrested.

In the state of Morelos, in February, 1909, the Democrats attempted to elect Patricio Leyva in opposition to Pablo Escandon, a slave-holding Spaniard whom Diaz had selected for the place. For accepting the Democratic candidacy Leyva was dismissed from his government position as Inspector of Irrigation in the Department of Fomento. The president and vice-president of the Free Suffrage Club at Jojutla and the officers of a similar club at Tiaquiltenango, as well as many others, were jailed on charges of sedition, while the authorities were reported as having killed several. Police placed in possession of the polls prevented many from voting, and finally the vote as actually cast was falsified in favor of Escandon, who became governor.

In July, 1909, many arrests occurred at Fuerte, Sinaloa, and the town was filled with federal *rurales*. In January, 1910, sixteen men arrested some time before on suspicion of being in a plot against the government at Viesca, were sentenced to be shot, the supreme court sitting at the capital pronouncing the decree.

While such incidents were going on the press situation was being manipulated, also. The government bought or subsidized news-papers, on the one hand, and suppressed them on the other. Some thirty or forty daily and weekly publications espoused the Democratic cause. I do not know of one of them which the government did not compel to suspend operations. Despite the fact that they were careful of their utterances, they were put out of business, the majority of them by imprisonment of their editors, seizure of their printing plants, or both.

April 16, 1909, Antonio Duch, editor of Tierra, of Merida, was escorted aboard a steamer at Veracruz by the Mexican secret police and compelled to leave the country under the charge of being a "pernicious foreigner." His paper was suppressed.

July 15, 1909, Francisco Navarro, editor of La Libertad, organ of the Club Democratico of Guadalajara, was jailed for criticizing the sabreing of Reyist students. His paper was stopped, his office closed, a *gendarme* was placed on guard and it was officially announced that were an attempt made to issue the paper from another shop, it, also, would be closed.

August 3, 1909, Felix Vera, correspondent of Democratic papers at Guadalajara, was taken to Belem prison, where he remains at this writing, though so far no formal charge has been filed against him.

In October, 1909, Manuel M. Oviedo, editor of La Hoja Suelta and president of the Anti-re-electionist Club of Torreon, was sent to prison and his paper was suppressed. Action was taken because Oviedo asked for a fair state election following the forced retirement of Governor Cardenas.

In November, 1909, Martin Stecker, a native of Germany, editor of El Trueno, Linares, Nuevo Leon, was jailed on a charge of "def-

amation" and his newspaper was suppressed. Stecker was only a
very mild Reyist. The real reason for his arrest was that Linares is
a good newspaper field and members of the Diaz machine wished
the sole privilege of exploiting it. Just previous to the suppression of
El Trueno Governor Reyes had been banished from the country and
his friends put out of the municipal government at Linares.

In November, 1909, Revista de Merida, of Merida, Yucatan, was
suppressed by the government. Editor Menendez and other writers
were imprisoned on the charge of sedition.

About the same time two other Merida newspapers were suppressed. One was Yucatan Nuevo. Its editors, Fernando M. Estrada
and Ramon Peovide, are at this writing still in jail. The other was
La Defensa Nacional. Its editors, Calixto M. Maldonado and Caesar
A. Gonzalez, were charged with "provocation of rebellion." The
evidence produced in court against them consisted of copies of a
circular sent out by the National Anti-re-electionist Club, which
they were passing among their friends.

In February, 1910, Heriberto Frias, editor of El Correo de la
Tarde, was driven out of Mazatlan because he published the statement that in the so-called election in Sinaloa boys of ten and twelve
were permitted to vote the administration ticket, while men of forty
¿ nd fifty of the opposition party were turned away on the ground
that they were too young to vote.

In October, 1909, Alfonso B. Peniche, editor of La Redencion,
Mexico City, was arrested for "defamation" of a minor employe of
the government. Despite his imprisonment, Peniche succeeded in
continuing his publication for a time, although in order to do so he
was compelled to smuggle his copy through the bars of the prison.
After remaining in Belem a short time he published an article asking for an investigation into the conditions of Belem, alleging that
an instrument of torture called "the rattler" was used upon the
prisoners. This undoubtedly had something to do with the extreme
severity of the punishment that was meted out to Peniche, for after

remaining five months in Belem he was sentenced to banishment to the penal colony on the Tres Marias Islands for four long years.

Undoubtedly the charge against Peniche was only a subterfuge to get him out of the way. The story of his "defamation," according to Mexico Nuevo, the most conservative democratic daily, was:

In his paper Redencion, now suspended, he published a statement signed by various merchants, making charges against a tax collector of the federal district, relating to acts committed in his official capacity. The Bureau of Taxation took action in the matter, ordering an investigation, and, as a result, the charges were sustained and the tax collector was removed by the Secretary of Hacienda, with the approval of the President of the Republic, for "not deserving the confidence of the government"; moreover, he was arraigned before the first judge of the district, for an inquiry into the supposed fraud of the treasury, and this inquiry is now pending.

This being the case, there were many reasons to suppose that Peniche, in publishing the accusation, was working in the public interest and was not committing any crime. Instead of this, he is convicted of defamation, an even more serious offense than libel.

El Diario de Hogar, an old and conservative daily paper of the capital, which has espoused the cause of the Democrats, printed an account of Peniche's banishment also, the article appearing under the caption "Newspaper Men Watch Out." The authorities at once forced the suspension of the paper. The owner, Filomeno Mata, an aged man who had retired from active life; Filomeno Mata, Jr., managing editor, and the mechanical foreman, were taken to prison. A month afterwards it was reported that father and son were still in jail and that Mata, Sr., was dying of ill treatment received from the jailers.

Some time later, in March, 1910, the government forced the suspension of Mexico Nuevo. It was revived later, however, and is the only Democratic paper which survived the Reyes campaign.

Paulino Martinez was one of the oldest and best-known newspaper men in Mexico. His papers were the only ones in opposition to the policy of the administration which succeeded in weathering the storm of press persecutions of past years. For several years his papers, La Voz de Juarez and El Insurgente, were the only opposition papers in Mexico. Martinez kept them alive, so he told me himself, by refraining always from making direct criticisms of high officials or acts of General Diaz.

But with the campaign against the Democratic movement Martinez's papers went with the rest. When the government began action against him his papers numbered four, La Voz de Juarez, El Insurgente, El Chinaco, all weeklies, and El Anti-Re-eleccionista, a daily. All were published in the capital.

The first blow fell upon La Voz de Juarez (The Voice of Juarez). August 3, 1909, that paper was suppressed and the plant confiscated. "Slandering the army," was the charge. The police looked for Martinez, but failed to find him. All minor employes found about the shop were jailed, and it was announced that the plant would be sold.

September 3rd the secret police descended upon El Insurgente and El Chinaco, also upon El Paladin, a weekly paper published by Ramon Alvarez Soto. The type forms of all three publications were seized and taken to the offices of the secret police as "pieces de conviction." Soto, Joaquin Pina, Martinez's managing editor of El Chinaco, Joaquin Fernando Bustillos, another editor, five printers, two other employes and Mrs. Martinez, were taken to jail. After five days the reporters and printers were released. But Mrs. Martinez and Enrique Patino, a member of El Paladin staff, who had been apprehended later, were held on charges of sedition.

El Anti-Re-eleccionista, the last of the Martinez papers, succumbed September 28th. The office was closed, the plant seized and sealed with the seal of the court, and twenty-two employes found about the office were all taken prisoner and charged with sedition. The list consisted of three members of the office executive force, one reporter, fifteen typesetters and three bindery girls.

How long these twenty-two remained in prison is not recorded. Six months later I saw a report that at least one of the Martinez editors, D. Feliz Palavicini, was still in prison. Mrs. Martinez remained in jail for several months. Her husband succeeded in escaping to the United States, and when Mrs. Martinez joined him neither of them had a dollar. Mrs. Martinez, by the way, is a native of the United States.

Most remarkable of all was the treatment meted out to the nominee of the Democratic Party, General Bernardo Reyes, governor of the state of Nuevo Leon. Doubly, trebly remarkable was that treatment in view of the fact that General Reyes not only did not accept the nomination of the Democratic Party, but that he repudiated it. Four times he repudiated it. Not only that, but during the months in which calamities were being heaped upon him and his friends he never gave utterance to one word or raised his little finger in the most insignificant act that might be construed as an offense to President Diaz, to Vice-President Corral, or to any of the members of the Diaz government. By its military bluster the government tried to create the impression that Reyes was on the verge of an armed revolt, but of that there is not the slightest evidence.

As a candidate, General Reyes did not perfectly fit the ideal of the leaders of the Democratic movement, for he had never before appeared in any way as a champion of democratic principles. Doubtless the Democrats chose him, as a government organ charged, because of their belief in his "ability to face the music." Reyes was a strong figure, and it requires a strong figure to rally the people when their fears are strong. It was for this reason that the Democratic leaders pinned their faith to him, and they launched their campaign on the assumption that when he discovered that the people were almost unanimous for him, he would accept the nomination.

In this the Democrats were mistaken. Reyes chose not to face the music. Four times he repudiated the nomination publicly. He re-

tired to his mountain resort and there waited for the storm to blow
over. He put himself out of touch with his partizans and with the
world. He made no move that might give offense to the government.

And yet—what happened to Reyes?

Diaz deposed the head of the military zone, which includes the
state of Monterey, and placed in command General Trevino, a personal enemy of Reyes. Trevino marched upon Reyes' state at the
head of an army. He stopped on his way at Saltillo and, by a display
of arms, compelled the resignation of Governor Cardenas of Coahuila merely because the latter was a friend of Reyes. He threw his
army into Monterey and overturned the local government, as well
as all the municipal government in the entire state. Diaz ordered a
fine of a third of a million dollars placed upon Reyes' financial associates, in order that they, as well as he, might be dealt a crushing
blow financially. Trevino surrounded Reyes in his mountain resort
and compelled him to return, a virtual prisoner, and to hand in his
resignation. Finally, Reyes was sent out of the country, ostensibly
on a "military mission" to Europe—actually, banished from his
native country for two years, or longer, should the ruler so decide.

So perished Reyism, as the government papers derisively called
the opposition. The Democratic movement was demoralized for the
time being, and the government doubtless imagined that the end of
Reyes meant the end of the Democratic movement.

But not so. The democratic ambitions of the people had been
aroused to a high pitch, and they would not be denied. Instead of
intimidating them, the banishment of Reyes and the high-handed
acts that went before it only served to make the people bolder in
their demands. From daring to nominate a candidate merely for
vice-president, they passed to nominating a candidate for president.
The pseudo opposition party became an opposition party indeed.

In Francisco I. Madero, the party found its new leader. Madero
was a distinguished citizen of Coahuila, a member of one of the
oldest and most respected families in Mexico. The Maderos had

never involved themselves in Diaz politics; they were rich farmers, well educated, cultured and progressive. Madero's first notable interest in democracy was shown in his book, "La Sucesion Presidencial," which he published in 1908. It was a thoughtful but mild criticism of the Diaz regime, and in the end it urged the people to insist upon the right to engage in the elections of 1910.

Madero's book is said to have been suppressed in Mexico, but only after it had gained wide circulation, and its influence was no doubt considerable in prompting the launching of the Democratic Party. After the nomination of Reyes, Madero went about the country in his own private car, addressing public meetings, not campaigning for Reyes, but confining himself chiefly to the dissemination of the A, B, C's of popular government.

The banishment of Reyes did not stop Madero's speech-making, and before the end of 1909 it was announced that the Democratic and Reyist clubs would reorganize as "Anti-Re-electionist" clubs, and that a national convention would be held at which the Anti-Re-electionist Party would be organized and nominations made for president and vice-president of the republic.

The convention was held in the middle of April, 1910; Madero was named for president and Dr. Francisco Vasquez Gomez for vice-president. The scattered elements of the interrupted campaign were got together and Madero and such others of the Democratic leaders as were out of jail went on with their speech-making—careful, as ever, to criticize but sparingly and to encourage no breaches of the peace.

The result was instantaneous. The nation was again in a fervor of enthusiasm over the idea of actually exercising their constitutional right of franchise. Had the movement been small, it would have been allowed to go its way and spend itself. But the movement was tremendous. It put on a parade in the national capital such as Diaz, with all his powers of coercion and of hire, had never been able to equal in his own behalf. Every marcher in that parade knew that in walking with that throng he was laying himself liable to persecution, to ruin, perhaps to death, but yet so great was the throng that the government organs themselves were forced to admit that the parade was a triumph for the "Maderists," as the Democrats were now called.

Before the convention and during the convention the Diaz press pooh-poohed Madero, his program and his party as too insignificant to be noticed. But before the delegates had returned to their homes the movement had assumed such grave proportions that the government proceeded against it as it had proceeded against the "Reyists" before the banishment of Reyes. Everywhere members of Anti-Re-electionist clubs were thrown into jail; such progressive newspapers as remained and dared to espouse the Democratic cause were suppressed, and the police power was used to break up the clubs, stop public meetings and prevent receptions being accorded the party's candidates as they traveled through the country.

So severe was this persecution that, May 21st, Attorney Roque Estrada, one of the most prominent of the Anti-Re-electionist speakers, addressed an open letter to Diaz, begging him to interfere in behalf of constitutional rights. This was followed by a letter from Madero himself, couched in a similar vein. In recounting some of the outrages which had been heaped upon his friends, Estrada said in part:

When the delegate of Cananea, Sonora, returned to his home, he was imprisoned, just as were some presidents of clubs; in Alamos, Sonora, independent citizens were arrested, and a journalist and his family were martyred; in Torreon, Coahuila, in Monterey, and in Orizaba the rights of association and reunion have been impudently violated; finally, in the tormented City of Puebla, immediately after the visit which the candidates of the people made on the 14th and 15th of the current month, an epoch of terror was begun, capable of destroying the reputation of the most sane and solid administration. In the City of Zaragoza many independent citizens were confined in prison, others were consigned to the army, as in the case of Senor Diaz Duran, president of an Anti-Re-electionist club; and others have felt the necessity of abandoning their homes in order to escape the fury of authority.

Some of the outrages recounted in Madero's letter follow:

At Coahuila the public officials have arbitrarily forbidden demonstrations in our honor, preventing also the spread of our principles. The same has happened in the states of Nuevo Leon, Aguascalientes and San Luis Potosi. . . . In the States of Sonora and Puebla the conditions are serious. In the former state an independent journalist, Mr. Caesar del Vando, was thrown into jail. . . . At Cananea the prosecutions are extreme against the members of my party, and according to late news received therefrom more than thirty individuals have been imprisoned, among them the full board of directors of the Club Anti-Re-eleccionista de Obreros (workers), three of whom were forcibly enlisted in the army.

At Puebla, Atlixco and Tlaxcala, where untold outrages have been committed against my followers, reigns intense excitement. The last news received shows the conditions of the working classes to be desperate; that they may at any moment resort to violent means to have their rights respected.

In June, the month of election, matters became very much worse. Estrada and Madero themselves were arrested. On the night of June 6 they were secretly taken and secretly held in the penitentiary at Monterey until the truth became noised about, when charges were formally preferred against them. Estrada was charged with "sedition." Madero was first accused of protecting Estrada from arrest, but soon afterwards this charge was dropped and he was accused of "insulting the nation." He was removed from the penitentiary of Nuevo Leon to the penitentiary of San Luis Potosi, and here he remained *incommunicado* until after "election."

The presidential campaign ended amid many reports of government persecutions. A reputable dispatch dated June 9th said that in breaking up a gathering at Saltillo, following the news of the arrest of Madero, the police rode down the crowds, injuring more than two hundred people. Another, dated June 14th, said that in the cities of Torreon, Saltillo and Monterey more than one hundred persons were arrested on the charge of "insulting" the government; that at Ciudad Porfirio Diaz forty-seven prominent citizens were arrested in one day, and that a big exodus of citizens of the border towns, fearing arrest, was taking place to the United States. Still another dispatch, dated June 21st, said that more than four hundred arrests had been made in northern Mexico the previous day and that 1,000 political prisoners were being held *incommunicado*, where they would remain until after the election.

"Election day" found soldiers or *rurales* in every town and hamlet. Booths were actually put up here and there and a farce of an election was gone through with. Soldiers held the polls and every man who dared cast a ballot for any but the administration ticket knew that he was risking imprisonment, confiscation of property, even death, in doing so. Finally, the government went through the form of counting the vote, and in due course of time the world was told that the Mexican people had proved "practically unanimous" in their choice of Diaz and Corral.

Four Mexican Strikes

On the line of the Mexican Railway, which climbs, in one hundred odd miles of travel, from the port of Veracruz 10,000 feet to the rim of the valley of Mexico, are situated a number of mill towns. Nearing the summit, after that wonderful ascent from the tropics to the snows, the passenger looks back from his car window through dizzying reaches of empty air, sheer a full mile, as the crow might dare to fly a score of them, down to the uppermost of these mill towns, Santa Rosa, a gray checkerboard upon a map of green. Just below Santa Rosa, but out of sight behind the titanic shoulder of a mountain, nestles Rio Blanco, largest of the mill towns, scene of the bloodiest strike in the labor history of Mexico.

In altitude half way between the shark-infested waters of Veracruz harbor and the plateau of the Montezumas, Rio Blanco, which in Spanish means White River, is not only a paradise in climate and scenery, but it is also perfectly situated for water-power manufactories. A bountiful supply of water, provided by the copious rains and the snows of the heights, gathers in the Rio Blanco and with the speed of Niagara rushes down the mountain gorges and into the town.

It is said to be a favorite boast of Manager Hartington, the steel-eyed, middle-aged Englishman who oversees the work of the 6,000 men, women and children that the mill at Rio Blanco is not only the largest and most modern cotton manufactory in the world, but that it pays the richest profits on the investment.

Certainly the factory is a big one. We saw it—De Lara and I—from A to Z, following the raw cotton from the cleaner through all its various processes and treatments until it finally came out neatly folded in fancy prints or specially colored weaves. We even descended five iron ladders down into the bowels of the earth, saw the great pin and caught a glimpse of the swirling black waters which turn every wheel in the mill. And we observed the workers, too, men, women and children.

They were Mexicans with hardly an exception. The men, in the mass, are paid thirty-seven and one-half cents a day in our money, the women from one dollar and a half to two dollars a week, the children, who range down to seven and eight, from ten to twenty-five cents a day. These figures were given us by an officer of the mill who showed us about, and they were confirmed in talks with the workers themselves.

Thirteen hours a day—from 6 until 8—are long for labor in the open air and sunshine, but thirteen hours in that roar of machinery, in that lint-laden air, in those poisonous dye rooms—how very long that must be! The terrible smell of the dye rooms nauseated me and I had to hurry on. The dye rooms are a suicide hole for the men who work there, for it is said that they survive, on an average, only a twelve-month. Yet the company finds that plenty of them are willing to commit the suicide for the additional inducement of seven and one-half cents a day over the regular wage.

The Rio Blanco mill was established sixteen years ago—sixteen years, but in their history the mill and the town have just two epochs—before the strike and after the strike. Wherever we went about Rio Blanco and Orizaba, the latter being the chief town in that political district, we heard echoes of the strike, although its bloody story had been written nearly two years before our visit.

In Mexico there are no labor laws in operation to protect the workers—no provision for factory inspection, no practical statutes against infant labor, no processes through which workmen may recover damages for injuries sustained or death met in the mine or at the machine. Wage-workers literally have no rights that the employers are bound to respect. Policy only determines the degree of exploitation, and in Mexico that policy is such as might prevail in the driving of horses in a locality where horses are dirt cheap, where profits from their use are high, and where there exists no Society for the Prevention of Cruelty to Animals.

Over against this absence of protection on the part of the governmental powers stands oppression on the part of the governmental powers, for the machinery of the Diaz state is wholly at the command of the employer to whip the worker into accepting his terms.

The six thousand laborers in the Rio Blanco mill were not content with thirteen hours daily in the company of that roaring machinery and in that choking atmosphere, especially since it brought to them only from twenty-five to thirty-seven and one-half cents. Nor were they content with paying out of such a sum the one American dollar a week that the company charged for the rental of the two-room, dirt-floor hovels which they called their homes. Least of all were they content with the coin in which they were paid. This consisted of credit checks upon the company store, which finished the exploitation—took back for the company the final *centavo* that the company had paid out in wages. A few miles away, at Orizaba, the same goods could be purchased for from twenty-five to seventy-five per cent less, but the operatives were unable to buy their goods at these stores.

The operatives were not content. The might of the company towered like a mountain above them, and behind and above the

company towered the government. Behind the company stood Diaz
himself, for Diaz was not only the government, he was also a heavy
stockholder in the company. Yet the operatives prepared to fight.
Secretly they organized a union, "El Circulo de Obreros," which
means "The Circle of Workers," holding their meetings not en
masse, but in small groups in their homes, in order that the authorities might not learn of their purposes.

Immediately upon the company learning that the workers were
discussing their troubles it took action against them. Through the
police authorities it issued a general order forbidding any of the
operatives from receiving any visitors whatsoever, even their own
relatives being barred, the penalty for violation being the city jail.
Persons who were suspected of having signed the roll of the union
were put in prison at once, and a weekly newspaper which was
known to be friendly to the workers was swooped down upon, suppressed and the printing plant confiscated.

At this juncture a strike was called in the cotton mills in the city
of Puebla, in an adjoining state. The mills of Puebla were owned by
the same company as owned the Rio Blanco mills, and the operatives
thereof were living under similar conditions to those at Rio Blanco.
The Puebla workers went on strike and the company, knowing that
they had no resources behind them, decided, as one of its agents told
me, "to let nature take its course"; that is, to starve out the workers,
as they believed this process could be accomplished inside of a fort-
night.

The strikers turned for aid to those of their fellow-craftsmen who
were at work in other localities. The Rio Blanco workers themselves
were already preparing to strike, but thereupon they decided to wait
for a time longer, in order that they might collect from their meager
earnings a fund to support their brothers in the city of Puebla. Thus
were the ends of the company defeated for the moment, for by living
on half rations both workers and strikers were able to eke out their

existence. But no sooner had the company learned the source of
strength of the Puebla strikers than the mills at Rio Blanco were
shut down and the workers there locked out. Other mills in other
localities were shut down and other means taken to prevent any
help reaching the Puebla strikers.

Locked out, the Rio Blanco workers promptly assumed the of-
fensive, declared they were on strike and formulated a series of
demands calculated in some measure to alleviate the conditions of
their lives.

But the demands were unheard, the machinery of the mill roared
no more, the mill slept in the sun, the waters of the Rio Blanco
dashed unharnessed through the town, the manager of the company
laughed in the faces of the striking men and women.

The six thousand starved. For two months they starved. They
scoured the surrounding hills for berries, and when the berries were
gone they deceived their gnawing stomachs with indigestible roots
and herbs gleaned from the mountain sides. In utter despair, they
looked to the highest power they knew, Porfirio Diaz, and begged
him to have mercy. They begged him to investigate their cause, and
for their part they promised to abide by his decision.

President Diaz pretended to investigate. He rendered a decision,
but his decision was that the mills should reopen and workers go
back to their thirteen hours of dust and machinery on the same
terms as they had left them.

True to their promise, the strikers at Rio Blanco prepared to
comply. But they were weak from starvation. In order to work they
must have sustenance. Consequently on the day of their surrender
they gathered in a body in front of the company store opposite the
big mill and asked that each of their number be given a certain
quantity of corn and beans so that they might be able to live through
the first week and until they should be paid their wages.

The storekeeper jeered at the request. "To these dogs we will not even give water!" is the answer he is credited with giving them.

It was then that a woman, Margarita Martinez, exhorted the people to take by force the provisions that had been denied them. This they did. They looted the store, then set fire to it, and finally to the mill across the way.

The people had not expected to riot, but the government had expected it. Unknown to the strikers, battalions of regular soldiers were waiting just outside the town, under command of General Rosalio Martinez himself, sub-secretary of war. The strikers had no arms. They were not prepared for revolution. They had intended no mischief, and their outburst was a spontaneous and doubtless a natural one, and one which an officer of the company afterwards confided to me could easily have been taken care of by the local police force, which was strong.

Nevertheless, the soldiers appeared, leaping upon the scene as if out of the ground. Volley after volley was discharged into the crowd at close range. There was no resistance whatsoever. The people were shot down in the streets with no regard for age or sex, many women and children being among the slain. They were pursued to their homes, dragged from their hiding places and shot to death. Some fled to the hills, where they were hunted for days and shot on sight. A company of rural guards which refused to fire on the crowd when the soldiers first arrived were exterminated on the spot.

There are no official figures of the number killed in the Rio Blanco massacre, and if there were any, of course they would be false. Estimates run from two hundred to eight hundred. My information for the Rio Blanco strike was obtained from numerous widely different sources—from an officer of the company itself, from a friend of the governor who rode with the *rurales* as they chased the fleeing strikers through the hills, from a labor editor who escaped after being hotly pursued for days, from survivors of the strike, from others who had heard the story from eye witnesses.

"I don't know how many were killed," the man who rode with

the *rurales* told me, "but on the first night after the soldiers came I saw *two flat cars piled high with dead and mangled bodies, and there were a good many killed after the first night.*"

"Those flat cars," the same informant told me, "were hauled away by special train that night, hurried to Veracruz, where the bodies were *dumped in the harbor as food for the sharks.*"

Strikers who were not punished by death were punished in other ways scarcely less terrible. It seems that for the first few hours death was dealt out indiscriminately, but after that some of those who were caught were not killed. Fugitives who were captured after the first two or three days were rounded up in a bull pen, and some five hundred of them were impressed into the army and sent to Quintana Roo. The vice-president and the secretary of the "Circulo de Obreros" were hanged, while the woman orator, Margarita Martinez, was among those sent to the prison of San Juan de Ulua.

Among the newspaper men who suffered as a result of the Rio Blanco strike are Jose Neira, Justino Fernandez, Juan Olivares and Paulino Martinez. Neira and Fernandez were imprisoned for long terms, the latter being tortured until he lost his reason. Olivares was pursued for many days, but escaped capture and found his way to the United States. None of the three had any connection with the riot. The fourth, Paulino Martinez, committed no crime more heinous than to comment mildly in his newspaper in favor of the strikers. He published his paper at Mexico City, a day's ride on the train to Rio Blanco. Personally he had been no nearer the scene of the trouble than that city, yet he was arrested, carried over the mountains to the mill town, imprisoned and held *incommunicado* for five months without even a charge being preferred against him.

The government made every effort to conceal the facts of the Rio Blanco massacre, but murder will out, and when the newspapers did not speak the news flew from mouth to mouth until the nation was shuddering at the story. It was a waste of blood, indeed, yet, even from the viewpoint of the workers, it was not wholly in vain.

For in the story the company store held a prominent place, and so great a protest was raised against it that President Diaz decided to make one concession to the decimated band of operatives and to abolish the company store at Rio Blanco.

Thus where before the strike there was but one store in Rio Blanco, today there are many; the workers buy where they choose. Thus it would seem that by their starvation and their blood the strikers had won a slight victory, but it is a question whether this is so, since in some ways the screws have been put down harder than ever before. Provision has been made against a repetition of the strike, provision that, for a country that claims to be a republic, is, to speak mildly, astounding.

The provision consists, first, of eight hundred Mexican troops— six hundred regular soldiers and two hundred *rurales*—who are encamped upon the company property; second, of a *jefe politico* clothed with the powers of a cannibal chief.

When we visited the barracks, De Lara and I, the little captain who showed us about informed us that the quarters were furnished, ground, house, light and water, by the company, and that in return the army was placed directly and unequivocally at the call of the company.

As to the *jefe politico*, his name is Miguel Gomez, and he was promoted to Rio Blanco from Cordoba, where his readiness to kill is said to have provoked the admiration of the man who appointed him, President Diaz. Regarding the powers of Miguel Gomez, I can hardly do better than to quote the words of an officer of the company, with whom De Lara and I took dinner one day:

"Miguel Gomez has orders direct from President Diaz to censor the reading of the mill workers and to allow no radical newspapers or Liberal literature to get into their hands. More than that, he has orders to kill anyone whom he suspects of having evil intentions. Yes, I said kill. It is *carte blanche* with Gomez, and no questions asked. He asks no one's advice and no court sits on his action, either before or after. *And he does kill!* If he sees a man on the street and gets any whimsical suspicion of him, dislikes his dress or his face, it is enough. That man disappears. I remember a laborer in the dye-mixing room who spoke some words friendly to Liberalism; I remember a spool tender who mentioned strike; there have been others —many others. They have disappeared suddenly, have been swallowed up and nothing heard of them but the whispers of their friends!"

Of course, it is impossible in the nature of things to verify this statement, but it is worth noting that it does not come from a revolutionist.

The trade unionists of Mexico are, of course, by far the best paid workers in the country. Because of the opposition of both employers and government, as well as the deep degradation out of which it is necessary for the Mexican to climb before he is able to pluck the fruits of organization, unionism is still in its infancy in Mexico. It is still in its swaddling clothes and, under the circumstances as they exist today, its growth is slow and fraught with great hardship. So far, there is no Mexican Federation of Labor.

The principal Mexican unions in 1908, as set forth to me by Felix Vera, president of the Grand League of Railroad Workers, and other organizers, were as follows:

The Grand League of Railroad Workers, 10,000 members; the Mechanics' Union, 500 members; Boilermakers' Union, 800 members; Cigarmakers' Union, 1,500 members; Carpenters' Union, 1,500 members; the Shop Blacksmiths' Union, with headquarters at Ciudad Porfirio Diaz, 800 members; Steel and Smelter Workers' Union, of Chihuahua, 500 members.

These are the only permanent Mexican unions, and an addition of their membership shows that they total under 16,000. Other unions have sprung up, as at Rio Blanco, at Cananea, at Tizapan and other places in response to a pressing need, but they have been crushed either by the employers or by the government—usually by both working in conjunction, the latter acting as the servant of the former. In the two years since 1908 there has been practically no advance in organization. Indeed, for a time the largest union, the railroad workers, having been beaten in a strike, all but went out of existence. But recently it has revived to almost its former strength.

All the unions mentioned are Mexican unions exclusively. The only branch of American organization which extends to Mexico consists of railroad men, who exclude Mexicans from membership. Hence the Grand League itself is a purely Mexican union.

As to pay, the boilermakers received a minimum of 27½ cents an hour in American money; the carpenters, who are organized only in the capital and have as yet no scale, from 75 cents to $1.75; the cigarmakers, from $1.75 to $2; the shop blacksmiths, 22½ cents an hour, and the steel and smelter workers, 25 cents an hour.

Among these trades there have been several strikes. In 1905 the cigarmakers enforced their own shop rules. A little later the union mechanics in the railroad shops at Aguascalientes struck because they were being gradually replaced by Hungarian unorganized men at lower wages. The strikers not only won their point, but secured a five-cent per day raise of wages besides, which so encouraged the boilermakers that the latter craftsmen made a demand all over the country for a five-cent raise and got it.

Besides several short strikes of less importance still, this is the extent of the labor victories in Mexico. Victory has been the exception. Intervention by the government, with blood and prison for the strikers, has been the rule.

The strike of the Grand League of Railway Workers occurred in the spring of 1908. The league consists principally of brakemen, who received $37.50 per month in American money, and shop mechanics, who received twenty-five cents an hour. Early in 1908 the bosses at San Luis Potosi began discriminating against union men, both in the shops and on the trains. The unions protested to General Manager Clark, and the latter promised to make reparation within two months. At the end of two months nothing had been done. The union then gave the manager twenty-four hours in which to act. At the end of twenty-four hours still nothing had been done. So the entire membership on the road, consisting of 3,000 men, walked out.

The strike tied up every foot of the Mexican National Railway, consisting of nearly one thousand miles of road running from Laredo, Texas, to Mexico City. For six days traffic was at a standstill. Recognition of the union, which is the necessary prerequisite for successful peace in any struggle along union lines, seemed assured. The great corporation seemed beaten, but—the men had not reckoned with the government.

No sooner did Manager Clark discover that he was beaten on the economic field of battle than he called to his aid the police power of Diaz.

President Vera of the Grand League was waited upon by the governor of the State of San Luis Potosi and informed that if the men did not return to work forthwith they would all be rounded up and thrown in jail and prosecuted for conspiracy against the government. He showed Vera a telegram from President Diaz which in significant terms reminded Vera of the massacre at Rio Blanco, which had occurred but a year previously.

Vera hurried to the national capital, where he interviewed Vice-President Corral and attempted to secure an audience with Diaz. Corral confirmed the threats of the governor of San Luis Potosi. Vera pleaded that the strikers were keeping perfect order; he begged that they be fairly treated. But it was no use. He knew that the government was not bluffing, for in such matters the Mexican government does not bluff. After a conference with the executive board of the union the strike was called off and the men went back to work.

Of course that demoralized the union, for what, pray, is the use of organization if you are not permitted to pluck the fruits of organization? The strikers were taken back to work, as agreed, but they were discharged one after another at convenient times. The membership of the league fell off, those remaining upon the roll remaining only in the hope of a less tyrannical government soon replacing the one that had foiled them. Vera resigned the presidency. His resignation was refused, he still remained the nominal head of the organization, but there was nothing that he could do. It was at this juncture that I met and talked with him about the railroad strike and the general outlook for Mexican unionism.

"The oppression of the government," said Vera, in his last few words to me, "is terrible—terrible! There is no chance for bettering the condition of labor in Mexico until there is a change in the administration. Every free laborer in Mexico knows that!"

Vera organized the Grand League of Railway Workers of Mexico in 1904, and since that time he has passed many months in prison for no other reason than his union activities. Not until early in 1909 did he engage in anything that smacked of political agitation. The hardships imposed by the government upon union organization, however, inevitably drove him into opposition to it. He became a newspaper correspondent, and it was because he dared to criticize the despot that he again found his way into that awful pit, Belem.

August 3, 1909, Vera was arrested at Guadalajara and carried to Mexico City. He was not taken before a judge. Nor was any formal charge lodged against him. He was merely told that the federal government had decided that he must spend the next two years in prison, serving out a sentence which had four years previously been meted out to him for his union activities, but under which he had been pardoned after serving one year and seven months.

Though a permanent cripple, Vera is a brave and honest man and a fervent organizer. Mexican liberty will lose much by his imprisonment.

Strikes in Mexico so far have usually been more the result of a spontaneous unwillingness on the part of the workers to go on with their miserable lives than of an organization of labor behind them or an appeal by agitators. Such a strike was that of Tizapan.

I mention the strike of Tizapan because I happened to visit the spot while the strikers were starving. For a month the strike had been going on, and though 600 cotton mill operatives were involved and Tizapan was only a score of miles from the palace of Chapultepec, not a daily newspaper in the capital, as far as I have learned, mentioned the fact that there was a strike.

I first heard of the Tizapan strike from Paulino Martinez, the editor, who is now a political refugee in the United States. Martinez cautioned me against saying that he told me, since, though he had not heard of the strike himself until after it had been called, he thought the telling might result in his arrest. The next day I took a run out to Tizapan, viewed the silent mill, visited the strikers in their squalid homes, and finally had a talk with the strike committee.

Except for Valle Nacional, I never saw so many people—men, women and children—with the mark of acute starvation on their faces, as at Tizapan. True, there was no fever among them, their eyes were not glazing with complete exhaustion from overwork and insufficient sleep, but their cheeks were pale, they breathed feebly and they walked unsteadily from lack of food.

These people had been working eleven hours a day for wages running from fifty cents to three dollars a week in our money. Doubtless they would have continued to work for it if they were really paid it, but the bosses were always devising new means to rob them of what little they were entitled to. Dirt spots on the calico meant a loss of one, two and sometimes even three *pesos*. Petty fines were innumerable. Finally, each worker was taxed three *centavos* per week to pay for the food of the dogs belonging to the factory. That was the last straw. The toilers refused to accept partial wages, the mill was closed and the period of starvation began.

When I visited Tizapan three-fourths of the men had gone away seeking work and food in other parts. Being wholly without means, it is quite likely that a large percentage of them fell into the hands of labor agents and were sold into slavery in the hot lands. A few men and the women and children were staying and starving. The strike committee had begged the national government to redress their wrongs, but without avail. They had asked President Diaz to reserve for them a little land out of the millions of acres which he was constantly signing away to foreigners, but they had received from him no reply. When I asked them if they hoped to win the strike, they told me no, that they had no hope, but they did not care; they preferred to die at once and in the open air than to go back to such miserable treatment as had been accorded them in the factory. Here is a translation of a pitiful appeal which these Tizapan strikers sent out to mill centers in other sections of the country:

Fellow Countrymen:

By this circular we make known to all the workers of the Mexican Republic that none of the factories which exist in our unfortunate country have exhibited men so avaricious as the manufacturers of "La Hormiga," Tizapan, since they are worse than highway robbers; not only are they robbers, but they are tyrants and hangmen.

Let us make it plain to you. Here are we robbed in weights and measures. Here are we exploited without mercy. Here are we fined two and three *pesos* and down to the very last of our wages, and we are dismissed from our work with kicks and blows. But what is the most disgusting, ridiculous and vile part of it all is the discount that is made on the workers of three cents weekly for the maintenance of the lazy dogs of the factory. What a disgrace!

Who can live such a sad and degraded life? Whereupon it does not appear that we live in a republic conquered by the blood of our forefathers, but rather that we inhabit a land of savage and brutal slavedrivers. Who can subsist on wages of three and four pesos weekly and discounted from that fines, house rent, and robbery in weights and measures? No, a thousand times, no! Because of such circumstances we petition our dear country for a fragment of land to cultivate, so that we may not continue to enrich the foreigner, trader and exploiter, who piles up gold at the cost of the devoted toil of the poor and unfortunate worker!

We protest against this order of things and we will not work until we are guaranteed that the fines will be abolished and also the maintenance of dogs, for which we ought not to pay, and that we shall be treated as workers and not as the unhappy slaves of a foreigner.

We hope that our fellow workers will aid us in this fight.

THE COMMITTEE.

Tizapan, March 7, 1909.

The Tizapan strike was lost. When it was ready to do so, the company reopened the mill without difficulty, for, as corporation prospectuses of the country say, there is labor aplenty in Mexico and it is very, very cheap.

The Cananea strike, occurring as it did, very close to the border line of the United States, is perhaps the one Mexican strike of which Americans generally have heard. Not having been a witness, nor even having ever been upon the ground, I cannot speak with personal authority, and yet I have talked with so many persons who were in one way or another connected with the affair, several of whom were in the very thick of the flying bullets, that I cannot but believe that I have a fairly clear idea of what occurred.

Cananea is a copper city of Sonora, situated several score of miles from the Arizona border. It was established by W. C. Greene, who secured several million acres along the border from the Mexican government at little or no cost, and who succeeded in forming such intimate relations with Ramon Corral and other high Mexican officials that the municipal government established upon his property was entirely under his control, while the government of the Mexican town close beside it was exceedingly friendly to him and practically under his orders. The American consul at Cananea, a man named Galbraith, was also an employe of Greene, so that both the

Mexican and United States governments, as far as Cananea and its vicinity was concerned, were—W. C. Greene.

Greene, having since fallen into disrepute with the powers that be in Mexico, has lost most of his holdings and the Greene-Cananea Copper Company is now the property of the Cole-Ryan mining combination, one of the parties in the Morgan-Guggenheim copper merger.

In the copper mines of Cananea were employed six thousand Mexican miners and about six hundred American miners. Greene paid the Mexican miners just half as much as he paid the American miners, not because they performed only half as much labor, but because he was able to secure them for that price. The Mexicans were getting big pay, for Mexicans—three *pesos* a day, most of them. But naturally they were dissatisfied and formed an organization for the purpose of forcing a better bargain out of Greene.

As to what precipitated the strike there is some dispute. Some say that it was due to an announcement by a mine boss that the company had decided to supersede the system of wage labor with the system of contract labor. Others say it was precipitated by Greene's telegraphing to Diaz for troops, following a demand of the miners for five *pesos* a day.

But whatever the immediate cause, the walkout was started by a night shift May 31, 1906. The strikers marched about the company's property, calling out the men in different departments. They met with success at all points, and trouble began only at the last place of call, the company lumber yard, where the parade arrived early in the forenoon. Here the manager, a man named Metcalfe, drenched the front ranks with water from a large hose. The strikers replied with stones, and Metcalfe and his brother came back with rifles. Some strikers fell, and in the ensuing battle the two Metcalfes were killed.

During the parade, the head of the Greene detective squad, a man named Rowan, handed out rifles and ammunition to the heads of departments of the company, and as soon as the fight started at the lumber yard the company detective force embarked in automobiles and drove about town, shooting right and left. The miners, unarmed, dispersed, but they were shot as they ran. One of the leaders, applying to the chief of police for arms with which the miners might protect themselves, was terribly beaten by the latter, who put his entire force at the service of the company. During the first few hours after the trouble some of the Greene men were put in jail, but very soon they were released and hundreds of the miners were locked up. Finding that no justice was to be given them, the bulk of the miners retired to a point on the company's property, where they barricaded themselves and, with what weapons they could secure, defied the Greene police.

From Greene's telegraph office were sent out reports that the Mexicans had started a race war and were massacring the Americans of Cananea, including the women and children. Consul Galbraith sent out such inflammatory stories to Washington that there was a flurry in our War Department; these stories were so misleading that Galbraith was removed as soon as the real facts became known.

The agent of the Department of Fomento of Mexico, on the other hand, reported the facts as they were, and through the influence of the company he was discharged at once.

Colonel Greene hurried away on his private car to Arizona, where he called for volunteers to go to Cananea and save the American women and children, offering one hundred dollars for each volunteer, whether he fought or not. Which action was wholly without valid excuse, since the strikers not only never assumed the aggressive in the violent acts of Cananea, but the affair was also in no sense an anti-foreign demonstration. It was a labor strike, pure and simple, a strike in which the one demand was for a raise of wages to five *pesos* a day.

While the false tales sent out from Greene's town were furnishing a sensation for the United States, Greene's Pinkertons were sent about the streets for another shoot-up of the Mexicans. Americans had been warned to stay indoors, in order that the assassins might take pot shots at anything in sight, which they did. The total list of killed by the Greene men—which was published at the time—was twenty-seven, among whom were several who were not miners at all. Among these, it is said, was a boy of six and an aged man over ninety, who was tending a cow when the bullet struck him.

By grossly misrepresenting the situation, Greene succeeded in getting a force of three hundred Americans, rangers, miners, stockmen, cowboys and others, together in Bisbee, Douglas and other towns. Governor Yzabal of Sonora, playing directly into the hands of Greene at every point, met this force of men at Naco and led them across the line. The crossing was disputed by the Mexican customs official, who swore that the invaders might pass only over his dead body. With leveled rifle this man faced the governor of his state and the three hundred foreigners, and refused to yield until Yzabal showed an order signed by General Diaz permitting the invasion.

Thus three hundred American citizens, some of them government employes, on June 2, 1906, violated the laws of the United States, the same laws that Magon and his friends are accused of merely *conspiring* to violate, and yet not one of them, not even Greene, the man who knew the situation and was extremely culpable, was ever prosecuted. Moreover, Ranger Captain Rhynning, who accepted an appointment of Governor Yzabal to command this force of Americans, instead of being deposed from his position, was afterwards promoted. At this writing he holds the fat job of warden of the territorial penitentiary at Florence, Arizona.

The rank and file of those three hundred men were hardly to be blamed for their act, for Greene completely fooled them. They thought they were invading Mexico to save some American women and children. When they arrived in Cananea on the evening of the second day, they discovered that they had been tricked, and the following day they returned without having taken part in the massacres of these early days of June.

But with the Mexican soldiers and *rurale* forces which poured into Cananea that same night it was different. They were under the orders of Yzabel, Greene and Corral, and they killed, as they were told to do. There was a company of cavalry under Colonel Barron. There were one thousand infantrymen under General Luis Torres, who hurried all the way from the Yaqui river to serve the purposes of Greene. There were some two hundred *rurales*. There were the Greene private detectives. There was a company of the *acordada*.

And all of them took part in the killing. Miners were taken from the jail and hanged. Miners were taken to the cemetery, made to dig their own graves and were shot. Several hundred of them were marched away to Hermosillo, where they were impressed into the Mexican army. Others were sent away to the penal colony on the islands of Tres Marias. Finally, others were sentenced to long terms in prison. When Torres' army arrived, the strikers who had barricaded themselves in the hills surrendered without any attempt at resistance. First, however, there was a parley, in which the leaders were assured that they would not be shot. But in spite of the fact that they persuaded the strikers not to resist the authorities, Manuel M. Dieguez, Esteban E. Calderon and Manuel Ibarre, the members of the executive board of the union, were sentenced to four years in prison, where they remain to this day—unless they are dead.

Among those who were jailed and ordered shot was L. Gutierrez De Lara, who had committed no crime except to address a meeting of the miners. The order for the shooting of De Lara, as well as for the others, came direct from Mexico City on representations from Governor Yzabal. De Lara had influential friends in Mexico, and these, getting word through the friendship of the telegraph operator and the postmaster of Cananea, succeeded in securing De Lara's reprieve.

The end of the whole affair was that the strikers, literally hacked to pieces by the murderous violence of the government, were unable to rally their forces. The strike was broken, and in time the surviving miners went back to work on more unsatisfactory conditions than before.

Such is the fate the Czar of Mexico metes out to workingmen who dare demand a larger share of the products of their labor in his country. One thing more remains to be said. Colonel Greene refused to grant the demand of the miners for more wages, and he claimed to have a good excuse for it.

"President Diaz," said Greene, "has ordered me not to raise wages, and I dare not disobey him."

It is an excuse that is being offered by employers of labor all over Mexico. Doubtless President Diaz did issue some such order, and employers of Mexican labor, Americans with the rest of them, are glad to take advantage of it. American capitalists support Diaz with a great deal more unanimity than they support Taft. American capitalists support Diaz because they are looking to Diaz to keep Mexican labor always cheap. And they are looking to Mexican cheap labor to help them break the back of organized labor in the United States, both by transferring a part of their capital to Mexico and by importing a part of Mexico's laborers into this country.

Critics and Corroboration

The first five chapters of this book, which, in a little less extended form, were published serially in The American Magazine in the fall of 1909, called forth a considerable measure of comment both in the United States and Mexico. Both the magazine and myself were deluged with letters, many of which asserted that the writers themselves had witnessed conditions similar to those which I described. On the other hand, there were many who flatly averred that I was a fabricator and a slanderer, declaring, variously, that nothing akin to slavery or even to peonage existed in Mexico, that, if it did, it was the only practical way to civilize Mexico, anyhow, that the Mexican working people were the happiest and most fortunate on the face of the earth, that President Diaz was the most benign ruler of the age, that a long enough hunt would discover cases of barbarities even in the United States, and we would better clean our own house first, that there were $900,000,000 of American capital invested in Mexico—and so on and so on.

The remarkable thing, indeed, about the discussion was the headlong manner in which certain magazines, newspapers, book publishers and private individuals in this country rushed to the defense of President Diaz. These individuals evidently acted on the theory that a charge of slavery in his domain was an aspersion on the rule of President Diaz, and quite correctly so. Wherefore, they proceeded to denounce me in the most vigorous terms, on the one hand, and to let loose a flood of adulatory literature concerning President Diaz, on the other. I imagine that it would require a very long freight train to carry all the flattering literature that was circulated in this country by the friends of Diaz in the six months following the first appearance of my articles upon the news stands.

The perusal of those articles and this other literature also would drive anyone inevitably to the conclusion that somebody was deliberately distorting the truth. Who was distorting the truth? Who —and why? Since the who as well as the why are peculiarly a part of this story I may be pardoned for pausing for a few pages to reply, first, to the question, "Who?"

It would give me pleasure to present here some hundreds of letters which, among them, corroborate many times all the essential features of my account of Mexican slavery. But did I do so there would be little room left in the book for anything else. I can merely say that in most cases the writers claimed to have spent various numbers of years in Mexico. The letters were unsolicited, the writers were paid by no one; in many cases they were endangering their own interests in writing. If I am the liar, all of these persons must be liars, also, a proposition which I doubt if anyone could believe were they to read the letters.

But I am not printing these letters and I do not ask the reader to consider them in my favor. Samples of them, and a large enough number to be convincing, are to be found, however, in the November, December and January numbers of The American Magazine.

I shall pass over, also, the published testimony of other writers, well-known investigators, who have corroborated my story in more or less detail. For example, the account of the slavery of the

American rubber plantations, written by Herman Whitaker and printed in The American Magazine for February, 1910; the accounts of the slavery of Yucatan by the English writers, Arnold and Frost, in the book, "An American Egypt," which was quoted at length in The American Magazine of April, 1910. The corroboration which I shall present here is taken almost entirely from my critics themselves, persons who started out to deny the slavery or to palliate it, and who ended by admitting the existence of the essential features of that institution.

To begin with the least important class of witnesses, I shall take up first the statements of several American planters who rushed into print to defend the system of their friend Diaz. There is George S. Gould, manager of the San Gabriel rubber plantation, on the Isthmus of Tehuantepec. In various newspapers Mr. Gould was quoted extensively, especially in the San Francisco Bulletin, where he speaks of the "absolute inaccuracy" of my writings. Here are some of his explanations taken from that paper:

As general manager of the San Gabriel, I send $2,500 at a certain season to my agent in the City of Oaxaca. He opens an employment office and calls for a quota of seventy-five men. . . .

The laborer is given an average of fifty cents (Mexican) a week until the debt he owes the company is liquidated. The company is not obliged to pay him this amount, but does so to keep him contented. He is usually contracted for for periods ranging from six months to three years. In three years, if he is reasonably industrious and saving, he will not only have paid off his debt money, but he will draw his liquidation with money in his pocket. . . .

The sum total is this: The peon slavery in Mexico might be called slavery in the strictest sense of the word, but as long as the laborer is under contract to the plantation owner he is being done an inestimable good. It is the plantation owners who prevent the peon—ordinarily worthless humans with no profession—from becoming public charges. Unwittingly perhaps they block a lawless and irresponsible element by teaching the peon to use his hands and brain.

Mr. Edward H. Thompson was for many years the American consul in Yucatan. Mr. Thompson owns a *henequen* plantation, and, though I did not visit it, I was informed that he held slaves under exactly the same conditions as do the *henequen* kings. Immediately following the publication of my first article Mr. Thompson issued a long statement that was published in so many papers that I imagine a news syndicate was employed to circulate it. Mr. Thompson began by denouncing my article as "outrageous in its statements and absolutely false in many details." But read what Mr. Thompson himself says are the facts:

Reduced to its lowest terms and looking at the matter without the desire to produce a sensational magazine article, the so-called slavery becomes one of simple contract convenience to both parties. The native needs the money, or thinks he does, while the planter needs the labor of the native servant.

The indebted servant is held more or less strictly to the terms of the verbal and implied contract, according to the personal equation of the planter or his representative. This general fact is equally true in all of the great industries of our country as well as in Yucatan.

I do not seek to defend the system of indebted labor. It is bad in theory and worse in practice. It is bad for the planter because it locks up capital that could otherwise be employed in developing the resources of the plantation. It is worse for the servant, because by reason of it he learns to lean too much on the powerful protection of his creditor-employer.

Reading those lines with discrimination, you will observe that Mr. Thompson admits that debt slavery is prevalent in Yucatan, admits that a similar system exists all over Mexico, and admits that it is a system that cannot be defended. Then why does he defend it?

Mr. C. V. Cooper, an American land promoter, writing in the Portland Oregonian, says that he read my articles with "amusement mixed with indignation," and decided that they were "grossly exaggerated." But he made some admissions. Said he:

The Mexican peon law provides that if a servant for any reason is indebted to his employer, he must remain and work out the debt at a wage agreed upon between the employer and the employe.

But, Mr. Cooper, if the employe *must* remain, how can he have any say as to how much the wage which you declare is "agreed upon" shall be?

Very naively Mr. Cooper explains the freedom of the peon. Says he:

There is nothing compulsory in his service at all. If he does not like his surroundings or his treatment, he is at perfect liberty to obtain the amount of his debt from anyone else and leave the property.

From whom else, Mr. Cooper? Oh, the sweet, sweet liberty of Mexico!

It is too bad that Mr. Cooper should have marred such a rosy picture as he paints by admitting the man-hunting part of the system. But he does:

Should a man run away, we can have him brought back if the amount of the debt involved is worth while. The expense of his capture is paid by the plantation and added to his account.

Yet Mr. Cooper finally avers:

The peons are perfectly free to come and go as they choose, with the only legal proviso that they do not swindle any one out of money that has been advanced them in good faith.

Mr. Cooper thought so well of his defense of the Diaz system that he—or someone else—went to the expense of having it printed in pamphlet form and circulated about the country. There were other pamphleteers besides Mr. Cooper, too, who rushed to the defense of Mexico. One was Mr. E. S. Smith of Tippecanoe, Iowa, the man who wired President Taft begging him to deny The American

Magazine the mails, and that before my first article went to press. Mr. Smith wrote "The Truth About Mexico," which The Bankers' Magazine printed, and the same matter was afterwards put into a pamphlet. Mr. Smith was so extravagant in his denials of imperfections in Mexican institutions and so glowing in his descriptions of Mexico's "ideal" government that one of that government's warmest defenders, The Mexican Herald, was revolted by the production and printed a long editorial in which it prayed that Mexico might be delivered of such friends as Mr. Smith.

Mr. Guillermo Hall, another American who is interested in Mexican properties, considers my articles a "great injustice," inasmuch as, since the poor Mexican knows nothing of freedom, he must be perfectly well off as a slave. The Tucson, Arizona, Citizen quoted Mr. Hall as follows:

> The cold facts stated in black type might seem preposterous to the Americans of this country, whose training and environment are so different. . . . In the lower country along the border, for instance, the so-called peon has no conception of the liberty we enjoy in America. He absolutely doesn't know what it means. The property owners there are compelled by force of circumstances to maintain, at present, a sort of feudalism over him.

Mr. Dwight E. Woodbridge, a planter and writer, wrote at length in defense of Mexican slavery in the Mining World, the organ of the American Mine Owners' organization. Here are some excerpts:

> Unquestionably there are brutalities and savageness in Mexico. Outrages are committed there, both on the prisoners taken from confinement to haciendas and on the Yaquis. . . . I am interested in a large plantation in southern Mexico, where we have some 300 Yaqui laborers.
>
> Throughout the Yaqui country I have seen such things as are pictured in the magazine, passed the bodies of men hanging to trees, sometimes mutilated; have seen hundreds of tame Yaquis herded in jails to be sent to the plantations of Yucatan, or Tabasco, or Veracruz; have heard of worse things.

There is a certain sort of peonage in Mexico. One may call it slavery if he will, and not be far from the truth. It is, in fact, illegal, and no contracts under it can be enforced in the courts. The slave is a slave so long as he is working out his debt.

Of course none of the defenders of Mexico admit all of my assertions, and all of them, naturally, seek to minimize the horrors of the slave system—otherwise they could not be defending it. But you will see that one admits one thing and another another until the whole story is confessed as true.

Among the American publishers who rushed to the defense of Diaz was Mr. William Randolph Hearst. Mr. Hearst sent a writer, Otheman Stevens, to Mexico to gather material to prove that Mexico is not barbarous. Valiantly did Mr. Stevens attempt to carry out his trust, but in dealing with the contract slavery system he succeeded in admitting most of the essential points, and was able to defend only on the plea of capitalistic "necessity." Some of his admissions, as they appeared in the Cosmopolitan Magazine of March, 1910, are:

To offset these prospects of early industrial advances is the contract labor system, and the contract labor system in Mexico is a bad institution.

Its repulsive feature to our eyes is the fact that, while the laborer enters voluntarily into the contract, the law gives the employer a right over the workman's person in the enforcement of the contract. Theoretically, there is no argument to be made for contract labor.

If an enganchado rebels or is insolent or lazy, the lithe rod in the hands of the 'boss' of the gang winds around him, and he soon understands that he must fulfill his part of the contract. If he runs away, a reward of ten dollars is paid to whoever brings him back. His clothes are taken away from him, and he is clad in a gunny sack with holes cut for arms and legs.

Mr. Stevens' defense of this system, as published in the same number of the same magazine, is:

Outside of the restrictions of dogmatic controversy there is only one phase that makes a wrong right, and that is necessity. A legal enforcement of a contract by using physical force over the person is in itself wrong. On the other hand, legislation now prohibiting contract labor would work a greater wrong, for it would destroy millions of investments, would retard a most beneficient and rapid development of the richest region on this continent, if not in the world, and would, by reflexes, work more harm to the very people it would intend to aid than an indefinite continuance of the present conditions.

This is exactly the logic the slave-driving cotton planters of our southern states used before the Civil War. It will hardly "go" with anyone who has not money invested in Mexican plantations which use *enganchados*.

I do not wish to tire the reader, but, aside from the fact that I have been most violently attacked, I have a reason for wishing to go a little deeper into this matter of critics and corroboration. Let us get right down into Mexico itself, down to the very newspapers that are paid a specified sum each week in exchange for manufacturing public opinion favorable to President Diaz and his system. In Mexico City there are two daily newspapers printed in English, the Herald and the Record. Both are prosperous and well edited, and both are open defenders of the Mexican government. The Herald, especially, repeatedly denounced my articles. I believe that I can show as many as fifty clippings from this paper alone which, in one way or another, attempted to cast doubt upon my statements. Nevertheless, in the course of the daily publication of the news, or in the very campaign of defense, both of these papers have since the first appearance of "Barbarous Mexico," printed matter which convincingly confirmed my charges.

October 23, 1909, the Daily Record dared to print an article from the pen of Dr. Luis Lara y Pardo, one of the best-known of Mexican writers, in which he admitted that my indictment was true. A few lines from the article will suffice. Said Dr. Pardo:

The regime of slavery continues under the cloak of the loan laws. Peons are sold by one hacendado to another under the pretext that the money that has been advanced must be paid. In the capital of the Republic itself traffic in human flesh has been engaged in.

On the haciendas the peons live in the most horrible manner. They are crowded into lodgings dirtier than a stable and are maltreated. The hacendado metes out justice to the peon, who is even denied the right to protest.

A widespread fear among the common people of being ensnared as *enganchados* would argue not only that the system is extensive, but that it is fraught with great hardship. January 6, 1910, the Mexican Daily Record published a news item which indicated that this is true, and also suggested one way in which the government plays into the hands of the labor snarers. Shorn of its headlines, the item is:

Five hundred contract laborers intended to work at construction camps on the Veracruz and Pacific railroad, are encamped near Buenavista station as a result of their unwillingness to sign a formal contract, and the law prohibiting their being taken into another state without such contract.

Governor Landa y Escandon yesterday afternoon refused to grant the request of R. P. Davis and F. Villademoros, signers of a petition to him to allow the laborers to be shipped out. With their wives, children, and all their worldly possessions they form a motley camp near the station.

In their petition, Davis and Villademoros claim that the railroad company is suffering large losses by the detention of the laborers and that many of the latter fear *if they sign contracts they will be shipped to sugar and coffee plantations and held until the expiration of the specified terms.*

Governor Landa refused the request on the ground that the law requires such a formality to protect the laborers, while the reason for waiving it did not appear logical.

The Mexican Herald furnishes more corroboration than the Mexican Record. Commenting editorially upon the announcements of "Barbarous Mexico," it said, August 27, 1909:

In this journal during recent years, and in many Mexican papers as well, the abuses of the peonage system, and the ill-treatment of *los enganchados* or contract laborers in some regions, have been most frankly dealt with. The enlightened Governor of Chiapas has denounced the evils of peonage in his state and has received the thanks of the patriotic press of the country. That there are dark spots in agricultural labor conditions, no fair-minded person of wide information seeks to deny.

About the same time Paul Hudson, general manager of the paper, was quoted in a New York interview as saying that my exposures "do not admit of categorical denial." And in the Mexican Herald of May 9, 1910, J. Torrey Conner, writing in praise of General Diaz, says: "Slavery, doubtless, is known to exist in Mexico—that is generally understood." In February, 1909, in an editorial item upon the political situation in the state of Morelos, the Mexican Herald went so far as to admit the killing of debt laborers by their masters. To quote it exactly:

It is undeniable that their (the planters') management is at times severe. When angry they heap abuse on the peons and even maltreat them physically. In some instances they have, in times not so distant, even taken the lives of native laborers who have incensed them, and have gone scot free.

August 27, 1909, in an article on "The *Enganchado*," the Herald said, in part:

The *enganchados* are guarded most carefully, for there is the ever present danger of their running away on the slightest opportunity. Often the *cabos* are cruel in their treatment, a fact which is to be condemned. . . . It is not in keeping here to mention the abuses which are alleged to have been practiced against the *enganchados*, the treatment of men so shamelessly that they die, the raping of the women, the deprivation of the laborers of any means of bathing, and the unsanitary condition of their houses, leading on to noxious diseases. . . . No planter who knows the real history of the system, or the inside facts of the neighboring plantations, will deny for a moment the worst stories of the *enganchado* are true.

Plantation men do not take the *enganchado* labor because they like it. Nor do they prefer it to any other, even the lowest. But there is a certain advantage in it, as one planter said to the writer, with a queer thrill in his voice: '*When you've got 'em they're yours, and have to do what you want them to do. If they don't, you can kill them.*'

Such corroboration from a subsidized supporter of the system itself would seem rather embarrassing to those individuals who were so zealous as publicly to announce that my portrayal of Mexican slavery was a fabrication. It will be seen that my exposures of Mexican slavery were not the first to be circulated in print; they were merely the first to be circulated widely, and they went into considerably more detail than anything that had gone before. The little item that I have just quoted admits practically all the worst features which I dealt with in my articles.

Here is an ordinary news item clipped from the Mexican Herald of May 30, 1909:

Angel Contreras, an *enganchado*, belonging to a good family, is reported to have been brutally killed by being beaten to death with staves at the nearby San Francisco sugar mills in the El Naranjal municipality. Local newspapers state that other similar crimes have been committed at that place.

This is the first information I have had that men are beaten to death in the sugar mills of Mexico.

I present a news item from the Mexican Herald which describes better than I did in my fourth chapter one of the methods pursued by labor snarers to get their fish into the net. The newspaper prints the story as if the occurrence were unusual; I reprint it in full because it is typical. The only difference is that in this particular case the

victim was rescued and the labor agent was jailed for a day or two
only because it chanced that the victim had been an employe of the
national Department of Foreign Relations. Had the authorities
wished to stop this sort of man-stealing, as the Herald would have
us believe, why did they not arrest the keepers of the other *"casas
de enganchadores"* which they found, and liberate the prisoners?
But here is the item, headlines and all:

BOY OF 16
TRAPPED HERE.

ALAMEDA SCENE OF BOLD
KIDNAPPING BY
SPANIARD.

TO GO TO OAXAQUENA.

CONTRACTORS PLANNED TO SEND
BOY TO AMERICAN
PLANTATION.

When Felipe Hernandez, agent of a company of labor contractors,
commonly referred to in Mexico as 'enganchadores,' met sixteen-year-
old Benito Juarez in the Alameda on Wednesday afternoon and induced
him by brilliant promises of work and wages to accompany him to a
house on la Calle de Violeta, he (Hernandez) made one of the serious
mistakes of his life. By refusing to allow young Benito to go out of the
house after he had once entered it, Hernandez violated one of the federal
statutes and he is now being held in the fifth comisaria to answer a
charge of illegal detention.

Hernandez claims that he is the employe of one Leandro Lopez, who
is securing laborers for the Oaxaquena Plantation Company, an American concern operating an extensive hacienda on the Isthmus of Tehuantepec, on the state boundary of Veracruz, not far from Santa Lucrecia. Both men are Spaniards. The whereabouts of the boy, Benito
Juarez, was not definitely ascertained until yesterday afternoon, when
his release was secured upon the demand of Subcomisario Bustamante

of the fifth comisaria, who subsequently arrested Hernandez after the lad's statement had been placed on record at the comisaria.

THE BOY'S SEDUCTION.

On Wednesday afternoon, at about 2 o'clock, young Benito, who had been working with his mother, a bread vendor, was sitting on one of the benches in the Alameda, when, according to his account, Hernandez happened along and in a benevolent way asked him if he wanted a job at $1.50 a day. The man explained that the work was at an alcohol factory near the city and that the position was something in the character of time-keeping or other clerical work. The lad agreed and was induced to accompany his new-found friend to Calle Violeta, where the details of his engagement were to be arranged.

On the way they stopped at a cheap clothing store, where Hernandez purchased a twenty-cent straw hat, a fifty-cent blouse, a pair of sandals and a pair of trousers. Arrived at the house on Calle Violeta young Juarez received orders to put on the peon clothing and to relinquish his own suit of good apparel. In the house where he found himself he encountered three or four other men in the same situation with himself who apprized him of the fact that he was now a contract laborer destined for a plantation in the hot country.

HIS FRIENDS TRACE HIM.

Until a short time ago Benito had been employed as a mozo in the office of the department of foreign relations on the Paseo de la Reforma and it was a fairly good suit of clothing that he had worn while working there that he exchanged for the peon's outfit. It was also through the charity of his former employer in the government office that he was released from his unwilling detention in Calle Violeta.

The boy's mother, Angela Ramos, who lives at No. 4 Calle Zanja, had expected to meet him at the Alameda, where he was waiting when Hernandez came along. Not seeing him, she started inquiry, which elicited the information that he had been seen going away with a man who was supposed to be a labor contractor, and she forthwith hunted up

Ignacio Arellano, who is employed in the foreign relations building, and explained to him her trouble.

POLICE APPEALED TO.

Mr. Arellano, accompanied by Alfredo Marquez, an employe of the department of fomento, secured the addresses of three establishments commonly known as 'casas de enganchadores,' located variously at Calle de Moctezuma, 7a Calle de Magnolia, and la de Violeta. Their experience as related yesterday to a representative of The Herald was much the same at each place and was about as follows:

At each of the labor contractors' 'offices' where they sought admission they were refused, being told that they had no such individual as the boy in question in their charge. At each place the assertion was made that they never contracted persons under age. Finding their efforts fruitless, Arellano and Marquez took the matter to the fifth comisaria, where it was explained to Subcomisario Bustamante, who detailed an officer and two secret service men to the places in question with orders to search them thoroughly.

SEARCHING THE HOUSE.

No particular resistance was made to the entrance of the officers at either the Moctezuma or Magnolia street places. In the former were about a dozen men who had signed contracts to go out of the city to work on plantations, while in the latter were about twice the same number. These men are said to have claimed that they were refused permission to leave the place where they were lodged while waiting transportation to their ultimate destinations.

At Calle Violeta, however, the door-keeper at first refused the officers admission, only submitting when threatened with the arrest of every person in the house. Here young Juarez was found and was taken to the fifth comisaria for examination. As soon as his statement had been taken the arrest of Hernandez was ordered, and after his identification by the boy, the latter was set at liberty.

THE BOY'S ACCOUNT.

Recounting his own adventure last night, young Juarez described the meeting in the Alameda and the exchange of clothing, and continued:

'After I entered the house I learned from one of the men who was already there that I had been fooled in the promise of pay at $1.50 as time-keeper in an alcohol factory, and when I asked the man with whom I had come if his promises were not correct he said that of course they were not and that I was to go to work as a peon on the Oaxaquena plantation at fifty cents per day. Then I asked him to let me go, as I did not want to do such work, but he would not let me leave the house, saying that I owed him five pesos for the clothes he had given me.

'Before that I had told him that I would have to ask my mother's permission before I could go. He told me he was in a great hurry, so I wrote her a note and gave it to him to be delivered. Later he told me my mother had read the note and had given her permission, but I have found out since that she never received it and was hunting for me at the time.

'I was given a peso and five cents as an advance on my pay and the next morning I was given twenty-five cents with which to buy food, which was sold in the house. All this money was charged up against me, to be paid after I went to work, as I learned before I left the place. Breakfast, which cost thirteen cents, consisted of chile and chicharrones (the crisp residue of dried-out pork fat), while dinner, a bowl of soup, cost twelve cents. There was no supper.

'After I was brought into the house there was brought in a man, and a woman who had a year-old baby with her. They are there yet. The people in the house still have my clothes, but I am pretty glad to get out of going to the hot country, anyway. I did not sign any sort of a contract. I did not even see one and I do not know whether the others in the place had signed contracts or not. They all said they had been refused permission to leave the house unless they paid back the money which they were told they owed.'

GOOD WORK OF THE POLICE.

From the time that the first notice of the infraction of the labor law was received by the police officials at the fifth comisaria until the prosecution of Hernandez was put under way their activity has demonstrated

beyond any question how far the government authorities are from connivance in labor abuses with which this country has been charged.

The Mexican law provides punishment by five years imprisonment
for offenses of this character against minors, and expressly forbids the
signing of contracts by persons under legal age binding themselves to
work. As there is no legal detention without process of law, the prospects
for a severe punishment of the man Hernandez, if the assertions of the
lad are found correct, seems certain, as he is likely to be made an example of for the benefit of other labor contractors disposed to be careless
of their methods.

I doubt if I could do better than to end this chapter with quotations
from official reports of the United States government itself. Cold-
bloodedly as were the succeeding paragraphs written, the statements
that they contain are yet exceedingly corroborative. They are from
Bulletin No. 38 of the United States Department of Labor, published
in January, 1902. I should like to quote more extensively, but I take
only a few paragraphs from pages 42, 43 and 44.

In a great many (Mexican) states where tropical products are raised
the native residents are employed under a contract which is compulsory
on their part, owing to their being in debt to the planter. . . .

The system of enforced labor is carried out to its logical sequence in
the sisal-grass plantations of Yucatan. There, on each large plantation,
is to be found a body of peons, called *criados* or *sirvientes* (servants),
who, with their families, live on the plantations, and in many cases
have been born there. These *criados* are bound to the soil by indebtedness, for although a mere contract to perform certain services does not
impose specific performance, it is held in Yucatan that where an advance payment has been made either the repayment of the money or, in
default thereof, the specific performance may be exacted.

The system of labor enforced by indebtedness seems to work in Yucatan to the satisfaction of the planter. The peon is compelled to work
unless he is able to pay off his constantly increasing debt, and any attempt at flight or evasion is followed by penal retribution. The peon
rarely, if ever, achieves independence, and a transference of a workman

from one employer to another is only effected by means of the new employer paying to the former one the amount of the debt contracted. The system thus resembles slavery, not only in the compulsion under which the peon works, but in the large initial expense required of the planter when making his first investment in labor.

In the State of Tabasco the conditions of forced labor are somewhat different and the difficulty of the labor problem, especially from the point of view of the planter, is exceedingly aggravated. In Tabasco the law does not permit the same remedy as in Yucatan, namely, the enforcement of the specific performance of a contract upon which an advance payment has been made, but this drawback is more apparent than real, since the governmental authority is vested in the hands of the landowning planting classes, and the obligation of contracted peons to work for the planters is virtually enforced.

Is it necessary to ask again, who has been distorting the truth, myself or the other fellow? Is there slavery in Mexico, and is it widespread? Are men bought and sold like mules, locked up at night, hunted down when they try to run away, starved, beaten, killed? Surely these questions have been answered to the satisfaction of every honest reader. But I have not yet answered that other question, why—why are so many Americans so ready to distort the truth about Mexico?

The Diaz-American Press Conspiracy

If there is any combination of Interests in the United States that exercises so powerful an influence over the press of this country as does President Diaz of Mexico I should like to know its name.

In a previous chapter I asserted that no publication in Mexico dares, no matter what the circumstances, to criticize President Diaz directly. While the same thing cannot, of course, be said of the United States, at least this can be said, that there exists a strange, even an uncanny, unwillingness on the part of powerful American publishers to print anything derogatory to the ruler of Mexico; that, also, there is manifested a remarkable willingness to print matter flattering to the Mexican dictator.

At this writing I do not know of a single book, regularly published and circulated in the United States, which seriously criticizes President Diaz, the man or his system; while I could name at least ten which flatter him most extravagantly. Indeed, I do not know of any book that has ever been circulated in the United States—that is, one put out by one of the regular publishing houses—which attempted an extended criticism of President Diaz.

And the situation with the magazines is exactly the same. While the number of articles containing praise of Diaz which have been published in magazines—not to mention newspapers—during the past several years have undoubtedly run into the hundreds, I do not know of one prominent magazine that has prosecuted a criticism of the Mexican dictator.

Is it not an astonishing situation? And what is the reason for it? Is it because the system of Diaz is beyond reproach? Or is it because by some mysterious power that personage is able to control the press in his favor?

Look about you. Is there any other statesman or politician of the present day, American or foreign, who has been accorded a larger proportion of praise and a smaller proportion of blame by prominent American publishers than President Diaz?

I say that I do not know of one prominent magazine that has prosecuted a criticism of Diaz. Then how about The American Magazine? The American Magazine began a criticism, truly. And it planned to carry it out. Repeatedly it promised its readers that it would deal with the political conditions behind the slavery of Mexico. It hinted that Diaz would be shown in a new light. It had the material in its hands—most of the material of this book—and it was very bold and unequivocal in its announcements. And then—

The American Magazine proved the point that I am making more convincingly than any other instance than I can cite. Suddenly my articles were stopped. The political investigation was stopped. Other articles were substituted, milder articles, good as corroborations of the exposures of slavery, but *in each and every one of these articles there was contained a suggestion that President Diaz was not personally to blame for the barbarous conditions that had been held up to the light.*

Diaz controls all sources of news and the means of transmitting it. Papers are suppressed or subsidized at the pleasure of the government.

We know of some of the subsidies paid even to important Mexican papers printed in English. The real news of Mexico does not get across the border. Books that truly describe the present state of things are suppressed or bought up even when published in the United States. A great Mexico-Diaz myth has been built up by skilfully applied influence upon journalism. It is the most astounding case of the suppression of truth and the dissemination of untruth that recent history affords.

With these words the editors of The American Magazine heralded to the world the first of my articles under the title of "Barbarous Mexico."

"Skilfully applied influence upon journalism!" Little did the writer of that pregnant phrase realize how pregnant it was. Little did he imagine that before six short months were gone that phrase would be as applicable to his own publication as to any other.

What was the skilfully applied influence exerted upon The American Magazine? I am not pretending to say. But to anyone who will go back and read again the bold announcements of the September, October and November numbers of the magazine—1909 —read the enthusiastic comments of the editors on the interest aroused by the series, the delighted statements of jumping circulation, the letters of subscribers begging the editors not to fear, but to go on with the good work, and then note how the magazine sheered away from its program after the first of the year, the conclusion that there was some kind of "skilfully applied influence" will seem pretty well justified.*

But let us note some of the journalistic antics of some other lead-

---

* Since this matter was put in type The American Magazine has begun a second series of articles on Mexico, in which it promises to follow out the thread of exposure which it dropped several months previously. In the October issue, 1910, it prints under the name of Alexander Powell an article two-thirds of which had been written by me and furnished to The American fifteen months earlier. The alleged author did not even take the trouble to re-write the material, and it appears almost word for word as I originally wrote it. To my mind this is but a confirmation of my widely circulated charges: First, that The American failed

ing publishers. There is William Randolph Hearst, for example, proprietor of the Cosmopolitan Magazine and numerous daily newspapers in different parts of the country. There is no use of dwelling here upon the democratic and humanitarian professions of Mr. Hearst. Everybody knows that for the United States, and doubtless most other countries, he advocates democracy, freedom of speech, a free press, universal suffrage, regulation of predatory corporations, protection of labor. But Mr. Hearst's readers have just learned that for Mexico he is in favor of despotism, a police ruled press, no suffrage, unbridled corporations, and—slavery. I have never seen a more frantic apology for these institutions anywhere than is to be found in the March, April and May, 1910, numbers of the Cosmopolitan Magazine.

That Mr. Hearst was personally responsible for the publication of these articles is evidenced by an interview which he gave The Mexican Herald while in Mexico last March. Says that newspaper, under date of March 23:

In reference to the stories attacking Mexico, which have been largely circulated recently, Mr. Hearst stated that he had looked after defending the good name of this country to the best of his ability. He placed two of his staff, Otheman Stevens and Alfred Henry Lewis, at work on matter pertaining to Mexico and much of the material collected by them had already appeared in some of his newspapers.

So headlong was Mr. Hearst's hurry to the defense of Diaz that he did not take time to secure writers familiar with the most primary facts about their subject, nor give them time to compare notes and avoid contradictions, nor give his editors time to verify ordinary

---

to carry out its promise to the public because of "skilfully applied influence;" second, that it has gone back to the subject of Mexico only because its readers who have read my charges have whipped it into doing so. Finally, its publication at this late day of my original material is proof that it has not been "gathering new facts," as announced, and that the facts furnished by me in the first place are the most effective as well as the most reliable that have yet come into its possession.

statements. Mr. Lewis' article was prepared so literally at the last moment that, when it came, the magazine had already been paged and the article had to be put in as an insertion, with special paging. A laughable feature of the campaign was that, in introducing his knights of the defense, the editor of the Cosmopolitan moralized at length on the matter of permitting raw and untried writers—meaning myself—to handle important subjects, named a list of proven and guaranteed-to-be-reliable writers among whom was Mr. Alfred Henry Lewis. But when Mr. Lewis came to write! I pray that in all this book there is not one mistake one-half as ridiculous as any of a dozen in Mr. Lewis' short article.

Mr. Lewis modestly remarked, near the start, that: "Personally, I know as much of Mexico and Mexicans as any." But the burden of his story was that my writings were inspired by Standard Oil, which wanted revenge on Diaz for having been "kicked out of Mexico." Now how Mr. Lewis could have lived in the United States during the previous few months and read the newspapers without having learned of the oil war in Mexico, a war in which at the very time the lines were written, Standard Oil seemed on the point of forcing its only competitor to sell out to it on unfavorable terms, how Mr. Lewis could have failed to know that Standard Oil owns millions of dollars worth of oil lands and does a vast majority of the retail oil business in Diaz-land, how he could have been ignorant of the fact that H. Clay Pierce, head of the Standard Oil corporation in Mexico, is a director of the National Railways of Mexico, the government merged lines, so-called, and a close ally of President Diaz, is a little difficult to understand. Personally, Mr. Lewis knows as much of Mexico and Mexicans as any! Any—what?

Just one more of Mr. Lewis' all-embracing blunders in that article. Said he:

Search where you will, in every Mexican corner, from the Pacific to the gulf, from Yucatan to the Arizona line, you will meet no sugar trust to cheat the government with false scales, no coal trust to steal the fires from the poor man's chimney, no wool or cotton trust to steal the clothes off his back, no beef trust to filch the meat from his table, no leather trust to take the shoes off his feet. . . . The trusts do not exist in Mexico.

Which proves that Mr. Lewis does not know the first principle upon which Mexican finance and Mexican commercial life is based. Not only does the same financial ring which monopolizes the great industries of the United States monopolize those same industries in Mexico—I shall presently enumerate some of them—but every state and locality has its minor trusts which control the necessities of life in their field a great deal more completely than such necessities are controlled in this country. Mr. Lewis does not seem to know that the Mexican government is openly in the trust business, that by sale and gift of special privileges known as "concessions" it creates and maintains trusts of high and low degree. Personally, Mr. Lewis knows as much of Mexico and Mexicans as any!

Just a slip or two from Mr. Stevens, taken almost at random.

There is no terrifying labor question to make the investor hesitate. *A strike is unknown*, and there is no danger of a shortage of labor, skilled or unskilled.

And another:

No bank in Mexico can fail, no bank-note can be worthless, and no depositor can possibly lose his money, no matter what fatality may befall the bank in which he has his account.

As to the first statement, I have answered it in the chapter, "Four Mexican Strikes." Three of these strikes are famous and there is no excuse for Mr. Stevens' having heard of none of them. As to the second statement, there are some hundreds of Americans who are just now fervently wishing it were really true—fervently wishing that they could get a settlement on the basis of twenty-five cents on the dollar. In February, 1910, about the time Mr. Stevens was pen-

ning so glowingly, the United States Bank of Mexico, the largest
bank in the country which catered to Americans, was wrecked in
exactly the same way as most American bank wrecks are made—by
misappropriation of funds to support a speculative scheme. The bank
went to smash, the president went to jail, the depositors did not get
their money and at this writing there seems little chance of their
getting any of it. Certainly they will never get all or half of it. And
this was not the only disaster of the sort that has lately occurred in
Mexico. About May 1, 1910, another American bank, the Federal
Banking Company, went to smash and its cashier, Robert E. Crump,
went to jail. The fact is that there was no ground for Mr. Stevens'
statement whatsoever.

To quote all of Mr. Stevens' blunders would be to quote most of
his three articles. He went to Mexico to prepare a defense of Diaz
and he did not take the trouble to put a liberal sprinkling of facts in
his defense. He was taken in charge by agents of Diaz and he wrote
down what they told him to write. He was even taken in on the
little yarn about the Yucatan slave who got his master into jail, a
yarn which had done duty before. The story runs that a *henequen*
king beat one of his laborers, the laborer appealed to a justice of
the peace, who arrested and fined the master. The truth of the incident was—and my authority is most reliable—that the slave had
run away, was caught by a planter other than his owner, who attempted to hold him quietly as his own. In the course of the day's
work the slave was badly beaten, and it was in this condition that
his real owner found him. The real owner secured the arrest of the
would-be thief, in the name of the slave, and so the story of the
"equality before the law" of the slave and master went out to the
world.

The important thing, however, is not the laughable mistakes of
Mr. Hearst's writers, but the wherefore of Mr. Hearst's putting his
printing presses so unreservedly into the service of a man and a

system such as he would not defend for a moment were they to be found in any other country.

But let us mention a few more publications which have put themselves in the same class as Mr. Hearst's magazine. There is Sunset Magazine. In February, 1910, it began a series of articles by "Gasper Estrada Gonzalez," who is announced as "a statesman who is very close to Diaz." There were three articles of fawning flattery. Followed an article by Herman Whitaker, in which he praised Diaz to the skies and absolved him from all blame for the slave atrocities of Mexico. Then came an article by a man named Murray, who wrote to justify Diaz's extermination of the Yaquis.

Moody's Magazine ran a series of articles under the title, "Mexico as it Is," in which the writer attempted to neutralize the effect of "Barbarous Mexico" upon the public conscience. I have already mentioned defenses which were published in the Bankers' Magazine and in the Mining World. In addition, The Overland Monthly, The Exporter, many newspapers—like the Los Angeles Times—and various smaller publications, as well as many private individuals and a book publisher or two took up the work of defending their friend Diaz.

As to the book defense against "Barbarous Mexico," little has appeared so far, doubtless because of the shortness of time, but there are reports that several books are on their way. One of these, it is said, is to be by James Creelman, who left the employ of Pearson's Magazine at the call of Diaz, hurried to Mexico from Turkey, and spent several weeks going over the route I described in my articles, in order that he might be able to "refute" me with verisimilitude, no doubt.

The book "Porfirio Diaz," written by Jose F. Godoy, whom Diaz recently appointed as his minister to Cuba, though it does not refer to my exposures in any way, was quite likely hurried out because of them. Here is a very expensively printed book, containing nothing that has not been printed repeatedly before, except—*seventy pages of endorsements of Diaz written by prominent Americans.* Here we have the case of a man, Mr. Godoy, who actually went about—or sent about—among senators, congressmen, diplomats and cabinet officers, *soliciting* kind words for President Diaz. And he got them. In looking over this book it seems to me that almost any discriminating persons would be moved to inquire *what moved G. P. Putnam's Sons to issue that book.* Surely it was not entirely the hope of profitable sales to the general public.

I know of only one book of criticism of the Diaz system that was put out by a regular American publisher, and the criticism in that book was so veiled and so interspersed with flattery that the American reviewers took it for one of the old adulatory sort. Only one of them, so the author himself told me, was discerning enough to see that it was a book of criticism. "I wrote the book that way," the author said to me, "in the hope that it would be allowed to circulate in Mexico."

But the officials of the Mexican government were more discerning than the American book reviewers and the book was not allowed to circulate. Not only that, but quite suddenly and mysteriously it disappeared from the stores in this country and very soon was not to be had. Had the book disappeared because it was bought by the public, the publishers would be expected to print a second edition, but this they declined to do and, though flatly asserting that the work was not again to appear, they also declined to give the author or other inquirers further satisfaction. The book I refer to was the one entitled "Porfirio Diaz," written by Rafael DeZayas Enriquez and issued by D. Appleton & Co., in 1908.

Carlo de Fornaro, a Mexican newspaperman, or rather, a native of Italy who had spent two years in newspaper work in Mexico City, also wrote a book, "Diaz, Czar of Mexico," printing it himself because he could not find a regular publisher. It was refused circulation in Mexico and action for criminal libel was at once begun against Fornaro in the New York courts. To bring this suit, the editor of Diaz's leading newspaper, El Imparcial, with Joaquin Casasus, the most prominent lawyer of Mexico and former ambassador to the United States, hurried from the Mexican capital. Among the American lawyers employed as special prosecutors was Henry W. Taft, brother of the president and counsel of the National Railways of Mexico. Fornaro, being without the means to bring witnesses from Mexico to support the charges made in his book, was convicted, sent to prison for one year and the book was thereafter not circulated in the regular way. In fact, immediately after the arrest of Fornaro for some reason the New York book stores, at least, refused longer to handle the work. The Fornaro incident occurred in 1909.

Perhaps even a more remarkable incident still was that of the suppression of "Yucatan, the American Egypt," written by Tabor and Frost, Englishmen. After being printed in England this book was put out in this country by Doubleday, Page & Co., one of our largest and most respectable publishers. It was put out in expensive form and, in the natural course of the book trade, should have been purchasable for years after it left the presses. But within six months the publishers, replying to a would-be purchaser, asserted that the book *"has gone out of print and absolutely no copies are available!"* I have the letter myself. The book was almost entirely about the ancient ruins of Yucatan, but it contained a score or so of pages exposing the slavery of the *henequen* plantations—and it had to go. What sort of argument was used upon our esteemed and respectable publishers to cause them to withdraw the book can be imagined.

These instances are added to the others to show what happens when a writer does succeed in getting an expose of the Diaz system into print. In this book which I am writing I am doing my best to bring out the most important facts and at the same time avoid giving valid grounds for action at libel. When it appears there will be no legal reason why it should not be circulated as the majority of books are circulated. Nevertheless, if it is extensively offered for sale in the usual way it will be the first extended criticism of Diaz and his system to be put squarely before the American people. And the reason for its being the first will be not because there have not been facts that begged to be printed and writers that desired to print those facts, but because of that "skilfully applied influence upon journalism" which General Diaz exerts in our land of free speech and free press.

Again I come back to the question: What is the source of that "influence upon journalism?" Why do citizens of the United States, who profess a reverence for the principles for which their forefathers of '76 fought, who claim to revere Abraham Lincoln most of all for his Emancipation Proclamation, who shudder at the labor-baiting of the Congo, at the horrors of Russia's Siberia, at the political system of Czar Nicholas, apologize for and defend a more cruel slavery, a worse political oppression, a more complete and terrible despotism—in Mexico?

To this question there is only one conceivable answer, that for the sake of sordid profits principles of decency and humanity, principles which are universally conceded as being best for the progress of the world, have been set aside.

By this I do not mean that all of the Americans who have expressed admiration for General Diaz have been directly bribed to do so by gifts of so many dollars and so many cents. By no means. Some publishers and some writers have undoubtedly been bought in this way. But the vast majority of the active flatterers of Diaz have been moved by nothing more than "business reasons," which, by some persons, will be considered as little different from bribery. As to the great mass of the Americans who think well of Diaz, and sometimes speak well of him—as distinct from what I have called the "active flatterers"—they have simply been fooled, deceived by the consistent press campaign which the others have kept up for, lo, these many years.

Such American planters as those whom I have quoted as defending the Diaz system of slavery may have been moved by nothing
more reprehensible than a desire to prevent my exposures from
"hurting the country," or "hurting business," meaning their business. In fact, I was much surprised that so many actual residents of
Mexico came forward in support of my statements as did, inasmuch
as nearly every American in Mexico has some land which he has
obtained for a very low price—or for nothing at all—and which he
wishes to sell at a profit. Or he has a stock-selling scheme, in a rubber
plantation, for example, with which he is trying to secure the good
money of widows and orphans, poor school teachers, small business
men and working people. Just as the average American real estate
boomer "boosts his town," decries exposures of political corruption
as "hurting business," even suppresses news of plague, earthquake
fatalities and such things, so the American in Mexico, knowing that
exposures of slavery and political instability will frighten away investments and perhaps lose him some profitable deals, seldom hesi-
tates to argue that political and industrial conditions in the country
are ideal. The more property a man owns in Mexico the less likely
is he to tell the truth about the country.

As to the American publishers, the "business reasons" are usually
found either in the interest of the publisher himself in some property
or "concession" in Mexico, or in his business connection with some
other persons of means who hold such properties or such concessions. And through one or the other of these avenues undoubtedly
nearly all of our largest publishers, of books, magazines or newspapers, are touched. The situation in my home town may be a little
exceptional, but from it may be guessed the extent of the "skilfully
applied influence" of Diaz that probably extends over the whole
country. I reside in Los Angeles, California, where there are five
daily newspapers. At the time of the high-handed persecutions of
Magon, Villarreal and Rivera, Sarabia, De Lara, Modesto Diaz,
Arizmendez, Ulibarri and other Mexicans, political enemies of Diaz,

in 1907, it became plain that the muzzle was on all of those newspapers. Suspicion was confirmed by a managing editor of one of
them, who said in confidence to me and to others:

*"The newspapers of this town could get those men out of jail in
twenty-four hours if they went at it. But they won't go at it because
the owners of all five are interested in concessions in Mexico. You
see we're up against it. We don't dare to say a word, for if we did
Diaz would get back at us."*

Two of these newspaper owners were Mr. Hearst himself and
Harrison Gray Otis, the latter proprietor of the well known Los
Angeles Times. Each of these men own more than a million acres of
Mexican land, which they are generally credited with securing from
the Mexican government for nothing or practically nothing. In
addition to owning a magnificent stock ranch, Mr. Hearst owns vast
oil lands and, in addition, is credited with being involved financially
with the Southern Pacific Railroad Company, which is one of the
hugest beneficiaries of the Diaz government. As to the magnificence
of Mr. Hearst's stock ranch, permit me to reproduce an item which
was published in the Mexican Herald, August 24, 1908.

IS WONDERFUL ESTATE.
HEARST HOLDINGS IN CHIHUAHUA
SMALL EMPIRE.
IS OVER MILLION ACRES.

WITHIN THE ENCLOSURE GRAZE 60,000 HEREFORDS AND 125,000 HEAD OF
SHEEP—THOUSANDS OF HORSES AND HOGS ARE RAISED THERE.

"With over a million acres of the finest agricultural and grazing land,
with large herds of blooded cattle, horses and sheep, roaming over this
vast domain, the big Hearst cattle ranch and farm in Chihuahua is the
peer of any such estate in the world, whether it lies in the great corn
belt of Illinois or Kansas, or stretches for miles across the wind-swept
prairies of Texas or Oklahoma. Two hundred and fifty miles of barbed
wire fence enclose a portion of this vast ranch and within the enclosure

graze 60,000 thoroughbred Herefords, 125,000 fine sheep, and many thousand head of horses and hogs. A modern, up-to-date ranch and farm, whose crops are unexcelled in the world, and whose stock is famous from end to end of the Republic, this ranch is convincing evidence of the great future which is in store for the agricultural and stock raising industry of Mexico."

Thus spoke E. Kirby Smith, a well-known planter of Campeche, who is spending a few days in the city. Mr. Kirby Smith has just returned from an extended trip into Chihuahua, where he spent several days on the great Hearst ranch.

"This ranch," said Mr. Kirby Smith, "is typical of the great modern stock farms and presents a glorious picture as to what may be expected from enterprises of this character, if properly conducted, in this Republic. The stock is of the best. Imported jacks and stallions, thoroughbred brood mares and thoroughbred cattle dot the ranch from end to end.

"Vast amounts of corn and potatoes are raised, and in potatoes alone fortunes are going to be made by the farmers of northern Mexico."

As to the Sunset Magazine, it is owned outright by the Southern Pacific Railroad company, and Moody's Magazine, the Bankers' Magazine, The Exporter, and the Mining World are all known to be dominated by Wall Street Interests. And what, pray, have the Southern Pacific Railroad and Wall Street to do with Diaz and Mexico?

The answer is—everything. While Wall Street has more or less conflicting interests in the looting of the United States, Wall Street is ONE when it comes to the looting of Mexico. This is the chief reason why American publishers are so nearly one when it comes to the flattering of Diaz. Wall Street and Diaz are business partners and the American press is an appendage of the Diaz press bureau. Through ownership and near ownership of magazines, newspapers and publishing houses, and through the power of shifting advertising patronage, Wall Street has up to this moment been able to suppress the truth and maintain a lie about Diaz and Mexico.

The American Partners of Diaz

The United States is a partner in the slavery of Mexico. After freeing his black slaves, Uncle Sam, at the end of half a century, has become a slaver again. Uncle Sam has gone to slave-driving in a foreign country.

No, I shall not charge this to Uncle Sam, the genial, liberty-loving fellow citizen of our childhood. I would rather say that Uncle Sam is dead and that another is masquerading in his place—a counterfeit Uncle Sam who has so far deceived the people into believing that he is the real one. It is that person whom I charge with being a slaver.

This is a strong statement, but I believe that the facts justify it. The United States is responsible in part for the extension of the system of slavery in Mexico; second, it is responsible as the determining force in the continuation of that slavery; third, it is responsible knowingly for these things.

When I say the United States I do not mean a few minor and irresponsible American officials. Nor do I mean the American nation —which, in my humble judgment, is unjustly charged with the crimes of some persons over whom, under conditions as they exist, it has no control. I use the term in its most literal and exact sense. I mean the organized power which officially represents this country at home and abroad. I mean the Federal Government and the Interests that control the Federal Government.

Adherents of a certain political cult in this country are wont to declare that chattel slavery was abolished in the United States because it ceased to be profitable. Without commenting on the truth or fallacy of this assertion, I aver that there are plenty of Americans who are prepared to prove that slavery is profitable in Mexico. Because it is considered profitable, these Americans have, in various ways, had a hand in the extension of the institution. Desiring to perpetuate Mexican slavery and considering General Diaz a necessary factor in that perpetuation, they have given him their undivided support. By their control of the press they have glorified his name, when otherwise his name should be by right a stench in the nostrils of the world. But they have gone much farther than this. By their control of the political machinery of their government, the United States government, they have held him in his place when otherwise he would have fallen. *Most effectively has the police power of this country been used to destroy a movement of Mexicans for the abolition of Mexican slavery and to keep the chief slave-driver of Barbarous Mexico, Porfirio Diaz, upon his throne.*

Still another step can we go in these generalizations. By making itself an indispensable factor in his continuation in the governmental power, through its business partnership, its press conspiracy and its police and military alliance, the United States has virtually reduced Diaz to a political dependency, and by so doing has virtually *transformed Mexico into a slave colony of the United States.*

As I have already suggested, these are generalizations, but if I did not believe that the facts set forth in this and the succeeding chapter fully justified each and every one of them, I would not make them.

Pardon me for again referring to the remarkable defense of

Mexican slavery and Mexican despotism which we find in the
United States, inasmuch as it is itself a strong presumption of
guilty partnership in that slavery and despotism. What publication
or individual in the United States, pray you, was ever known to
defend the system of political oppression in Russia? What publication or individual in the United States was ever known to excuse
the slave atrocities of the Congo Free State? How many Americans
are in the habit of singing paeans of praise to Czar Nicholas or the
late King Leopold?

Americans of whatever class not only do not dare to do these
things, but they do not care to do them. But what a difference when
it comes to Mexico! Here slavery is sacred. Here autocracy is deified.

It will not do to deny the honesty of the comparison between
Mexico and Russia or the Congo. For every worshipper of Diaz
knows that he is an autocrat and a slave-driver and enough of them
admit it to leave no ground for doubt that they know it.

What, then, is the reason for this strange diversion of attitude?
Why do so many prostrate themselves before the Czar of Mexico
and none prostrate themselves before the Czar of Russia? Why is
America flooded with books hailing the Mexican autocrat as the
greatest man of the age while it is impossible to buy a single book,
regularly published and circulated, that seriously criticizes him?

The inference is inevitable that it is because Diaz is the Golden
Calf in but another form, that Americans are profiting by Mexican
slavery and are exerting themselves to maintain it.

But there are easily provable facts that carry us far beyond any
mere inference, however logical it may be.

What is the most universal reply that has been made to my criticisms of Mexico and Mexico's ruler? That there are $900,000,000
of American capital invested in Mexico.

To the Powers that Be in the United States the nine hundred
million dollars of American capital form a conclusive argument

against any criticism of President Diaz. They are an overwhelming defense of Mexican slavery.

"Hush! Hush!" the word goes about. "Why, we have nine hundred million dollars grinding out profits down there!" And the American publishers obediently hush.

In that $900,000,000 of American capital in Mexico is to be found the full explanation not only of the American defense of the Mexican government, but also of the political dependency of Diaz upon the Powers that Be in this country. Wherever capital flows capital controls the government. This doctrine is recognized everywhere and by all men who have as much as half an eye for the lessons that the world is writing. The last decade or two has proved it in every country where large aggregations of capital have gathered.

No wonder there is a growing anti-American sentiment in Mexico. The Mexican people are naturally patriotic. They have gone through tremendous trials to throw off the foreign yoke in past generations and they are unwilling to bend beneath the foreign yoke today. They want the opportunity of working out their own national destiny as a separate people. They look upon the United States as a great colossus which is about to seize them and bend them to its will.

And they are right. American capital in Mexico will not be denied. The partnership of Diaz and American capital has wrecked Mexico as a national entity. The United States government, as long as it represents American capital—and the most rampant hypocrite will hardly deny that it does today—will have a deciding voice in Mexican affairs. From the viewpoint of patriotic Mexicans the outlook is melancholy indeed.

Let us cast our eyes over Mexico and see what some of that $900,000,000 of American capital is doing there.

The Morgan-Guggenheim copper merger is in absolute control of the copper output of Mexico.

M. Guggenheim Sons own all the large smelters in Mexico, as well as vast mining properties. They occupy the same powerful position in the mining industry generally in Mexico as they occupy in the United States.

The Standard Oil company, under the name of the Waters-Pierce, with many subsidiary corporations, controls a vastly major portion of the crude oil flow of Mexico. It controls a still greater portion of the wholesale and retail trade in oil—ninety per cent of it, so its managers claim. At the present writing there is an oil war in Mexico caused by an attempt of the only other oil distributing concern in the country—controlled by the Pearsons—to force the Standard to buy it out at a favorable price. The situation predicts an early victory for the Standard, after which its monopoly will be complete.

Agents of the American Sugar Trust have just secured from the Federal and State governments concessions for the production of sugar beets and beet sugar so favorable as to insure it a complete monopoly of the Mexican sugar business within the next ten years.

The Inter-Continental Rubber company—in other words, The American Rubber Trust—is in possession of millions of acres of rubber lands, the best in Mexico.

The Wells-Fargo Express company, the property of the Southern Pacific Railroad, through its partnership with the government, holds an absolute monopoly of the express carrying business of Mexico.

E. N. Brown, president of the National Railways of Mexico and a satellite of H. Clay Pierce and the late E. H. Harriman, is a member of the board of directors of the Banco Nacional, which is by far the largest financial institution in Mexico, a concern that has over fifty branches, in which all the chief members of the Diaz financial camarilla are interested and through which financial deals of the Mexican government are transacted.

Finally, the Southern Pacific Railroad and allied Harriman heirs, despite the much vaunted government railway merger, own outright or control by virtue of near-ownership, three-fourths of the main line railway mileage of Mexico, which enables it today to impose as absolute a monopoly in restraint of trade as exists in the case of any railway combination in the United States.

These are merely some of the largest aggregations of American capital in Mexico. For example, the Harriman heirs own two and one-half millions acres of oil land in the Tampico country, and a number of other Americans own properties running into the millions of acres. Americans are involved in the combinations which control the flour and meat trades of Mexico. The purely trade interests are themselves considerable. Eighty per cent of Mexican exports come to the United States and sixty-six per cent of Mexican imports are sent to her by us, the American trade with Mexico totaling some $75,000,000 a year.

So you see how it is in Mexico. The Americanization of Mexico of which Wall Street boasts, is being accomplished and accomplished with a vengeance.

It were hardly worth while to pause at this juncture and discuss the question why Mexicans did not get in on the ground floor and control these industries. It is not, as numerous writers would have us believe, because Americans are the only intelligent people in the world and because God made Mexicans a stupid people and intended that they should be governed by their superiors. One very good reason why Diaz delivered his country into the hands of Americans was that Americans had more money to pay for special privileges. And Americans had more money because, while all Mexicans were becoming impoverished by the war for the overthrow of the foreigner, Maximilian, thousands of Americans were making fortunes by means of grafting army contracts involved in our Civil War.

Let me present an instance or two of the way in which Americans are contributing to the extension of slavery.

Take the Yaqui atrocities, for example. Vice-president Corral, who was then in control of the government of the state of Sonora, stirred up a Yaqui war because he saw an opportunity to get the Yaqui lands and sell them at a good price to American capitalists. The Yaqui country is rich in both mining and agricultural possibilities. American capitalists bought the lands while the Yaquis were still on them, then stimulated the war of extermination and finally instigated the scheme to deport them into slavery in Yucatan.

But American capital did not stop even there. It followed the Yaqui women and children away from their homes. It saw families dismembered, women forced into wifehood with Chinamen, men beaten to death. It saw these things, encouraged them and covered them up from the eyes of the world because of its interest in the price of sisal hemp, because it feared that with the passing of slave labor the price of sisal hemp would rise. The American Cordage Trust, a ramification of Standard Oil, absorbs over half the henequen export of Yucatan. The Standard Oil press declares there is no slavery in Mexico. Governor Fred N. Warner, of Michigan, publicly denied my expose of slavery in Yucatan. Governor Warner is interested in contracts involving the purchase annually of half a million dollars worth of sisal hemp from the slave kings of Yucatan.

Also, Americans work the slaves—buy them, drive them, lock them up at night, beat them, kill them, exactly as do other employers of labor in Mexico. And they admit that they do these things. In my possession are scores of admissions by American planters that they employ labor which is essentially slave labor. All over the tropical section of Mexico, on the plantations of rubber, sugar-cane, tropical fruits—everywhere—you will find Americans buying, beating, imprisoning, killing slaves.

Let me quote you just one interview I had with a well known and popular American of Diaz's metropolis, a man who for five years ran a large plantation near Santa Lucrecia.

"When we needed a lot of *enganchados*," he told me, "all we had to do was to wire to one of the numerous *enganchadores* in Mexico, saying: 'We want so many men and so many women on such and such a day.' Sometimes we'd call for three or four hundred, but the *enganchadores* would never fail to deliver the full number on the dot. We paid fifty *pesos* apiece for them, rejecting those that didn't look good to us, and that was all there was to it. We always kept them as long as they lasted.

"It's healthier down there than it is right here in the city of Mexico," he told me. "If you have the means to take care of yourself you can keep as well there as you can anywhere on earth."

Less than five minutes after making this statement he told me:

"Yes, I remember a lot of three hundred *enganchados* we received one Spring. *In less than three months we buried more than half of them.*"

The hand of the American slave-driver of Mexico has been known to reach out for its victims even as far as his own home—the United States. During my travels in Mexico, in order to become better acquainted with the common people, I spent most of my traveling days in second or third class cars. Riding in a third class car between Tierra Blanca and Veracruz one night, I spied an American negro sitting in a corner.

"I wonder if they ever caught *him* down here?" I said to myself. "I'll find out."

Tom West, a free-born Kentucky negro of twenty-five, hesitated to admit that he had ever been a slave. But he confessed gradually.

"Ah was workin' in a brick yahd in Kaintucky at two dollahs a day," was the way Tom put it, "when anothah cullahd man come along an' told me he knowed where Ah cud get three seventy-five a day. Ah said 'Ah'm with ye.' So he hands me one o' them book prospectuses an' the next day he tuk me to the office o' the company an' they said the same thing—three seventy-five American money, or seven an' a half Mex! So Ah come with eighty othah cullahd folks by way o' Tampa, Florida, and Veracruz, down here to a coffee and rubbah plantation at La Junta, near Santa Lucrecia, Oaxaca.

"Seven and a half a day! Huh! Seven an' a half! That's just what they paid me when they let me go—after two yeahs! Ah run away twict, but they ketched me and brung me back. Did they beat me? Naw, they beat lots o' othahs, but they nevah beat me. Ah yeh, they batted me a few times with a stick, but Ah wouldn't a let 'em beat me; no suh, not me!"

The plantation that caught Tom West, Kentuckian, was an American plantation. Some months after talking with Tom I happened to hold a conversation with a man who identified himself as Tom's master after I had told him Tom's story.

"Those niggers," this American told me, "were an experiment that didn't turn out very well. They must have been ours, for I don't know of anybody else down that way that had them at the time of which you speak. The seven and a half a day? Oh, the agents told 'em anything to get them. That was none of our business. We simply bought them and paid for them and then made them work out their purchase price before we gave them any money. Yes, we kept them under lock and key at night and had to guard them with guns in the daytime. When they tried to make a break we'd tie 'em up and give 'em a good dressing down with a club. The authorities? We chummed with the authorities. They were our friends."

The partnership of American capital with President Diaz not only puts at its disposal a system of slave labor, but also permits it to utilize the system of peonage and to beat the class of wage-laborers down to the lowest point of subsistence. Where slavery does not exist in Mexico you find peonage, a mild form of slavery, or you find cheap wage-labor. Diaz's *rurales* shot Colonel Greene's copper miners into submission and threats of imprisonment put an end to the great strike on an American-Mexican railroad. American capitalists boast of the fact that their Diaz "does not permit any foolishness on the part of these labor unions." In such facts as these are found the reason for their hysterical defense of him.

I shall briefly outline the railroad situation in Mexico, and tell the story of the railway merger.

Today the main lines of Mexican railroads aggregate 12,500 miles. Of this mileage the Southern Pacific company controls and will probably soon own 8,941 miles, or nearly three-fourths of the total. These lines consist of:

The Southern Pacific in Mexico, 950 miles; the Kansas City, Mexico and Orient, 279 miles; the Pan-American, 296 miles; the Mexican, 327 miles; the National Railways of Mexico, 7,089 miles.

Of these the Southern Pacific is the only one that is being operated openly as the property of the Harriman heirs. The Orient road is operated under the presidency of A. E. Stilwell, a Harriman ally, whose vice-president, George H. Ross, is a director of the Chicago & Alton road, a Harriman property with which the Orient road has traffic agreements. Construction is still going on on both of these roads and they are drawing from the Diaz government about $20,000 of subsidy for every mile built, or nearly enough to build the road.

The Pan-American railroad was recently acquired by David H. Thompson, who is the nominal president. Thompson was the United States ambassador to Mexico, where he seems to have represented the Harriman interests first and the other American interests afterwards. After securing the road, he resigned the ambassadorship. It is a pretty generally accepted fact that Thompson was acting for Harriman in securing the road. Harriman men are associated with him as directors of the road. The especial purpose of Thompson's securing the road was to incorporate it as a part of Harriman's plan to make an all-rail route from the Arizona border to Central America.

The only control exercised by the Harriman interests over the

"Mexican Railway," as far as the writer knows, is that involved in
the pooling of interests, in both freight and passenger traffic, of the
Mexican road and the National Railways of Mexico. It is the inside
story of the Mexican merger—a story which I obtained from
unimpeachable sources while working as a reporter of the Mexican
Daily Herald in the Spring of 1909.

Briefly, the story is this: The consolidation under nominal government control of the two principal railroad systems in Mexico,
the Mexican Central and the Mexican National, was brought about,
not, as is officially given out, to provide against the absorption of
the Mexican highways by foreign capitalists, but to provide *for* that
very thing. It was a deal between E. H. Harriman, on the one hand,
and the government financial camarilla, on the other, the victim in
the case being Mexico. It was a sort of deferred sale of the Mexican
railroads to Harriman, the members of the camarilla getting as their
share of the loot millions and millions of dollars through the
juggling of securities and stock in effecting the merger. On the
whole, it constitutes perhaps the most colossal single piece of
plundering carried out by the organized wreckers of the Mexican
nation.

In this deal with Harriman, Limantour, Minister of Finance, was
the chief manipulator, and Pablo Macedo, brother of Miguel Macedo, Sub-secretary of the Department of the Interior, was first
lieutenant. As a reward for their part in the deal, Limantour and
Macedo are said to have divided $9,000,000 gold profits between
them, and Limantour was made president and Macedo vice-president of the board of directors of the merged roads, which positions
they still hold. The other members of the board of directors of the
merged roads are Guillermo de Landa y Escandon, governor of the
Federal District of Mexico, Samuel Morse Felton, former president
of the Mexican Central, who was Harriman's special emissary in
Mexico to work on Diaz to secure his consent to the deal, E. N.

Brown, former vice-president and general manager of the Mexican National lines, and Gabriel Mancera. Each of these four men is said to have made a personal fortune for himself out of the transaction.

The National Railways of Mexico, as they are officially known, have, in addition to a general board of directors, a New York board of directors. Note the Harriman timber to be found among these names: William H. Nichols, Ernest Thallmann, James N. Wallace, James Speyer, Bradley W. Palmer, H. Clay Pierce, Clay Arthur Pierce, Henry S. Priest, Eban Richards and H. C. P. Channan.

Whether the Mexican railroad steal was conceived in the brain of Limantour or of Harriman is not known, but Limantour seems to have attempted to bring about the merger originally without the aid of Harriman. Some four years ago Limantour and Don Pablo Martinez del Rio, owner of the Mexican Herald and manager of the Banco Nacional, went into the market and bought heavily of Mexican Central and Mexican National stock, after which they broached the merger scheme to Diaz. Diaz turned the proposition down pointblank and Limantour and del Rio both lost heavily, del Rio's losses so bearing down upon him that he died soon afterwards.

It was at this point that Limantour is supposed to have turned to Harriman, who immediately fell in with the scheme and carried it to an exceedingly successful termination for himself.

Harriman owned some Mexican Central stock, but fifty-one per cent of this property was in the personal possession of H. Clay Pierce. When the first rumblings of the 1907 panic were heard Pierce was persuaded to hypothecate his entire holdings to Harriman.

After getting control of from eighty to eighty-five per cent of the Mexican Central property Harriman sent Samuel Morse Felton, one of the ablest railroad manipulators in the United States, to talk Diaz over to the merger scheme. Where Limantour had failed

Felton succeeded and the world was informed that the Mexican
government had accomplished a great financial feat by securing
the ownership and control of its railroad lines.

It was announced that the government had actually secured fifty-
one per cent of the stock of the company. Also the government was
put in nominal control of the situation.

But—in the deal Harriman succeeded in placing such heavy obligations upon the new company that his heirs are almost sure to
foreclose in the course of time.

The Mexican Central and Mexican National systems are both
cheaply built roads; their rolling stock is of very low grade. Their
entire joint mileage at the time of the merger was 5,400 miles, and
yet under the merger they were capitalized at $615,000,000 gold,
or $112,000 per mile. Oceans of water there. The Mexican Central
was 30 years old, yet had never paid a penny. The Mexican National was over 25 years old, yet it had paid less than two per cent.
Yet in the over-capitalized merger we find that the company binds
itself to pay *four and one-half per cent on* $225,000,000 *worth of
bonds and four per cent on* $160,000,000 *worth of bonds, or*
$16,525,000 *interest a year, and pay it semi-annually!*

Out of the merger deal Harriman is supposed to have received, in
addition to merger stocks and bonds, a cash consideration and
special secret concessions and subsidies for his west coast road.
Harriman dictated the contract as to the payment of interest on
those merger bonds and his successors will compel payment or
foreclose. As long as Diaz remains in power, as long as the Mexican
government is "good;" that is, as long as it continues in partnership
with American capital, the matter can be arranged—if in no other
way, by paying the deficiency out of the Mexican treasury. But the
moment there is trouble it is expected that the government will be
unable to pay and the railroad will become American in name as
well as in fact.

Trouble! That word is an exceedingly significant one here. A Mexican revolution will probably mean trouble of this particular sort, for every revolution of the past in Mexico has seen the necessity of the government's repudiating all or a part of the national obligations for a time. Thus the final step in the complete Americanization of Mexico's railways will be one of the clubs held over the Mexican people to prevent them from overturning a government that is particularly favorable to American capital.

Trouble! Trouble will come, too, when Mexico attempts to kick over the traces of undue American "influence." The United States will intervene with an army if necessary, to maintain Diaz or a successor who would continue the special partnership with American capital. In case of a serious revolution the United States will intervene on the plea of protecting American capital. American intervention will destroy the last hope of Mexico for an independent national existence. Mexican patriots cannot forget this, for it is daily paraded before them by the Diaz press itself. Thus the threat of an American army in Mexico is another of the American influences which keep Mexico from revolution against the autocracy of Diaz.

American capital is not at present in favor of political annexation of Mexico. This is because the slavery by which it profits can be maintained with greater safety under the Mexican flag than under the American flag. As long as Mexico can be controlled—in other words, as long as she can be held as a slave colony—she will not be annexed, for once she is annexed the protest of the American people will become so great that the slavery must of necessity be abolished or veiled under less brutal and downright forms. The annexation of Mexico will come only when she cannot be controlled by other means. Nevertheless, the threat of annexation is today held as a club over the Mexican people to prevent them from forcibly removing Diaz.

Do I guess when I prophesy that the United States will intervene in case of a revolution against Diaz? Hardly, *for the United States has already intervened in that very cause.* The United States has not waited for the revolution to assume a serious aspect, but has lent its powers most strenuously to stamping out its first evidences. President Taft and Attorney General Wickersham, at the behest of American capital, have already placed the United States government in the service of Diaz to aid in stamping out an incipient revolution with which, for justifiable grounds, our revolution of 1776 cannot for an instant be thought of in comparison. Attorney General Wickersham is credited with being a heavy stockholder in the National Railways of Mexico; Henry W. Taft, brother of the president, is general counsel for the same corporation. Thus it will be seen that these officials have a personal as well as a political interest in maintaining the system of Diaz.

Three times during the past two years the United States government has rushed an army to the Mexican border in order to crush a movement of Liberals which had risen against the autocrat of Mexico. Constantly during the past three years the American government, through its Secret Service, its Department of Justice, its Immigration officials, its border rangers, has maintained in the border states a reign of terror for Mexicans, in which it has lent itself unreservedly to the extermination of political refugees of Mexico who have sought safety from the long arm of Diaz upon the soil of the "land of the free and the home of the brave."

American Persecution of the Enemies of Diaz

America, Cradle of Liberty, has joined hands with Porfirio Diaz, the most devastating despot that rules a nation, in stamping out that portion of the world movement for democracy which is today attempting to secure the common rights of human beings for the Mexican people.

In previous chapters I have shown how the United States is a voluntary partner in the slavery and political oppression of Diazland. I have shown how, by its commercial alliance, its press conspiracy and its threat of intervention and annexation, it has supported the military dictatorship of Diaz. This chapter I shall devote to the story of how the United States has delivered its military and civil resources into the hands of the Tyrant and with that power has held him in his place when otherwise he would have fallen; and thus has been the final determining force in the continuation of the system of slavery which I have described in the early chapters of this book.

When I say the United States here I mean the United States government chiefly, though state and local governments along our

Mexican border are also involved. Numerous instances go to show
that, in order to exterminate the enemies of Diaz who have come as
political refugees to this country, public officials from the president
down have set aside American principles cherished for generations,
have criminally violated some laws and stretched and twisted others
out of all semblance to their former selves, and have permitted,
encouraged and protected law-breaking on the part of Mexican
officials and their hirelings in this country.

For the past five years the law of our border states, as far as Mexican citizens are concerned, has been very much the law of Diaz.
The border has been Mexicanized. In numerous instances our
government has delegated its own special powers to agents of Mexico
in the form of consuls, hired attorneys and private detectives. Mexican citizens have been denied the right of asylum and the ordinary
protection of our laws. By the reign of terror thus established the
United States has held in check a movement which otherwise would
surely have developed sufficient strength to overthrow Diaz, abolish
Mexican slavery and restore constitutional government in the country to the south of us.

Three times during the past two years, twice as Secretary of War
and once as President, William Howard Taft has ordered troops to
the Texas border to aid Diaz in wreaking vengeance upon his enemies. He also—at the same time as well as at other times—ordered
posses of United States Marshals and squads of Secret Service operatives there for the same purpose.

The first time Taft ordered troops to the border was in June, 1908,
the second time in September, 1908, the third time in July, 1909.
The troops were commanded to drive back into the hands of pur-
suing Mexican soldiers or to capture and detain any fugitives who
attempted to cross the Rio Grande and save their lives upon Texas
soil.

That this action on the part of President Taft was an undue
stretching of the laws it would appear from dispatches sent out from

Washington, June 30, 1908. From one of these dispatches published throughout the country, July 1, 1908, I quote the following:

The employment of American troops for this purpose, by the way, is almost without precedent in recent years, and the law officers of the War Department, as well as the Attorney-General himself, have been obliged to give close study to the question of the extent to which they may exercise the power of preventing persons from entering the United States across the Mexican border.

Under the law no passports are required except in the case of Chinese and Japanese, and about the only other reasonable ground for detention of fugitives seeking to cross the line would be some presumable violation of the immigration or health-inspection laws.

So it will be a delicate task for the army officers, who are charged with the duty of policing this international boundary line, to avert clashes with the civil courts if they undertake to make promiscuous arrests of persons fleeing from Mexico into the United States.

The troops obeyed orders. Fleeing Liberals were turned back to be pierced by the bullets of Diaz's soldiers. Was our government justified in causing the death of those unfortunate men in such a manner? If not, would it be improper to characterize the action as executive murder?

During the past five years hundreds of Mexican refugees have been imprisoned in the border states, and there have been numerous attempts to carry refugees across the line, in order that the Diaz government might deal with them after its own summary methods, and many of these attempts have been successful. Some of the schemes employed in this campaign of deportation are, first, to institute extradition proceedings under charges of "murder and robbery;" second, to deport through the Immigration Department under charges of being "undesirable immigrants;" third, to kidnap outright and feloniously carry across the line.

Some members of the Liberal Party whose extradition was sought on charges of "murder and robbery" during the space of a few months were Librado Rivera, Pedro Gonzales, Crescencio Villarreal, Trinidad Garcia, Demetrio Castro, Patricio Guerra, Antonio I. Villarreal, Lauro Aguirre, Ricardo Flores Magon and Manuel Sarabia. There were others, but I have not definite knowledge of their cases. Some of the prosecutions occurred at St. Louis, others at El Paso, Texas, others at Del Rio, Texas, and others at Los Angeles, Cal.

An uprising of a Liberal club at Jimenez, Coahuila, formed the basis of the charges in all but one or two of the cases. During this uprising somebody was killed and the government postoffice lost some money. Wherefore every Mexican who could be convicted of membership in the Liberal Party, although he might never have been in Coahuila nor have ever heard of the rebellion, stood in danger of extradition for "murder and robbery." The United States government spent a good many thousands of dollars in prosecuting these manifestly groundless charges, but it is to the credit of certain Federal Judges that the prosecutions were generally unsuccessful. Judge Gray of St. Louis and Judge Maxey of Texas both characterized the offenses as being of a political nature. The text of the former's decision in the Rivera case follows:

The United States vs. Librado Rivera.
City of St. Louis, ss., State of Missouri.

I hereby certify that upon a public hearing had before me at my office in said city on this 30th day of November, 1906, the defendant being present, it appearing from the proofs that the offense complained of was entirely of a political nature, the said defendant, Librado Rivera, was discharged.

Witness my hand and seal.

JAMES R. GRAY,
United States Commissioner at St. Louis, Mo.

The scheme to deport political refugees through the Immigration Department was more successful. The immigration laws provide that, if it be discovered that an immigrant is a criminal or an anarchist, or if he has entered this country in an illegal manner, provided that such discovery is made within three years of his arrival here, the immigration officials may deport him. The question of the "undesirability" of the immigrant is not a subject for review by the courts, the immigrant may not appeal, and within two or three restrictions the immigration agent's word is law. It will be readily seen, therefore, that if the said official be not an honest man, if he be willing to accept a bribe or even yield to influence or blandishments, he may, with impunity, send many pure and upright men to an untimely death.

And exactly this thing has been done. Antonio I. Villarreal, secretary of the Liberal Party, was among those placed in danger of deportation "under the immigration laws." After various means had been used unsuccessfully to secure his extradition, he was turned over to the immigration officials at El Paso and was actually on his way to the line when he made a break for liberty and escaped.

Of a large number of Mexican Liberals arrested in Arizona in the fall of 1906, Lazaro Puente, Abraham Salcido, Gabriel Rubio, Bruno Trevino, Carlos Humbert, Leonardo Villarreal and several others were deported in one party by the immigration officials at Douglas. There is no legal excuse for deporting an immigrant because he is a political refugee. On the other hand, according to "American principles," so-called, he is entitled to especially solicitous care for this reason. And yet all of these men were deported because they were political refugees. All of them were peaceful, respectable persons. The law under no circumstances permits of deportation after the immigrant has been a resident of this country for more than three years. But several of this number had lived here for longer than that time and Puente, who was editing a paper in Douglas, claimed to have resided in the United States continuously for thirteen years.

Still another crime of officials may be cited in this particular case. When occasion arises for deportation the immigrant in ordinary cases is merely returned to the country whence he came. But in this case the group of Mexican Liberals was delivered over to the Mexican police in handcuffs, and the American handcuffs were not removed until the prisoners arrived at the penitentiary of Hermosillo, state of Sonora!

The Mexican government, by the way, found nothing against these men after it had got them except that they were members of the Liberal Party. Nevertheless, it sent each and every one of them to long terms in prison.

Many Americans will remember the case of L. Gutierrez De Lara, whom the Immigration Department seized for deportation in October, 1909, accusing him of being "an alien anarchist." De Lara had resided more than three years in this country, yet undoubtedly he would have been sent to his death had not the country sent up such a protest that the conspirators were frightened. It is supposed that De Lara's life was sought at this particular time because he accompanied me to Mexico and aided in securing material for my exposé of Mexican conditions.

When Diaz fails to gain possession of his enemies in the United States by other means he does not hesitate to resort to kidnapping and when he resorts to kidnapping he finds no trouble in securing the criminal assistance of American officials.

The most notable case of refugee kidnapping on record is that of Manuel Sarabia. The case is notable not because it is the only one of its kind, but because it is the one which was most successfully exposed.

Manuel Sarabia was second speaker of the Liberal junta. He was hounded about from place to place by Diaz detectives, finally bringing up in Douglas, Arizona, where he went to work quietly at his trade of printer.

On June 30, 1907, Antonio Maza, the Mexican consul at Douglas, saw Sarabia on the street and recognized him. That evening U. S.

Ranger Sam Hayhurst held up Sarabia at the point of a pistol and, without a warrant, put him in the city jail. At eleven o'clock that night Sarabia's door swung open, he was led outside, forced into an automobile, carried across the international boundary line and there turned over to Colonel Kosterlitzsky, an officer of Mexican *rurales*. The *rurales* tied Sarabia on the back of a mule, and telling him that he was to be shot on the road, made a hurried trip with him through the mountains, finally bringing up, after five days, at the penitentiary at Hermosillo, Sonora.

What saved Sarabia? Just one thing. As he was forced into the automobile he cried out his name and shouted that he was being kidnapped. The ruffians guarding him choked him into silence and then gagged him, but some one had heard and the story spread.

Even then Consul Maza had the audacity to try to hush up the matter and carry his plot to a successful conclusion. By some means he succeeded in muzzling the string of Arizona newspapers run by George H. Kelly, as Kelly afterwards admitted in court. But in Douglas at that time there was a newspaper man whom Maza could not bribe. It was Franklin B. Dorr, who was running the Douglas Daily Examiner.

In his paper Dorr raised a protest that stirred the blood of the people of Douglas. Street meetings were held to further arouse the people. Mother Jones was there. A crowd looked for Maza with a rope. Telegraphic appeals were sent to the state and national governments. And finally—Sarabia was shamefacedly returned.

What would have happened to Sarabia if his voice had not been heard on that night in June, 1907? Exactly what has happened to others whose frightened voices have not been heard. He would have dropped out of sight and no one would ever have been able to say for certain where he had gone.

And what, pray, happened to the kidnappers? Absolutely nothing. Consul Maza, Ranger Hayhurst, Lee Thompson, city jailer, Con-

stable Shorpshire, Henry Elvey, the chauffeur, and some private
detectives whose names were never given to the public seem plainly
to have been guilty of the crime of kidnapping, which is punishable
by imprisonment in the penitentiary. Those named were arrested
and the first four were duly held to answer to the upper court sitting
at Douglas. Elvey made a clean breast of the case and the evidence
seemed conclusive. But as soon as the excitement had blown over
every one of the cases was quietly dropped. It was not Sarabia's
fault, for an effort was made to bribe Sarabia to leave town and
Sarabia refused the bribe. Evidently the money which had bribed
Hayhurst, Thompson and Shorpshire was not all the money that
was used by Maza at that time.

Nearly every small town along the Mexican border harbors a
personage who enjoys the title of Mexican consul. Consuls are found
in villages hundreds of miles from the Mexican border. Consuls are
supposed to be for the purpose of looking after the interests of trade
between countries, but towns in California, Arizona, New Mexico
and Texas which do not do a hundred dollars worth of trade a year
with Mexico have consuls who are maintained by Diaz at the expense of tens of thousands of dollars a year.

Such consuls are not consuls at all. They are spies, persecutors,
bribers. They are furnished with plenty of money and they spend it
freely in hiring thugs and detectives and bribing American office-
holders. By the power thus gained they have repeatedly suppressed
newspapers and put their editors in jail, as well as broken up political clubs of Mexicans.

During the trial of Jose Maria Ramires and four other Liberals
in El Paso in October, 1908, a city policeman naively swore that his
chief had told him to obey the orders of the Mexican consul and the
chief of police of Juarez, a Mexican town.

When, after threats by the Mexican consul of Tucson, Arizona,
thugs destroyed the printing plant of Manuel Sarabia in that city

in December, 1908, Sarabia was unable to persuade the City Marshal to make an investigation of the affair or to attempt to bring the perpetrators to account.

City detectives of Los Angeles, California, have repeatedly taken orders from the Mexican consul there and have unlawfully placed in his hands property of persons whom they have arrested.

Antonio Lozano, the Mexican consul at Los Angeles, at one time had two fake employment offices running at the same time for the single purpose of hiring members of the Liberal Party and luring them to points in Mexico where they could be captured by the Diaz police. This same consul, after De Lara and I started on our trip to Mexico, offered bribes to various friends of De Lara to tell them where he had gone.

Such minor details would fill many pages. John Murray was arrested by Secret Service Chief Wilkie. Murray's offense consisted of raising money for the legal defense of the refugees. Robert W. Dowe, the American customs collector at Eagle Pass, Texas, was compelled to resign under charges of acting as a secret agent for the Mexican government, and receiving money for such service. The evidence in the case was suppressed by our Treasury Department, which reinstated Dowe after some months had passed and public indignation over the affair at Eagle Pass had blown over. In the District Court of Los Angeles, Cal., a warrant for the arrest of De Lara, his wife, Mrs. Mamie Shea, an American, Mrs. Marie Talavera and about twenty others, has been on file for many months, ready for service at any time. Those named are charged with violating the neutrality laws in having *circulated a manifesto printed by the Liberal Party*. Threats that this warrant was to be served have been made to various of the parties, with the evident purpose of deterring them from aiding in any way the movement for the regeneration of Mexico.

Only a few months ago newspapers reported that Major Elihu

Root of the U. S. Army had gone on a special mission to Mexico to confer with Diaz's War Department on the most practical means of entrapping the enemies of Diaz who are sojourning on our soil.

Only a short time ago the news was printed that Punto Rojo, an anti-Diaz labor paper of Texas, had been suppressed, that $10,000 reward had been offered for the capture of its editor, Praxedis Guerrero, that secret service men in pursuit of that reward had seized subscription books of the paper and from the books had secured names of men who would be at once proceeded against.

During the past three years persecution of this general character has directly caused the suspension of at least ten newspapers printed in Spanish along the border for Mexican readers.

To each of these persecutions and press suppressions there is an interesting story attached, but to attempt to detail all of them would require too great a proportion of this work. I shall detail but one case, that of Ricardo Flores Magon, president of the Liberal Party, and his immediate associates. This case, as well as being the most important of all, is typical. Its difference from the rest has been chiefly that Magon, having been able to gather about him greater resources, has been able to make a longer and more desperate fight for his life and liberty than others of his countrymen who have been singled out for persecution. For six and one-half years Magon has been in this country and during nearly the whole of that time he has been engaged in trying to escape being sent back to death beyond the Rio Grande. More than one-half of that time he has passed in American prisons, and for no other reason than that he is opposed to Diaz and his system of slavery and despotism.

The worst that can be said of Magon—as of any of his followers whom I know—is that he desires to bring about an armed rebellion against the established government of Mexico. In cases where reformers are given the opportunity of urging their reforms by democratic methods, armed rebellion in this day and age are indefensible. But when through the suppression of free speech, free press and such liberties, peaceable means of propaganda are impossible, then force is the only alternative. It was upon this principle that our revolutionary forefathers proceeded and upon which the Mexican Liberals are proceeding today.

Magon and his followers would never have come to this country to plot against Diaz had not their peaceable movement been broken up by gun and club methods and their lives seriously endangered at home. The propriety of citizens of despotic countries seeking refuge in another country, there to plan better things for their own, was for many decades recognized by the constituted powers of the United States, which protected political refugees.

A dozen years ago Palma established the Cuban revolutionary Junta in the city of New York, and instead of being arrested he was lionized. For more than a century political refugees from European countries, South America, and even China have found safety with us. Young Turks prepared for their revolution here. Irish societies raised money here for a movement to free Ireland. Jewish defense societies have been financed all over the country and none of the promoters have been turned over to the vengeance of the Czar. And these things have been done openly, not secretly. Today there are known to be Portuguese revolutionist headquarters in the United States. Porfirio Diaz himself—what historic irony!—when he turned revolutionist found safety on American soil and, though his cause was an extremely questionable one, no one arrested him. What is more, Diaz committed the identical crime which, through the legal machinery of the United States, he is now urging against many of the refugees, that of setting on foot a military expedition against a foreign power. On March 22, 1876, Diaz crossed the Rio Grande at Brownsville, Texas, with forty armed followers for the purpose of waging war upon President Lerdo de Tejada. He was driven back and, though all America knew of his exploit, no effort was made to imprison him.

But now the policy has been changed to accommodate President

Diaz. Action has been taken against political refugees of just one
other country, Russia, and it is safe to assume that those cases were
undertaken merely that the authorities might defend themselves
against the charge of using the machinery of government with par-
tiality against Mexicans.

Magon and a small group of followers, including his brother
Enrique and the Sarabias, crossed the Rio Grande in January, 1904,
and soon afterwards established their paper "Regeneracion" in San
Antonio. The paper had been going but a few weeks when a Mexican, a supposed hireling of the Mexican government, called at the
office and tried to reach the Liberal leader with a dirk-knife. Enrique
Magon grappled with the fellow, and in another moment four city
detectives rushed in and placed Enrique under arrest. The next day
he was fined $30 in the police court, while the supposed thug was
not even arrested.

The exiles looked upon this incident as a part of a conspiracy to
get them into trouble. They moved to St. Louis, where they re-estab-
lished their paper. They had hardly got into their new quarters
when they began to be annoyed by the Furlong Detective Agency.
They claim that the Furlong Detective Agency put an "operative"
into the office of "Regeneracion" in the role of an advertising solici-
tor, put "operatives" into the St. Louis postoffice to waylay the
letters of the exile, put "operatives" out to hunt somebody to bring
libel proceedings against "Regeneracion," put "operatives" at work
to harass the editors of the paper in every possible way.

Our Postoffice Department, called to aid in the suppression of
"Regeneracion," revoked the second class privileges which had been
properly secured at San Antonio. But this was insufficient, so two
different parties were brought from Mexico to institute charges of
criminal and civil libel against the editors. The editors were thrown
in jail, the publication stopped. Furlong detectives stole letters and
turned them over to the Mexican consul, and from these letters, the

refugees claim, was gleaned a list of names which resulted in the arrest of some three hundred Liberals in Mexico.

The editors got out of jail on bail, whereupon new charges were prepared to get them back again. But, having important work to do, they chose to pay their bail and flee from these charges. Magon and Juan Sarabia went to Canada and it was here that they carried on their final correspondence preparatory to launching an armed rebellion against Diaz. The first gun was to be fired October 20, 1906, and on the night of October 19 the Liberal leaders gathered at El Paso preparatory to crossing the line the following morning.

As set forth in a previous chapter, this rebellion was betrayed and was more or less of a fizzle. Of the refugee leaders, Juan Sarabia was betrayed into the hands of Diaz and with scores of others was soon afterwards sent to the military prison of San Juan de Ulua. Villarreal, as previously stated, was among those arrested by the American police. For a long time he fought extradition on the "murder and robbery" charge and was finally turned over to the immigration authorities. Immigration officers were in the act of leading him to the boundary line when he bolted and succeeded in escaping by running through the streets of El Paso. Librado Rivera, first speaker of the Liberal Junta, with Aaron Mansano, was kidnapped at St. Louis by city detectives, was hurried as far as Ironton, Missouri, but was there rescued and brought back through an exposé which was made by one of the St. Louis papers.

As for Magon, for months he was hunted by detectives from city to city. He went to California, but was still kept dodging and once masqueraded as a woman in order to escape the Diaz hounds. Finally, he revived his paper in Los Angeles under the name of "Revolucion" and here he was joined by Villarreal and Rivera. The three worked quietly together, keeping always indoors in the daytime and going out for their airing only at night and in disguise.

Early in August, 1907, the hiding-place of the Liberal leaders in

Los Angeles was located. The evidence seems to point to a plot to kidnap them much as Sarabia was kidnapped. First, the officers had plenty of time in which to procure a warrant, but they did not procure a warrant nor even attempt to do so. Second, they secreted an automobile in the vicinity and did not use it after the arrest. Third, when the three men, fearing a kidnapping plot, cried out at the top of their voices, the officers beat them with pistols most brutally, Magon being beaten until he lay bleeding and insensible on the ground. This circumstantial evidence of a kidnapping plot is borne out by the direct testimony of one of the hirelings of the Mexican consul at that time, who has since confessed that there was such a plot and that the Mexican consul was the man who hatched it.

Everything seems to have been arranged. The descent of the sleuths was made August 23, and Ambassador Creel came all the way from Washington to be on hand and see that things went off smoothly. On the night of August 22 Creel was given a banquet by Mexican concessionaires having headquarters in Los Angeles and the following day he sat in his hotel and waited for news that his thugs had gotten their victims as planned.

But the outcries of Magon and his friends collected a crowd and it became impossible to kidnap them. So unprepared were the officers for a mere arrest case that when they got their prisoners to jail they were at a loss to know what charge to place against them, so they put them down on the police books as *"resisting an officer!"*

Ambassador Creel then proceeded to hire some of the highest priced lawyers in Southern California to devise ways and means for getting the prisoners down into Mexico. These lawyers were ex-Governor Henry T. Gage, Gray, Barker and Bowen, partners of U. S. Senator Flint; and Horace H. Appel. When the cases came into court their names were announced by the public prosecutor as special counsel and always during the hearings one or more of them was personally in attendance.

The "officers" who beat the refugees nearly to death and then charged them with resisting an officer—although they had not even procured a warrant—were Thomas H. Furlong, head of the Furlong Detective Agency of St. Louis, chief refugee-hunter for Diaz, an assistant Furlong detective, and two Los Angeles city detectives, the notorious Talamantes and Rico.

For months previous to the arrest of Magon and his associates a card offering $20,000 for their apprehension was circulated about the United States. That the city detectives received their share of this reward is evidenced by sworn testimony given in the Los Angeles courts by Federico Arizmendez, a Los Angeles printer. After the arrest of Magon the sleuths repaired to the office of Magon's newspaper, where they took into custody the nominal editor, Modesto Diaz. Here they met Arizmendez and the following conversation ensued:

Talamantes—You'd better congratulate me; I just made a thousand dollars.

Arizmendez—How's that?

Talamantes—I've just caught Villarreal.

At this writing Rico and Talamantes are still members of the Los Angeles police force!

The identity of the employer of Talamantes et al. was confirmed beyond question and the astounding usurpation by that employer of American governmental powers was revealed when upon being released the day following the conversation quoted above, Modesto Diaz was informed that he would have to wait a few days for the papers taken from him at the time of his arrest, as they had been *placed in the hands of the Mexican Consul!*

If there is any doubt as to who hired Furlong and his henchmen to hunt down Magon the doubt will be dispelled by the reading of an excerpt from Furlong's sworn testimony taken in the Los Angeles courts. Here it is:

CROSS EXAMINATION.

By Mr. Harriman:

Q.—What is your business?

A.—I am the president and manager of the Furlong Secret Service Company, St. Louis, Missouri.

Q.—You helped to arrest these men?

A.—I did.

Q.—What right did you have?

Mr. Lawler—That is objected to as a conclusion of the witness.

Q.—By Mr. Harriman: Did you have a warrant?

A.—No, sir.

The Commissioner—The other question is withdrawn and now you ask him if he had a warrant?

Mr. Harriman—Yes, sir.

Q.—Arrested them without a warrant?

A.—Yes, sir.

Q.—You took this property away from them without a warrant?

A.—Yes, sir.

Q.—Went through the house and searched it without a warrant?

A.—How is that?

Q.—Went through the house and searched it without a warrant?

A.—Yes.

Q.—And took the papers from them?

A.—I didn't take any papers from them. I took them and locked them up and then went back and got the papers.

Q.—Took them from their house and kept them, did you?

A.—No, sir. I turned them over——

Q.—Well, you kept them, so far as they are concerned?

A.—Yes, sir.

Q.—Who paid you for doing this work?

A.—The Mexican government.

Nor was Furlong backward about confessing the purpose of the hunt. By a Los Angeles newspaper Furlong, in bragging about the arrest, was quoted as asserting that he had been "after" Magon and his friends for three years. During that period, he said, he had succeeded in "getting" 180 Mexican revolutionists and turning them over to the Diaz government, which "had made short work of them." According to an affidavit properly sworn to by W. F. Zwickey and on record in the Los Angeles courts, Furlong stated that he was "not so much interested in this case and the charges for which the defendants are being tried as in getting them over into Arizona; that all we (meaning by 'we' himself and the Mexican authorities) want is to get the defendants down into Arizona, and then we will see that they get across the line."

Attorney General Bonaparte seems to have had the same purpose as Furlong and the Mexican authorities, even at a time when the case in hand did not involve extradition to Mexico or even to Arizona. During a hearing before Judge Ross in San Francisco Mr. Bonaparte had the temerity to wire his district attorney in that city: "Resist habeas corpus proceedings in case of Magon et al. on all grounds, *as they are wanted in Mexico.*" This telegram was read in court. The incident was all the more remarkable in view of the fact that only a few days previously Bonaparte, in answer to a query from U. S. Senator Perkins, had replied by letter assuring the senator that the purpose of the prosecution of these men was *not* to send them back to Mexico.

Five separate and distinct charges were brought against Magon and his associates, one after another. First, it was "resisting an officer." Then it was the old charge of "murder and robbery." Later it was criminal libel. Still later it was murdering "John Doe" in Mexico. Finally it was conspiracy to violate the neutrality laws.

Undoubtedly the conspirators would have early succeeded in their purpose to railroad the men back to Mexico had not a number of Los Angeles organizations formed a defense committee, held mass meetings to arouse public sentiment, collected funds, and hired two

able attorneys, Job Harriman and A. R. Holston. These lawyers
after a long fight succeeded in driving the prosecution into a corner
where they were compelled to proceed only under action involving
imprisonment in this country.

During the early stages of the legal fight the Diaz agents were
suppressing the paper "Revolucion" in characteristic style. After
the arrest of its three editors, the editorial emergency was met by
L. Gutierrez De Lara, who had not previously been in any way
identified with the Liberal Party. Two weeks later De Lara was
keeping company with Magon, Villarreal and Rivera. His extradition was sought on the ground that he had committed robbery "on
the blank day of the blank month of 1906 in the blank state of
Mexico!"

Despite the passing of De Lara "Revolucion" continued to appear
regularly. As soon as the agents of the prosecution could locate the
new editor they promptly arrested him. He proved to be Manuel
Sarabia and he was charged with the same offense as happened to
stand against Magon, Villarreal and Rivera at the time.

Who was left to publish little "Revolucion"? There were the
printers. They—Modesto Diaz, Federico Arizmendez and a boy
named Ulibarri—rose to the occasion. But in less than a month
they, too, were led to jail, all three of them charged with criminal
libel. Thus the Mexican opposition newspaper passed into history.
Incidentally, Modesto Diaz died as a result of the confinement following that arrest.

"Revolucion" was not an anarchist paper. It was not a socialist
paper. It did not advocate the assassination of presidents or the abolition of government. It merely stood for the principles which Americans in general since the Declaration of Independence and the
Constitution of the United States came into being have considered
as necessary to the well-being of any nation. If an American newspaper of its ideals had been suppressed by one-tenth as brazen

methods, a righteous protest would have echoed and re-echoed across the continent. But it was only a Mexican newspaper, an opponent of President Diaz, and—it was suppressed.

The story of Lazaro Gutierrez De Lara well exemplifies the system of robbing the enemies of Diaz of their personal liberty in the United States, as practiced by the Department of Justice working in conjunction with Mexican agents in various parts of the West during the past five years.

De Lara was taken to jail on September 27, 1907, on telegraphic instructions from Attorney General Bonaparte. As before stated, he was charged with larceny committed on the blank day of the blank month of 1906 in the blank state of the Republic of Mexico, and on this awful indictment his extradition to Mexico was sought.

The extradition treaty between the United States and Mexico provides that the country asking extradition must furnish evidence of guilt within forty days of the arrest of the accused. In De Lara's case this little technicality was waived, and at the end of forty days a new complaint was filed containing the illuminating information that the alleged crime had been committed in the state of Sonora. This was considered sufficient ground upon which to hold the prisoner another forty days.

Nothing happened at the end of the second forty days, and on December 22 Attorney Harriman applied for a writ of habeas corpus. The writ was denied and the prosecution was given more time in which to file a third complaint. De Lara was then accused of *stealing uncut stove-wood in the state of Sonora, August 13, 1903!*

Several peculiar facts developed at the hearing. One was that De Lara had been tried and acquitted of the identical offense in Mexico more than four years previously. Another was that while at the trial in Mexico the value of the wood was fixed by the prosecution at four dollars, at the Los Angeles hearing its value was

placed at twenty-eight dollars. Because a thief cannot be extradited
for stealing less than twenty-five dollars the wood market had taken
a spectacular jump. But, by an oversight of the prosecution the
market even then did not jump quite high enough, for by discovering that the price of silver was a little lower than usual that year,
Attorney Harriman showed that the alleged value, fifty-six Mexican
pesos, did not come to twenty-eight dollars in American money,
but a little less than twenty-five dollars, and so on that technicality
the life of De Lara was saved.

The facts of the case were that De Lara had never stolen any
wood, but that, while acting as attorney for a widow whom a
wealthy American mine owner was trying to euchre out of a piece
of land, he had given the widow permission to cut some wood on the
land for her own use. The audacity of the prosecutors in this case
would be unbelievable were it not a matter of record. De Lara was
released, but only after one hundred and four precious days of his
life had been wasted in an American jail. He had been luckier than
many of his compatriots, he had won his fight against extradition,
but that three and one-half months were gone and could never be
brought back. Moreover, "Revolucion" had been suppressed and a
Mexican gentleman had been taught that he who opposes the tyrant
may be properly disciplined in the United States as well as in
Mexico.

Magon, Villarreal and Rivera remained in prison continuously
since August 23, 1907, for nearly three years. From early in July,
1908, to January, 1909, they were held *incommunicado* in the Los
Angeles county jail, which means that no visitors, not even newspaper men, were permitted to see them. For a time not even Mrs.
Rivera and her children were permitted to see the husband and
father. Only their local attorney saw them. Two attorneys who
were representing them in another state were excluded on the flimsy
ground that they were not attorneys of record in California.

The only excuse Oscar Lawler, United States District Attorney, had to offer for this severe isolation when, in July, 1908, I called upon him at his office and protested was:

"We are doing this at the request of the Mexican government. They have accommodated us and it's no more than right that we accommodate them."

Requests were also made by the Mexican government that the men be not admitted to bail and the requests were obeyed. The privilege of liberty on bail pending trial is guaranteed by the law to all accused persons below the murderer in cold blood, and yet Judge Welborn, sitting both as district and circuit judge, denied the men this privilege. Bail had previously been fixed as $5,000, ten times the amount required in similar cases that had previously come up. In the latter part of July, 1908, this amount was raised and presented in the most gilt-edged form, but it was not accepted. Judge Welborn's excuse was that a rule of the Supreme Court says that during habeas corpus proceedings the custody of a prisoner shall not be changed. This rule he strangely interpreted to mean that these particular prisoners should not be admitted to bail.

During their six months of *incommunicado,* when the prisoners were unable to make any public statement, Lawler took advantage of their enforced silence publicly to declare them guilty not only of the offenses charged, but of others, among them a plot to assassinate President Diaz, when, as a matter of fact, Lawler had no evidence whatsoever of such a plot.

After nearly two years in county jails Magon, Villarreal and Rivera, were adjudged guilty of conspiring to violate the neutrality laws by conspiring to set on foot a military expedition against Mexico. They were sentenced to eighteen months' imprisonment and were confined in the penitentiary at Florence, Arizona. Sarabia was not tried. Having waived extradition proceedings, he had been taken to Arizona ahead of the others. Here he was released on bail and soon afterwards was married to Miss Elizabeth D. Trowbridge, a Boston girl of old and wealthy family. His health broken by long confinement, believing that a trial would result in his imprisonment in spite of the lack of evidence against him, Sarabia was persuaded to pay his bail and with his wife flee to Europe. There he has since interested himself in writing for various English, French, Spanish and Belgian papers articles upon the democratic movements in Mexico.

The campaign to extradite the refugees on charges of "murder and robbery," generally failed. It succeeded insofar as it kept a good many Liberals in jail for many months, drained their resources, weakened their organization, and intimidated their friends, but it did not succeed in extraditing them. Most of the Liberals deported were deported by immigration officials or by kidnapping.

The "murder and robbery" campaign failed because it was so plainly in contradiction with American laws and American principles. The U. S. prosecuters must have known this from the start but, in order to accommodate Diaz, they went ahead with the prosecutions. That this campaign was not a mere blundering on the part of individual U. S. Attorneys, but that it was a policy of the highest officials of the government was shown, in 1908, when numerous published reports from various departments at Washington and from Oyster Bay expressed the desire of the administration to deport Mexican political refugees *as common criminals.*

Failing in its efforts to deport Mexican refugees wholesale "as common criminals," our Department of Justice concentrated its energies to secure their imprisonment for violation of the neutrality laws or conspiracy to violate the neutrality laws. It is a high misdemeanor to set on foot a military expedition against a "friendly power," or to conspire to set on foot a military expedition against a "friendly power." In addition to Magon, Villarreal, Rivera and Sarabia, some of the Liberal refugees who have been prosecuted under this law are Tomas de Espinosa, Jose M. Rangel, Casimiro

H. Regalado, Lauro Aguirre, Raymundo Cano, Antonio Aruajo, Amado Hernandez, Tomas Morales, Encarnacion Diaz Guerra, Juan Castro, Priciliano Silva, Jose Maria Martinez, Benjamin Silva, Leocadio Trevino, Jose Ruiz, Benito Solis, Tomas Sarabia, Praxedis Guerrero, Sirvando T. Agis, John Murray, Calixto Guerra, Guillermo Adan, E. Davilla, Ramon Torres Delgado, Amendo Morantes, Francisco Sainz, Marcelleno Ibarra and Inez Ruiz.

Most of the arrests occurred at San Antonio, Del Rio, El Paso, Douglas, or Los Angeles. This is by no means a complete list, but is a list of the most notable cases.

In nearly all of these cases the accused were kept in jail for month after month without an opportunity of proving their innocence. When the cases came to trial, they were usually acquitted. Convictions were secured in the cases of Espinosa, Aruajo, Guerra, Priciliano Silva, Trevino, Rangel, and Magon, Villarreal and Rivera. Prison sentences ranging from one and one-half to two and one-half years were given the convicted ones and they were confined either at Leavenworth, Kansas, or Florence, Arizona.

Were these men guilty? If not, how is it that they were convicted?

It is my opinion that not one was guilty within the proper interpretation of the statute, that the laws were stretched to convict them, that in some instances, at least, they were deliberately jobbed.

This is a bold statement, but I think the facts bear me out. That there exists on the part of our government a most incontinent desire to serve Diaz is shown by the circumstances that cases where the evidence of violation of the neutrality laws is ten times as clear— as American expeditions to aid revolutions in Central American or South American countries—have been and are habitually overlooked by our authorities. But this fact I do not need to urge in favor of the Mexican Liberals. The truth is that there has never been any adequate evidence to show a violation of the neutrality laws on their part.

Did they set on foot a military expedition against a friendly

power? Did they plan to do so? No. What did they do? They came
to this country and here planned to aid a revolutionary movement
in Mexico. Here they fled to save their lives, here they staid, planning to return and take part in a rebellion upon Mexican soil;
nothing more.

Did this constitute a violation of the neutrality laws?

Not in the opinion of U. S. Judge Maxey, of Texas, who reviewed
some of the cases. January 7, 1908, the San Antonio Daily Light
and Gazette, quotes Judge Maxey as follows:

"If Jose M. Rangel, the defendant, merely went across the river and
joined in the fight, he had every right to do so, and I will so tell the jury
in my charge. This indictment is not for fighting in a foreign country,
but for beginning and setting on foot an expedition in Val Verde
county."

The exact text of the law is as follows:

Every person who, within the territory or jurisdiction of the United
States, begins, or sets on foot, or provides or prepares the means for, any
military expedition or enterprise, to be carried on from thence against
the territory or dominions of any foreign prince or state, or of any
colony, district or people, with whom the United States are at peace,
shall be deemed guilty of a high misdemeanor, and shall be fined not
exceeding $3,000; and imprisoned not more than three years.

Magon, Villarreal and Rivera, the leaders, not only did not set on
foot an expedition against Mexico, but they did not even cross the
river and fight themselves. Their conviction was secured through
the palpably perjured testimony of a Mexican detective named
Vasquez, who presented the only direct evidence against them.
Vasquez claimed to be a spy who had penetrated a meeting of a
Liberal club. There, he declared, letters were read from Magon
ordering the club to constitute itself as a military body and invade
Mexico. At this meeting, said Vasquez, military appointments,

forwarded by Magon, were made. The names, said he, were written by a member named Salcido. The paper was produced, but handwriting experts brought by the defense proved the document to be a forgery. Vasquez then changed his testimony and swore that he wrote the names himself. This was a vital point in the testimony and, *had the public prosecutors been interested in upholding the law rather than in persecuting the political enemies of Diaz, they would have discharged the defendants and prosecuted Vasquez for perjury.*

The general persecution of Mexican political refugees continued unabated up to June, 1910, when the scandal became so great that the matter was presented to Congress, and the facts which I have set down here, but in more complete form, were testified to before the House Rules Committee. Resolutions providing for a general investigation of the persecutions are now pending in both houses.

Up to the initiation of congressional proceedings the government planned to continue the persecutions. Repeatedly it was announced that, when the terms of Magon, Villarreal and Rivera, at the Florence penitentiary, ended, they would be prosecuted on further charges. But on August 3 they were released and were not rearrested. Since that date there have been no prosecutions, to my knowledge. It is to be hoped that the laws of this country, and the great American principle of protection for political refugees, will not again be abused, for I fear that the conspirators are only waiting for the public to forget their past crimes.

There may be further persecutions and there may not. Even if there are not, Justice will not be satisfied; the friends of decency and of liberty cannot be content. For some of the victims are still enduring unjust punishment which it is in the power of the American people to end. There is Lazaro Puente, for example, the peaceful editor, thirteen years a resident of the United States, who was unjustly and unlawfully deported as an "undesirable immigrant"

by our immigration officials. Lazaro Puente is a prisoner in San
Juan de Ulua, the military fortress in Vera Cruz Harbor. He has
been a prisoner there for more than four years. Unjustly he was
yielded up to the Diaz police; in justice the American people should
demand that he be returned free to this country.

Diaz Himself

"But Diaz himself—isn't he a pretty good sort of fellow?"

It is a question that almost invariably rises to the lips of the average American when he learns for the first time of the slavery, peonage and political oppression of Mexico. Though the question is only another evidence that the Diaz press agents have done their work well, yet it is one that may very well be examined separately.

The current American estimate of Porfirio Diaz, at least up to the past year or two, has indeed been that he is a very good fellow. Theodore Roosevelt, in writing to James Creelman after the publication in Pearson's Magazine of the latter's famous laudatory article, declared that among contemporary statesmen there was none greater than Porfirio Diaz. In the same year, during a trip to Mexico, William Jennings Bryan spoke in the most eulogistic terms of Diaz's "great work." David Starr Jordan of Stanford University, in recent speeches, has echoed Creelman's assertion that Diaz is the greatest man in the western hemisphere. And hundreds of our most distinguished citizens have expressed themselves in a similar vein. On the part of prominent Americans traveling in Mexico, it has become a custom, a sort of formality of the trip, to banquet at Chapultepec castle—the lesser lights at Chapultepec cafe—and to raise the after-dinner voice in most extravagant praise, loudly to attribute to Porfirio Diaz the virtues of a superman, even of a demi-god.

Were not the facts overwhelmingly to the contrary, did not the easily provable acts of Porfirio Diaz tell an entirely different story, I would not presume to question the estimates of such men, especially when those estimates agree and are accepted generally as correct. But when the facts speak for themselves, it matters not how obscure may be the individual who brings them to light. It matters not, even, how distinguished the men who disregard those facts, for facts are greater than men. Current literature, in calling attention to the new conception of Porfirio Diaz that has of late been gaining ground in America, refers to Diaz as a man of mystery. "Is he a sublime statesman or is he a colossal criminal?" it inquires. To which I would reply that we have our ideals of statesmanship and our concepts of criminality; all we need upon which to base an estimate are the facts of the life of the man in question. Given the facts and the mystery dispels itself.

In judging the life of a man, especially of a man who has decided the fate of thousands, who has "saved a nation," or wrecked it, small virtues and small vices count for little; insignificant acts of good or ill are important only in the aggregate. A man may have committed grave crimes, yet if he has brought more joy to the world than sorrow, he should be judged kindly. On the other hand, he may be credited with laudable deeds, yet if he has locked the wheels of progress for a time to feed his own ambition, history will not acquit him of the crime. It is the balance that counts; it is the scales that decide. Will not Porfirio Diaz, when weighed in the balance of his good and evil deeds, be found wanting—terribly wanting? His friends may sing his praises, but when they, his best friends, begin to specify, to point out their reasons for selecting him for a high niche in the hall of good fame, is it not found that they themselves become, instead of his advocates, his prosecutors? Out of even their mouths is he not convicted and by those our ideals of statesmanship and our concepts of criminality will we not judge him, not a statesman, but a criminal, and because there is no individual man in the world who wields so much power over so many human beings, will we not judge him the most colossal criminal of our time?

It is curious, this almost universal feeling—in this country— that Porfirio Diaz is a very good fellow. But it can be explained. For one thing, individuals who have not had the opportunity to judge a particular man or thing for themselves, though they be college presidents and congressmen, are apt to accept the word of others as to that man or thing. Porfirio Diaz, knowing this and valuing the good opinions of men who do not know, has spent millions for printer's ink in this country. For another thing, most men are susceptible to flattery and Diaz is a good flatterer. As prominent Catholics journeying to Rome seek an audience with the Pope, so Americans traveling to Mexico seek an audience with General Diaz; they usually get it and are flattered. Still again, to paraphrase an old proverb, men not only do not look a gift horse in the mouth, but they do not look the giver in the mouth. Despite the ancient warning, men do not usually beware of the Greeks when they bring gifts; and Diaz is free with gifts to men whose good opinion is influential with others. Finally, there is nothing that succeeds like success, and Diaz has succeeded. Power dazzles the strong as well as the weak and Diaz's power has dazzled men and cowed them until they had not the courage to look steadily at the glare long enough to see the bones and carrion behind it. I do not for a minute imagine that any decent American approves of the acts of Porfirio Diaz. I merely guess that they—the decent ones— are ignorant of those deeds and are moved to strong praise by having accepted the word of others—and by the dazzle of success.

As for me, I do not come with a new ideal of statesmanship with which to change your opinions, but I come with facts. With those facts before you, if you hold Washington a great statesman, or Jefferson, or Lincoln, or any other enduring light of American political history, I am sure you cannot at the same time hold Porfirio Diaz a great statesman. What Porfirio Diaz has done, Washington, Jefferson, Lincoln, would have abhorred to do, and you yourself would abhor to do or see done, are you really an admirer of any or all of these men.

Porfirio Diaz is truly a striking figure. He must be a genius of a sort and there must actually be some traits of character about him to be admired. Let us examine some of his acts with a view to discovering whether or not he may justly be called the greatest living statesman or "the grandest man in the Americas."

First let us examine those broadly general allegations upon which is based his good fame abroad. Chief among these are three, that Diaz has "made modern Mexico," that he brought peace to Mexico and should therefore stand as a sort of prince of peace, and that he is a model of virtue in his private life.

Did Porfirio Diaz "make" modern Mexico? Is Mexico modern? Hardly. Neither industrially nor in the matter of public education, nor in the form of government is Mexico modern. Industrially, it is at least a quarter of a century behind the times; in the matter of public education it is at least a half century behind the times; in its system of government it is worthy of the Egypt of three thousand years ago.

True, Mexico has seen some advancement in some lines—especially industrially—during the past thirty-four years. But that mere fact does not argue any propelling force on the part of Porfirio Diaz. In order to show that Diaz was the special propelling force will it not be necessary to how that Mexico has advanced in that period faster than other countries? And should it be shown that Mexico has advanced more slowly than almost any other large nation in the world in the past thirty-four years, would it not be logical to attribute to Diaz at least some of that retarding force?

Consider the United States thirty-four years ago and then today, and then consider Mexico. Consider that the world has been built over, industrially, in the past thirty-four years. To make the comparison perfectly unassailable, disregard the United States and European countries and compare the progress of Mexico with other Latin-American countries. Among persons who have traveled extensively in Argentine, Chili, Brazil and even Cuba, and Mexico, there is a pretty good agreement that Mexico is the most backward of the five—in the matter of government, in the matter of public education, even industrially. Who made Argentine? Who made Chili? Who made Brazil? Why don't we find a "maker" of these countries? The fact is that whatever modernization Mexico has had during the past thirty-four years must be attributed to evolution— that is, to the general progress of the world—instead of to Porfirio Diaz. In general, Porfirio Diaz has been a reactionary force. His claims for being progressive are all based upon one fact—upon his having "encouraged" foreign capital.

"Diaz, the peace-maker, the greatest peace-maker alive, greater than Roosevelt!" chanted an American politician in a banquet at the Mexican capital recently. And the chant was only an echo of louder voices. I remember seeing, not long ago, a news item stating that the American Peace Society had made Porfirio Diaz an honorary vice-president, in consideration of his having brought peace to Mexico. The theory seems to be that since the history of Mexico before Diaz was full of wars and violent changes in the government and the history of Mexico under Diaz has been without violent upheavals of far-reaching effect, Diaz must necessarily be a humane, Christ-like creature who shrinks at the mention of bloodshed and whose example of loving-kindness is so compelling that none of his subjects have the heart to do anything but emulate him.

In answer to which it will only be necessary to refer the reader to my account of how Diaz began his career as a statesman by deliberately breaking the peace of Mexico himself, and how he has been breaking the peace ever since—by making bloody war upon the self-respecting, democratic elements among his people. He has kept the peace—if it can be called keeping the peace—by killing off his opponents as fast as their heads have appeared above the horizon. This sort of peace is what the Mexican writer DeZayas calls "mechanical peace." It has no virtue, because the fruits of legitimate peace fail to ripen under it. It neither brings happiness to the nation, nor prepares the nation for happiness. It prepares it only for violent revolution.

For more than twenty years before arriving at the supreme power in Mexico Diaz had been a professional soldier and almost continually in the field. The wars of those times were by no means unnecessary affairs. Mexico did not fight simply because it is the Mexican character to be looking always for trouble, for it isn't. Diaz fought in the Three Years War, in which the throttling grip of the Catholic church on the throat of the nation was broken and the nation secured a real republican constitution. Afterwards he fought in the War of Maximilian, which ended in the execution of the Austrian prince whom the armies of Napoleon Third had seated as emperor.

During these twenty odd years Diaz fought on the side of Mexico and patriotism. He probably fought no more wisely nor energetically than thousands of other Mexicans, but he had the good luck to have become acquainted in his youth with Benito Juarez, who, years later, as father of the constitution and constitutional president, guided the destinies of the country safely through many troublous years. Juarez remembered Diaz, watched his work and promoted him gradually from one rank to another until, at the downfall of Maximilian, Don Porfirio held a rank which in our country would carry the title of major-general. Note how Diaz repaid the favors of Juarez.

Following the overthrow of Maximilian, peace reigned in Mexico. Juarez was president. The constitution was put into operation. The people were sick unto death of war. There threatened neither foreign foe nor internal revolt. Yet the ambitious Diaz wantonly and without any plausible excuse stirred up rebellion after rebellion for the purpose of securing for himself the supreme power of the land.

There is evidence that Diaz began plotting to seize the presidency even before the fall of the empire. During those last days when Maximilian was penned up in Queretaro friends of Diaz approached several military leaders and proposed that they form a military party to secure the presidency by force of arms, which prize would be raffled off among Generals Diaz, Corona and Escobedo. General Escobedo refused to enter into the conspiracy and the plan consequently fell through. Diaz, who was at that time besieging Mexico City, then effected a secret combination with the church to overthrow the Liberal government. According to one writer, he intentionally delayed taking the metropolis and asked General Escobedo for two of his strongest divisions, which he planned to turn against Juarez. But Juarez received word of the plot in time and instructed General Escobedo to send two of his strongest divisions under command of General Corona and General Regules, respectively, with orders to destroy the treachery of Diaz, should it arise. When the reinforcements arrived Diaz tried to get them entirely in his power by appointing new officers, but Corona and Regules stood firm, and Diaz, realizing that he had been anticipated, abandoned his plot.

Immediately after the coming of peace Juarez appointed Diaz commander of that part of the army stationed in Oaxaca and Diaz used the power thus secured to control the state elections and impose himself as governor. After his defeat for the presidency Diaz started a revolution, known as "La Ciudadela," The Citadel, but the uprising was crushed in one decisive meeting with the government troops. Six weeks later Diaz started a second revolution, calling his friends to arms under what is known as the "Plan de Noria," a platform, in reality, in which the leading demand was for an amendment to the constitution absolutely forbidding the re-election of either president or governors. This rebellion also met with ignominious defeat on the battlefield at the hands of the government forces, and when Juarez died in July, 1872, Diaz was a fugitive from justice. During one of these little rebellions of the present superman Juarez is said to have captured and brought Diaz before him and told him that he deserved to be shot like a rebel, but that the country would take into consideration his services rendered during the War of Intervention.

After the death of Juarez, Diaz prosecuted a successful revolution, but only after four years more of plotting and rebelling. The people of the country were overwhelmingly against him, but he found one very definite interest upon which to play. That, far from being a peaceful and legitimate interest, was a military interest, the interest of the chiefs of the army and of those who had made their living by killing and plundering. The government of Juarez and the government of Lerdo both carried out, after peace came, a sweeping anti-militarist policy. They announced their intention of reducing the army and proceeded to reduce the army. Thereupon the chiefs thereof, seeing their glory departing from them, became fertile ground for the seeds of rebellion which Diaz was strewing broadcast. Diaz gave these army chiefs to understand that under him they would not be shorn of their military splendor, but, on the other hand, that they would be raised to positions of higher power.

Lerdo issued an amnesty to all revolutionists and Diaz was safe from prosecution as a rebel. But instead of employing the freedom thus given to useful and honorable pursuits, he used it to facilitate his plotting until, in January, 1876, he started his third revolution, issuing his "Plan de Tuxtepec," in which he again demanded a change prohibiting the re-election of the president.

For nearly a year Diaz prosecuted his third revolution, during that time issuing another manifesto, the "Plan de Palo Blanco," which gave his operations the aspect of still another and a fourth revolution. It was under this plan that the rebel leader finally gained a decisive victory over government troops and soon afterwards led his army into the capital and declared himself provisional president. A few days later he held a farcical election, in which he placed soldiers in possession of the polls and permitted neither rival candidates to appear nor opposition votes to be cast.

Thus in 1876, more than a generation ago, Porfirio Diaz came to the head of the Mexican state a rebel in arms. He broke the peace of Mexico to begin with, and he has continued to break the peace by periodical and wholesale butcheries of his people. General Porfirio Diaz, the "greatest living peace-maker," "prince of peace!" It is a sacrilege!

That the Mexican dictator has not fallen a victim to the physical debaucheries that sometimes over-tempt men suddenly risen to great power is undoubtedly true. But what of it? Certainly no one will argue that, since a man keeps clean physically, he has a right to misgovern a country and assassinate a people. Personal cleanliness, physical temperance and marital virtue do not in the least determine the standing a man deserves as a statesman.

Thus it will be seen that the allegations upon which the good fame of General Diaz is based have no foundation in fact. Moreover, none of his flatterers have so far discovered in him any claims for greatness any better substantiated than those mentioned.

Diaz has some personal abilities, such as a genius for organization, keen judgment of human nature, and industry, but these do not determine that his public acts shall be beneficent. Like the virtues the devout Methodist lady attributed to the Devil, industry and persistence, they merely render him more efficient in what he does. If he chooses to do good, they become virtues; if he chooses to do ill, they may very properly be incorporated with his vices.

The flatterers of Porfirio Diaz are wont to speak in generalities, for otherwise they would come to grief. On the other hand, a large book could be written recounting his evil deeds and contemptible traits. Ingratitude is one of the charges least worthy of mention that are made against him. Benito Juarez made the career of Porfirio Diaz. Every promotion which Diaz received was given him by the hands of Juarez. Nevertheless, Diaz turned against his country and his friend, started rebellion after rebellion and made the last days of the great patriot turbulent and unhappy.

Yet, to portray the other side, Diaz has shown gratitude to some of his friends, and in doing so he has at the same time exhibited his utter disregard for the public welfare. An Indian named Cahuantzi, illiterate but rich, was Diaz's friend when the latter was in rebellion against Juarez and Lerdo. Cahuantzi furnished the rebel with horses and money and when Diaz captured the supreme power he did not forget. He made Cahuantzi governor of Tlaxcala and sent him a teacher that he might learn to sign his name to documents of state. He retained Cahuantzi as governor of the state of Tlaxcala, giving him free rein to rob and plunder at will. He kept Cahuantzi there for thirty-four years, down to this day.

A similar case was that of Manuel Gonzalez, a *compadre* who aided the Diaz rebellions and whom Diaz substituted for himself in the presidential chair from 1880 to 1884. After Gonzalez had served his purpose in the federal government Don Porfirio presented him with the state government of Guanajuato, where he reigned until his death. Gonzalez was wont to boast that the government had killed all the bandits in Guanajuato but himself, that he was the only bandit tolerated in that state.

The flatterers of Diaz tell of his intellectual ability, but of his culture they dare say nothing. The question as to whether or not he is a cultivated man would seem important inasmuch as it would determine somewhat the distribution of culture among the people whom he controls so absolutely. Diaz is intelligent, but his intelligence may very well be denominated a criminal intelligence—such as is needed at the head of a great freebooter corporation or an organization such as Tammany Hall. In devising ways and means to strengthen his personal power Diaz's intelligence has risen even to genius, but of refinement and culture he possesses little or none. Despite the necessity of his meeting foreigners almost daily he has never learned English nor any other foreign language. He never reads anything but press clippings and books about himself and he never studies anything but the art of keeping himself in power. He is interested in neither music, art, literature nor the drama and the encouragement he gives to these things is negligible. Mexico's drama is imported from Spain, Italy and France. Her literature is imported from France and Spain. Her art and music are likewise imported. Within a century past art flourished in Mexico, but now her art is decadent—choked like her budding literature, by the thorns of political tyranny.

General education in Mexico is appallingly absent. The flatterers of Diaz tell of the schools that he has established, but the investigator fails to find these schools. They are mostly on paper. There is practically no such thing as country schools in Mexico, while towns of many hundreds of inhabitants often have no school whatsoever. Nominally there are schools in such towns, but actually there are none because the governors of the various states prefer to keep the expense money for themselves. While traveling in the rural districts of the state of Mexico, for example, I learned that scores of schools in small towns had been closed for three years because the governor, General Fernando Gonzalez, had withheld the money, explaining to the local authorities that he needed it for other purposes. The fact that there is no adequate public school system in Mexico is attested by the most recent official census (1900), which goes to show that but 16 per cent of the population are able to read and write. Compare this with Japan, an over-populated country where the people are very poor and where the opportunities for education seemingly ought not to be so good. Ninety-eight per cent of Japanese men and 93 per cent of Japanese women are able to read and write. The sort of educational ideals held by President Diaz is shown in the schools that are running, where a most important item in the curriculum is military study and training!

Is Diaz humane? The question is almost superfluous, inasmuch as few of his admirers credit him with this trait. All admit that he has been severe and harsh, even brutal, in his treatment of his enemies, while some of them even relate deeds of the most blood-thirsty cruelty—relate them with gusto, condemning not at all, but treating the incidents as if they were merely some excusable eccentricities of genius! The wholesale killings carried out by the orders of Diaz, the torture perpetrated in his prisons, the slavery of hundreds of thousands of his people, the heart-breaking poverty which he sees every time he leaves his palace, and which he could greatly ameliorate if he wished, are of themselves sufficient proof of his inhumanity.

Cruelty was undoubtedly a part of his inheritance, for his father, a horse-breaker by trade, was noted for it. Horses which did not yield readily Chepe Diaz, the father, killed, and others he chastised with a whip tipped with a steel star, which he landed on the belly, the most tender part of the poor brute. For this reason the people of Oaxaca, the birthplace of Diaz, patronized the father but little, and he was poor. That inherited trait showed itself in Porfirio at an extremely tender age, for while only a child Porfirio, becoming angry at his brother over a trivial matter, filled his brother's nostrils with gunpowder while he was asleep and touched a match to it. From that time Felix was known as "Chato" (Pug-nose) Diaz. "For Porfirio Diaz"—in the words of Gutierrez De Lara, "the people of Mexico have been the horse."

As a military commander Diaz was noted for his cruelty to his own soldiers and to any portion of the enemy that happened to fall into his hands. Several Mexican writers mention unwarranted acts of severity and executions of subordinates ordered in the heat of passion. Revenge is a twin brother of cruelty and Diaz was revengeful. Terrible was the revenge visited by the child upon his sleeping brother and terrible was the revenge visited upon the town where his brother many years later met a tragic death.

Accounts of the incident differ, but all authorities agree that the massacre at Juchitan, Oaxaca, was done in cold blood, indiscriminately and out of revenge. On becoming president, Diaz installed his brother "Chato" as governor of Oaxaca. "Chato" was a drunkard and a libertine and he was killed while over-riding the personal liberties of the people of the town of Juchitan. Many weeks later, long after the uprising of a day had passed, President Diaz sent troops to Juchitan who, according to one writer, suddenly appeared one evening in the public square where the people had gathered to listen to the music of a band, and poured volley after volley into the crowd, continuing to fire until all the people left in the square were dead or dying on the ground.

Such killings have been a recognized policy of the Diaz rule. The Rio Blanco massacre, the details of which were set forth in a previous chapter, took place after the town was entirely quiet. The executions in Cananea were carried out with little discrimination and after the alleged disturbance of the strikers was over. The summary executions at Velardena in the Spring of 1909 all took place after the so-called riot was over. And other instances could be given. It may be suggested that in some of these cases not Diaz, but an underling, was responsible. But it is well known that Diaz usually gave the orders for distributing indiscriminate death. That he approves of such a policy as a policy is shown by his remarkable toast to General Bernardo Reyes, after the Monterey massacre in 1903, when he said: "Senor General, that is the way to govern."

The inhuman methods used by Diaz to exterminate the Yaqui Indians have been exploited in a previous chapter. One of his famous Yaqui orders which, however, I did not mention, not only exhibits his rude and uncultured ideas of justice, but it paints his cruelty as most diabolical. Several years ago, after various employers of labor of the state of Sonora had protested against the wholesale deportation of the Yaquis because they needed the Yaquis as farm and mine laborers, Diaz, in order to pacify the aforesaid employers, modified his deportation decree to read substantially as follows: "No more Yaquis are to be deported except in case of offenses being committed by Yaquis. For every offense hereafter committed by any Yaqui 500 Yaquis are to be rounded up and deported to Yucatan."

This decree is attested to by no less a personage than Francisco I. Madero, the distinguished citizen of the state of Coahuila, who dared oppose Diaz in the presidential campaign of 1910. The decree was carried out, or at least the stream of Yaqui exiles kept on. Cruel and revengeful is the Mexican president and bitterly has his nation suffered as a result of it.

Is Diaz a brave man? In some quarters it has been taken for granted that he is a man of courage, inasmuch as he made a success as a soldier. But there are many distinguished Mexicans who, having watched his career, assert that he is not only not brave, but that he is a shrinking, cringing coward. And they point to numerous accepted facts to support their assertion. When the news of the uprising at Las Vacas reached him in the last days of June, 1908, Diaz was suddenly taken sick and for five days he staid in his bed. In high government circles it was whispered about—and the fact is alleged to have come from one of his physicians—that he was suffering from a common malady which comes upon one overpowered by acute and panicky fear.

The fact that when Diaz seized the power he carefully excluded from any part in the government each and every one of the most popular and able Mexicans of the day is attributed to fear. The fact that he maintains a large army which he distributes in every quarter of the country, and a huge secret police system armed with extraordinary power to kill on suspicion, the terrible way in which he gets rid of his enemies, his bloody massacres themselves, even his muzzling of the press, are all attributed to arrant cowardice. In his book "Diaz, Czar of Mexico," Carlo de Fornaro voices this belief in the cowardice of Diaz and reasons quite effectively upon it. He says:

Like all people quick to anger he (Diaz) is not really fearless, for as the jungle song says, 'Anger is the egg of fear.' Fearful and therefore ever vigilant, he was saved from destruction by this alertness, as the hare is preserved from capture by his long ears. He mistook cruelty for strength of character and consequently was ever ready to terrorize for fear of being thought weak. As a result of the outrageous nickel law and the payment of the famous English debt in the period of Gonzalez, there happened a mutiny. 'Knife them all,' suggested Porfirio Diaz to Gonzalez. But Gonzalez was not afraid.

Last year, on the 16th of September, as the Mexican students desired to parade on the streets of the capital, they sent their representative, a Mr. Olea, to beg the President's permission. Porfirio Diaz answered: 'Yes, but beware, for the Mexicans have revolutionary tendencies lurking in their blood.' Think of three score of youngsters parading unarmed being a menace to the republic, with 5,000 soldiers, rurales and policemen in the capital!

It is only by admitting this shameful well-hidden stigma on the apparently brave front of this man that we can logically explain such despicable and infamous acts as the massacres of Veracruz and Orizaba. He was then panic-stricken, like a wanderer, who shoots wildly at the fleeing phantoms of the night; he was so terrorized that the only means of relieving his blue funk was to terrorize in return.

Hand in hand with cruelty and cowardice often travels hypocrisy and of the three Diaz is not the least endowed with hypocrisy. Constantly is he foisting new shams and deceptions and farces upon the public. His election farces and his periodical pretense of wishing to retire from the presidency and then reluctantly yielding to a universal demand on the part of his people have already been referred to. Diaz's rule began in hypocrisy, for he went into office on a platform which he had no notion of carrying out. He pretended to consider the doctrine of non-re-election of president and governors of enough importance to warrant turning the nation over in a revolution, yet as soon as he had entrenched himself in power he proceeded to re-elect himself as well as his governors on to the end of time.

When Elihu Root went in to Mexico to see Diaz and to arrange some matters in regard to Magdalena Bay Diaz was desirous of showing Root that the Mexican people were not as poverty-stricken as they had been painted. He therefore, through his Department of the Interior, distributed the day before Root's arrival in the capital, 5,000 pairs of new pantaloons among that class of workmen who were habitually most prominently on the streets. In spite of orders that the pants were to be worn, the majority of them were promptly exchanged for food, and so Mr. Root was probably not very badly fooled. The incident merely goes to show to what extents the petty hypocrisy of the Mexican ruler sometimes goes.

Diaz is the head of the Masons in Mexico, yet he nominates every new bishop and archbishop the country gets. Church marriages are not recognized as legal, yet Diaz has favored the church so far as to refuse to enact a divorce law, so that today there is no such thing as divorce or re-marriage during the life of both parties in Mexico. Constantly is Diaz trying to fool the people as to his own motives. He brought about the merger under national control of the two leading railway systems of the country, ostensibly to put the railways where the government can use them best in time of war, but actually in order to give his friends an opportunity to make millions in the juggling of securities. Deceits of this class could be enumerated ad infinitum.

One of the most notable hypocritical antics of Diaz is his pretended concurrence in the overwhelmingly popular idolatry of the patriot Juarez. It will be remembered that when Juarez died Diaz was in revolution against him and that therefore if it is conceded that Juarez was a great statesman it must be admitted that Diaz was wrong in rebelling. Diaz undoubtedly recognized this fact and some ten years ago he is said to have aided secretly the publication and circulation of a book which attempted, by new and cleverly written interpretations of the acts of Juarez, to make out the father of the constitution a great blunderer instead of a great statesman. This failed to turn the tide against Juarez, however, and Diaz fell in with the tide until nowadays we see him every year, on the occasion of the birthday of Juarez, delivering a eulogistic speech over the tomb of the man against whom he rebelled. More than this, during each speech Diaz sheds tears—rains tears—and is wont to refer to Juarez as "my great teacher!"

The ability to shed tears freely and on the slightest provocation has, indeed, been named by Diaz's enemies as his greatest asset as a statesman. When a distinguished visitor praises Diaz or his work Diaz cries—and the visitor is touched and drawn toward him. When the "Circulo de Amigos de General Diaz" pays its formal call to tell its creator that the country once more demands his re-election he weeps—and the foreign press remarks upon how that man *does* love his country. Once a year, on his birthday, the president of Mexico goes down into the street and shakes hands with his people. The reception takes place in front of the national palace and all the while the tears are raining down his cheeks—and the soft-hearted people say to themselves: "Poor old man, he's had his troubles. Let him end his life in peace."

Diaz has always been able to cry. While striving against the Lerdist government in 1876, just before his day of success came, he was beaten in the battle of Icamole. He thought it meant an end of his hopes and he cried like a baby, while his subordinate officers looked on in shame. This gained him the nickname of "The weeper of Icamole," which still sticks to him among his enemies. In his memoirs Lerdo calls Diaz "The Man Who Weeps."

An oft-related incident which shows the shallowness of the feeling which accompanies the Diaz tears is told by Fornaro as follows:

When Captain Clodomoro Cota was sentenced by the military tribunal to be shot, his father sought the President, and on his knees, weeping, begged him to pardon his son. Porfirio Diaz also was weeping, but, lifting the despairing man, uttered this ambiguous phrase: 'Have courage and faith in justice.' The father left, consoled, believing that his petition had been answered. But on the following morning his son was shot. The tears of Porfirio Diaz are crocodile tears.

It is said that Diaz does not dissipate. At least he drinks deep and drunkenly of the wine of adulation. Both vanity and lack of refinement and taste are shown by the very coarseness and ridiculousness of the praise for which he pays and in which he revels.

Diaz is not noted for avarice, which is not surprising, inasmuch as the power that he wields by reason of the army and the rest of his machine is far greater than any power that money could buy in Mexico. To Porfirio Diaz money and other cashable goods are but a pawn in the game, and he uses them to buy the support of the greedy. Yet his enemies declare that he is the richest man in Mexico. He keeps his financial affairs so well hidden that few can guess how large a fortune he has. It is known that he has large holdings under aliases and in the names of dummies and that the various members of his family are all wealthy. But why should Porfirio Diaz care for mere money, when all Mexico is his—his with no strings upon it except the strings of foreign capital?

The picture sometimes drawn of the love match of Don Porfirio and Carmelita Romero Rubio de Diaz, while pretty, is not true; the truth is not at all flattering to the personal virtues of Diaz. The facts are that little Carmen was forced to marry Diaz for purposes of state. Her father, Romero Rubio, had held a high position in the Lerdist government and had a strong personal following; her god-father was Lerdo de Tejada himself, while little Carmen, together with the other feminine members of the family, was a devout Catholic. By marrying the girl Diaz hoped to kill three birds with one stone, to win the support of her father, to turn aside the enmity of the friends of Lerdo, and to assure to himself more actively than ever the support of the church. He knew that Carmen not only did not love him, but that she wanted to marry another man, and yet he was a party to her forced marriage. The marriage did give him the more active support of the church, it won Don Romero Rubio, but as for Lerdo, he was obdurate. In his memoirs Lerdo prints some letters from the unhappy Carmen, his god-child, to show how her youth and innocence were employed as merchandise in Diaz's mad barter for political security. One of these letters, which also gives an interesting side-light on the times, is as follows:

"Mexico City, Jan. 1, 1885.

"Sr. Lic. Don Sebastian Lerdo de Tejada.

"My Very Dear God-Father:—If you continue to be displeased with Papa, that is no reason why you should persist in being so with me; you know better than anyone that my marriage with General Diaz was the exclusive work of my parents, for whom, for the sake of pleasing them, I have sacrificed my heart, if it can be called a sacrifice to have given my hand to a man who adores me and to whom I respond only with filial affection. To unite myself with an enemy of yours has not been to curse you; on the contrary, I have desired to be the dove that with the olive branch calms the political torments of my country. I do not fear that God will punish me for having taken this step, as the greatest punishment will be to have children by a man whom I do not love; nevertheless, I shall respect him and be faithful to him all my life. You have nothing, God-father, with which to reproach me. I have conducted myself with perfect correctness inside the social, moral and religious laws. Can you blame the Archduchess Marie of Austria for uniting herself with Napoleon? Since my marriage I am constantly surrounded by a crowd of flatterers, so much the more contemptible since I do not encourage them. They do not fail in anything except in falling down on their knees and kissing my feet, as happened with the golden princesses of Perrault. From the deputation of beggars with whom I became acquainted yesterday to the minister who begged a *peseta* in order to dine, on the staircase ascending or descending, all mix together and trample each other under foot, entreating for a salute, a smile, a glance. The same who in a time not so very remote would have refused to give me their hand had they seen me fall on the sidewalk, today crawl like reptiles in my path, and would consider themselves happy if the wheels of my carriage should pass over their unclean bodies. The other night, while expectorating in the aisle of the theatre, a general who was at my side interposed his handkerchief, in order that the saliva, each precious pearl, should not fall on the tile floor. If we had been alone, surely the miserable creature would have converted his mouth into a cuspidor. This is not the exquisite flattery of educated folk; it is the brutal servility of the rabble in its animal and repulsive form, in that of a slave. The poets, the minor poets and the poetasters each martyr me after his own fashion; it is a waterspout of ink fit to blacken the ocean itself. This calamity irritates my nerves to such an extent that at times I have attacks of hysteria. Horrible, isn't it, dear God-father? And I say nothing to you of the paragraphs and articles published by the press that Papa has hired. Those who do not call me an angel say that I am a cherub; others raise me to the standard of a goddess; others place me in the firmament as a star, and still others put me down in botany, classifying me among the lilies, the marguerites and the jasmin. At times I myself do not know whether I am an angel, a cherub, a goddess, a star, a lily, a marguerite, a jasmin, or a woman. *Dios!* Whom am I that I am deified and enveloped in this cloud of fetid incense? Ah, my God-father, I am very unfortunate, and I hope that you will not deny me your pardon and your advice.

"CARMEN."

Is Diaz patriotic? Has he the welfare of Mexico at heart? The flatterers of Diaz swear by his patriotism, but the facts demand a negative answer. Diaz helped depose the foreign prince, but immediately afterwards he plunged a peaceful country into war to feed his own ambition. Perhaps it will be said that Diaz imagined that he could order the destinies of Mexico more for the benefit of

Mexico than could anyone else. Doubtless, but why has he not given his country progress? Is it possible that he believes that autocracy is better for a people than democracy? Is it possible that he considers illiteracy a condition of the greatest possible happiness for a people? Can he believe that a state of chronic starvation contributes to the welfare of a nation? He is an old man—eighty years old. Why does he not make some provision against political chaos after his death? Is it possible that he believes it to be best for his people never to attempt to govern themselves, and for this reason is wrecking his nation so as to prepare it for easy possession by foreigners?

It is impossible to believe these things of Diaz. It is eminently more reasonable to judge that whatever desire for the welfare of his country he possesses is overshadowed, wiped off the slate, by a personal ambition to maintain his rule for life.

This, in my judgment, is a key to the character and the public acts of Porfirio Diaz—to stay there—*to stay there!*

How will this move affect the security of my position? I believe this question has been the one test for the acts of Porfirio Diaz in all those thirty-four years. This question has always been before him. With it he has eaten, drank, slept. With it before him he was married. With it he built a machine, enriched his friends and disposed of his enemies, buying some and killing others; with it he has flattered and gifted the foreigner, favored the church, kept temperance in his body and learned a martial carriage; with it he set one friend against another, fostered prejudice between his people and other peoples, paid the printer, cried in the sight of the multitude when there was no sorrow in his soul and—wrecked his country!

Upon what thread hangs the good fame of Porfirio Diaz with Americans? Upon that one fact, that he has wrecked his country— and prepared it for easy possession by foreigners. Porfirio Diaz is giving to Americans the lands of Mexico; the people he is permitting them to enslave; therefore he is the greatest living statesman, hero of the Americans, the maker of Mexico! A wonderful man, that he is intelligent and far-seeing enough to appreciate the fact that, of all nations, the American is the only one with virtue and ability enough to lift Mexico out of its Slough of Despond! As for the Mexican, let him die. He is only fit to feed the grist mill of American capital, anyhow!

The Mexican People

Since, in the last analysis, all apologies for the Diaz system of economic slavery and political autocracy have their roots in assertions of ethnological inferiority on the part of the Mexican people, it would seem wise to end this book with an examination of the character of Mexicans and a discussion of the arguments upon which Americans are wont to defend a system in Mexico such as they would not for a moment excuse in any other country.

Every defense of Diaz is an attack upon the Mexican people. It must be so, since there is no other conceivable defense of despotism except that the people are so weak or so wicked that they cannot be trusted to take care of themselves.

The gist of the defense is that the Mexican must be ruled from above because he "is not fit for democracy," that he must be enslaved for the sake of "progress," since he would do nothing for himself or the world were he not compelled to do it through fear of the whip or acute starvation, that he must be enslaved because he knows nothing better than slavery and that he is happy in slavery, anyhow. All of which, in the end, resolve themselves into the simple proposition that because he is down he ought to be kept down. Incurable laziness, childish superstition, wanton improvidence, constitutional stupidity, immovable conservatism, impenetrable ignorance, an uncontrollable propensity for theft, drunkenness and cowardice are some of the vices attributed to the Mexican people by those same persons who declare their ruler to be the wisest and most beatific on the face of the earth.

Laziness, in the estimation of the American friends of Diaz, is the cardinal vice of the Mexican. Laziness has always been a cardinal vice in the eyes of the grinders of the poor. American planters actually expect the Mexican to work himself to death for the love of it! Or is it for the love of his master that he expects him to work? Or for the dignity of labor?

But the Mexican does not appreciate such things. And, failing to receive anything more tangible for his work, he "soldiers" on the job. Wherefore he is not only lazy, but stupid! Wherefore, it is right and proper that he should be driven to the field with clubs, that he should be hunted down, forced into *enganchado* gangs, locked up at night, and starved.

It may be information to some persons to tell them that Mexicans have been known to work willingly and effectively when they saw anything to work for. Tens of thousands of Mexicans have displaced Americans and Japanese on the railroads and in the fields of the American Southwest. As high an authority as E. H. Harriman said, in an interview published in the Los Angeles Times in March, 1909: "We have had a good deal of experience with the Mexican, and we have found that after he is fed up and gets his strength he makes a very good worker."

Note that. *"After he is fed up and gets his strength."* Which is saying, in effect, that the employers of Mexican labor, many of whom are estimable Americans, friends of Diaz, *starve them so chronically that they have not the actual strength to work effectively.* Thus we have a second reason why Mexicans sometimes "soldier" on the job. Worthless, worthless Mexicans! Virtuous, virtuous Americans!

The American promoter feels a personal grievance at the religious bigotry of the poor Mexican. It is because of the church *fiestas*, which give the Mexican a few extra holidays a month, when he is free to take them. Profits are lost on those *fiesta* days; hence the anguish of the American promoter. Hence the welcome which the American gives to a system of labor such as we find in Valle Nacional, where the cane of *bejuco* wood is mightier than the priest, where there are neither feast days nor Sundays, nor any days when the club does not drive the slave to the back-breaking labor of the field.

"They told us labor was cheap down here," an American once said to me in a grieved tone. "Cheap? Of course. Dirt cheap. But it has its drawbacks." He expected every "hand" to do as much work as an able-bodied American and to live on thin air besides!

Far be it from me to express approval of the influence of the Catholic church upon the Mexican. Yet it must be admitted that the church alleviates his misery somewhat by providing him with some extra holidays. And it feeds his hunger for sights of beauty and sounds of sweetness, which for the poor Mexican are usually impossible of attainment outside of a church. If the rulers of the land had been enlightened and had given the Mexican the barest glimpse of brightness outside of the church the sway of the priest might have been less pronounced than it is today.

Those *fiestas* which are such a thorn in the side of the American promoter are useful to him at least in that they furnish him with an excuse for paying the wage-earner so little that it is an extravagance, indeed, for the latter to take a day off. "They're so improvident that I have to keep them at the starvation point or they won't work at all." You'll hear Americans saying that almost any day in Mexico. In illustration of which numerous stories are virtuously recounted.

Improvident! Yes, the starving Mexican is improvident. He

spends his money to keep from starving! Yes, there are cases where he is paid such munificent wages that he is able to save a *centavo* now and then if he tries. And, trying, he finds that providence boots him nothing. He finds that the moment he gets a few dollars ahead he at once becomes a mark for every grafting petty official within whose ken he falls. If the masters of Mexico wished their slaves to be provident they should give them an opportunity to get something ahead and then guarantee not to steal it back again.

The poor Mexican is accused of being an inveterate thief. The way a Mexican laborer will accept money and then try to run away, instead of working for the rest of his life to pay off the debt, is, indeed, enough to bring tears to the eyes of the American grinder of *enganchados*. The American promoter steals the very life blood of the laborer and then expects the latter to be so steeped in virtue as to refrain from stealing any part of it back again. When a Mexican peon sees a trinket or a pretty thing that takes his fancy he is quite likely to steal it, for it is the only way he can get it. He risks jail for an article worth a few *centavos*. How often would he do it if the payment of those few *centavos* would not mean a hungry day for him? American planters steal laborers, carry them away by force to their plantations, steal their families away from them, lock them up at night, beat them, starve them while they work, neglect them when they are sick, pay them nothing, kill them at the last, and then raise their hands in righteous horror when a poor fellow steals an extra *tortilla* or an ear of corn!

In Mexico plowing is often done with a crooked stick or with the hoe. The backs of men take the place of freight wagons and express vehicles. In short, Mexico is woefully behind in the use of modern machinery. For which the Mexican is accused of being unprogressive.

But the common people do not choose how much machinery shall be used in the country. The master does that. American promoters in Mexico are little more progressive in the use of machinery than are Mexican promoters, and when they are they frequently lose money by it. Why? Because flesh and blood are cheaper in Mexico than machinery. A peon is cheaper to own than a horse. A peon is cheaper than a plow. A hundred women can be bought for the price of a grist mill. It is because the master has made it so. If by some means the price of flesh and blood were suddenly to be shoved up above that of dead steel, machinery would flow into Mexico as fast as it would flow into any new industrial field in the United States or any other country.

Do not think that the Mexican is too stupid to operate machinery when he is put to it. There are some lines in which machine labor is cheaper than hand labor and we have only to look to these lines to learn that the Mexican can handle machinery quite as easily as any other people. Native labor operates the great cotton mills of Mexico almost exclusively, for example. For that matter, mechanical cunning of a high order is shown in the many hand arts and crafts practiced by the natives, the blanket weaving, the pottery making, the making of laces, the manufacture of curios.

Ignorance is charged against the Mexican people as if it were a crime. On the other hand, we are told, in glowing terms of the public school system which Diaz has established. Charles F. Lummis in his book on Mexico remarks that it is doubtful if there is a single hamlet of one hundred Mexicans in all the country that has not its free public school. The truth is that the people are ignorant and that there are few schools. The sort of authority Mr. Lummis is may be gauged by the government statistics themselves, which, in the year Mr. Lummis issued his book, placed the number of Mexicans who could read and write at sixteen per cent of the population. In Mexico there are some public schools in the cities and almost none in the country districts. But even if they were there, can a hungry baby learn to read and write? What promise does study hold out for a youth born to shoulder a debt of his father and carry it on to the end of his days?

And they say the Mexican is happy! "As happy as a peon," has come to be a common expression. Can a starving man be happy? Is there any people on earth—any beast of the field, even—so peculiar of nature that it loves cold better than warmth, an empty stomach better than a full one? Where is the scientist that has discovered a people who would choose an ever narrowing horizon to an ever widening one? Depraved indeed are the Mexican people if they are happy. But I do not believe they are happy. Some who have said it lied knowingly. Others mistook the dull glaze of settled despair for the signature of contentment.

Most persistent of all derogations of Mexicans is the one that the Spanish-American character is somehow incapable of democracy and therefore needs the strong hand of a dictator. Since the Spanish-Americans of Mexico have never had a fair trial at democracy, and since those who are asserting that they are incapable of democracy are just the ones who are trying hardest to prevent them from having a trial at democracy, the suspicion naturally arises that those persons have an ulterior motive in spreading such an impression. That motive has been pretty well elucidated in previous chapters of this book, especially in the one on the American partners of Diaz.

The truth of the whole malignment of Mexicans as a people seems very plain. It is a defense against indefensible conditions whereby the defenders are profiting. It is an excuse—an excuse for hideous cruelty, a salve to the conscience, an apology to the world, a defense against the vengeance of eternity.

The truth is that the Mexican is a human being and that he is subject to the same evolutionary laws of growth as are potent in the development of any other people. The truth is that, if the Mexican does not fully measure up to the standard of the highest type of European, it is because of his history, a most influential part of which is the grinding exploitation to which he is subjected under the present regime in Mexico. Let us go back to the beginning and glance briefly at the Mexican as an ethnological being and compare his abilities and possibilities with that of the "free" American.

While nearly all persons of more than primary education nominally accept the theory of evolution as the correct interpretation of life upon this planet, not so many of us take advantage of its truths in estimating the people about us. We cling, instead, to the old error of existence by special creation, which supports us when we wish to believe that some men are created of superior clay, that some are inherently better than others and always must be better, that some are designed and intended to occupy a station of special rank and privilege among their fellow men. Forgotten is the scientific truth that all men are shoots from the same stalk, that intrinsically one man is no better than another, that in the fulness of time the possibilities of one race or people are no greater than those of any other. Whatever differences there are between men and races of men are due, not to inherent differences, but to the action of outside influences, to soil and climate, to temperature and rainfall, and to what may be denominated the accidents of history following naturally, however, in the train of these influences. "A man's a man for a' that and a' that."

But there are differences. There are differences in general between Americans and Mexicans. Let us see if there are any differences which justify the condemnation of Mexicans to slavery and government by a despot.

What is a Mexican? Usually the term is applied to the members of a mixed race, part native and part Spanish, who predominate in the so-called sister republic. Pure natives who long ago left the aboriginal state are also often included in the category and they seem to have a right to the name. In the government census of 1900 the proportion of races is given as 43 per cent mixed, 38 pure native and 19 of European or distinct foreign extraction. The Mexican Year Book thinks that the proportion of mixed peoples has greatly increased in the past ten years until it is far more than half the total today. The Mexican of today, then, is either all Spanish, all native, or a mixture of the two, most often the last; so the peculiar character of Mexicans can be said to be made up of a combination of the two elements.

Take the Spanish element, first. What are the peculiar attributes of the Spanish nature? In Spain we find much art and literature, but on the other hand, much religious bigotry and little democracy. We find a versatile people, but a people with swift passions and fickle energies. In its accomplishments along modern lines Spain stands at the foot of the countries of western Europe.

But—why?

The answer is to the credit of Spain. Spain sacrificed herself to save Europe. Standing upon the southern frontier, she bore the brunt of the Moslem invasion. Retarding the barbarian hordes, she saved the budding civilization of Europe and its religion, Christianity. Long after the issue was settled as far as the other nations were concerned, Spain was still engaged in that fight. And in that death-struggle to preserve their existence, it was inevitable that the power of the State should become more centralized and despotic, that the Church should come into closer union with the State, that the Church should become more unscrupulous of the methods it employed to annex power to itself, more sordid of gain, more dogmatic in its teachings and more ruthless in the treatment of its enemies.

Thus is revealed the prime cause for Spain's position as a laggard in the path of democracy and religious enlightenment. For the rest, it may be said that, while the magnificent scenery of the country has helped to make the Spaniard superstitious, it has also helped to make him an artist; that while the exuberance of the soil by enabling him to secure his living with comparatively little labor, has not forced him to habits of such regular industry as are found farther north, it has contributed to his cultivating the arts of music, painting and social intercourse; that the heat of the summer, by rendering hard labor at that season inadvisable, has also militated toward the same ends.

Of course I am not attempting to go into details on these matters. I am merely pointing out a few principles which underlie racial diversities. On the whole, a close examination of the Spanish people would show that there is nothing whatsoever to indicate that they are specially unfit or unworthy to enjoy the blessings of democracy.

As to the native element, which is more important, inasmuch as it undoubtedly predominates in the make-up of the average Mexican, especially the Mexican of the poorer class, an examination of its peculiar character will prove quite as favorable. Biologically, the aboriginal Mexican is not to be classed with any of the so-called lower races, such as the negro, the South Sea Islander, the pure Filipino, or the American Indian. The Aztec has been a long time out of the forest. His facial angle is as good as our own. In many ways he measures up to us. In some ways perhaps he even surpasses us, while the ways in which he falls below us can all be traced either to peculiar external influences, or the luck of history, or both.

It must be admitted that Mexico is not quite as well favored for the generation of physical and mental energy as is the great portion of the United States. The bulk of the population of Diaz-land lives upon a plateau ranging from 5,000 to 8,000 feet high. Here the air is thinner and for every foot-pound of energy expended there is a greater tax upon the heart and the human machine generally. Americans who take up their residence on that plateau find that they must live a little more slowly than in this country, that it is better to take the mid-day *siesta*, like the Mexicans. If they persist in keeping up the old gait they find that they grow old very fast, that it does not pay. If, on the other hand, they choose to live in the tropical belt they find that here, too, because of the greater heat and moisture, it is not wise for them to work as fast as they were wont to do at home.

If the average Mexican has less working capacity than the average American it is largely for this reason, and for the other reason that the Mexican laborer is invariably half starved. When the American laborer meets the Mexican on the latter's own ground he is quite often outdone. Few Americans engage in physical labor either on the plateau or in the tropics. The laborer of no nation can outdo the Mexican in carrying heavy loads or in feats of endurance, while in the tropics the Mexican, if he is not starved, is supreme. The American negro, the Asiatic coolie, the athletic Yaqui from the north, have all been tried out against the native of the tropical states and all have been found wanting, while there is no question as to the inferiority of the working capacity of men of European descent under tropical conditions.

So much for the working capacity of Mexicans, which, in this extremely utilitarian age, is placed high among the virtues of a people. As to intelligence, in spite of the fact that it was always the policy of the Spanish conquerers to hold the native Aztecs in subordinate positions, enough of the latter have succeeded in forcing their way to the top to prove that they were quite as capable in the higher functions of civilization as the Spaniards themselves. The most brilliant poets, artists, writers, musicians, men of science, military heroes and constructive statesmen in the history of Mexico were natives pure or natives but faintly crossed with the blood of Spain.

On the whole, the Mexicans seem to exhibit stronger artistic and literary tendencies than we and less inclination toward commerce and heavy mechanics. The mass of the people are illiterate, but that does not mean that they are stupid. There are undoubtedly several million Americans who are able to read but who don't read regularly, not even a newspaper, and they are no better informed, perhaps, and certainly no clearer thinkers, than the peons who pass the news of the day from mouth to mouth on their Sundays and their feast days. That these people are illiterate by choice, that they are poor because they want to be, that they prefer dirt to cleanliness is absurd.

"They choose that sort of life, so why should we bother ourselves about their troubles?" "They could improve their condition if they cared to make an effort." "They are perfectly happy, anyhow." Such expressions are sure to greet the traveler who remarks upon the misery of the common Mexican. The fact is, the ordinary Mexican chooses the life he lives about as nearly so as a horse chooses to be born a horse. As I suggested before, he cannot be happy, for no starving being can be happy. While as to improving his condition alone and unaided he has about as much chance of doing it as a horse has of inventing a flying machine.

Pick up a poor young Mexican in Mexico City, for example, where the opportunities are the best in the land. Take a typical Mexican laborer. He cannot read or write because he was probably born in a country district ten miles from the nearest school, or if he was born in the shadow of a public school he literally had to scratch the earth from the time he could crawl in order to get something to eat. He has no education and no special training of any kind because he has had no opportunity to secure either. Having had no special training all he is able to do is to carry heavy loads.

Probably at twenty-five he is a physical wreck from under-feeding, exposure and overwork. But suppose he is one of the few who has kept his strength. What can he do? Carry more heavy loads; that is all. He can get perhaps fifty cents a day carrying heavy loads and all the effort of a Hercules cannot better the price, for all he has is brawn, and brawn is cheap as dirt in Mexico. I have seen men "making an effort." I have seen them work until I could see the glazing of their eyes, I have seen them put forth such efforts that their chests rose and fell with explosive gasps, I have seen them carry such heavy weights that they tottered and fell in the street, in which way they are crushed to death, sometimes, by the thing above them. They were putting forth their best efforts in the only thing

they knew because they had never had an opportunity to learn anything else, and they were dying just as fast as those others who did
as little as possible to live. The point is that they never enjoyed the
opportunities at the start that we accept as a birthright. Imagine, if
you can, the majority of our American schools being suddenly
swept away, imagine a change from your condition of partial work
partial leisure to one of all work and no leisure, imagine your earning power as insufficient to feed any mouth but your own, imagine
each mouth in the family needing a separate pair of hands to feed it
and each new mouth needing its own hands while they are yet the
soft hands of a baby—imagine these things and you may faintly appreciate the difficulties which the common Mexican encounters in
trying to improve his condition. For all practical purposes they are
insurmountable.

And how about the capacity of Mexicans for democracy? The
assertion that democracy is not compatible with "the Spanish-American character" seems to be based wholly upon the fact that a considerable percentage of the Spanish-American countries—though
not all of them—are still ruled by dictators, and that changes in the
government come only through revolutions by which one dictator is
succeeded by another. This state of affairs was brought about by
the peculiar history of these countries rather than by "the Spanish-
American character." Ruled as slave colonies by foreigners, these
countries asserted enough valor and patriotism to overthrow the
foreigner and expel him. Their struggle for freedom was long and
bitter; moreover, being small countries, their national exi stence was
in danger for considerable periods after their independenc . Therefore, of necessity the military calling became a dominant profession
and militarism and dictatorships followed naturally. Today what
Spanish-American countries as are still ruled by dictators are ruled
by dictators largely because of the support accorded the latter by
foreign governments, which oppose democratic movements sometimes even with arms. Diaz is not the only Spanish-American dicta-

tor who is supported by the United States at the behest of Wall Street. During the past five years several of the most notorious of the Central American dictators have been held in their places only by a military demonstration on the part of this country.

But is Mexico ready for democracy? Does she not need to be ruled by a despot for awhile longer, until such a time as she shall have developed capacity for democracy? I repeat this absurd question only because it is so common. The only reasonable reply is that of Macaulay, that capacity for democracy can only increase with experience with the problems of democracy. Mexico is as ready for democracy as a country can be which has no democracy whatsoever. There is no chance of Mexico having complete democracy at this time. These things come only gradually, and there is no danger whatsoever of her suddenly getting more democracy than is good for her. Who will say that Mexico should not at once have just a little democracy, enough, say, to deliver her people from the mire of slavery and peonage?

Assuredly Mexico is behind us in the march of progress, behind us in the conquests of democracy. But, in considering her, be just and consider what the luck of history gave us in comparison to what it gave the Mexican. We were lucky enough not to have the rule of Spain imposed upon us for 300 years. We were lucky enough to escape the clutch of the Catholic church at our throats in our infancy. Finally, we were lucky enough not to be caught in our weakness at the end of a foreign war, caught by one of our own generals, who, in the guise of president of our republic, quietly and cunningly, with the cunning of a genius and the remorselessness of an assassin, built up a repressive machine such as no modern nation has ever been called upon to break. We were lucky enough to escape the reign of Porfirio Diaz.

Thus, whichever way we turn, we come finally back to the fact that the immediate cause of all the ills, the shortcomings, the vices of Mexico is the system of Diaz. Mexico is a wonderful country. The

capacity of its people is beyond question. Once its republican constitution is restored, it will be capable of solving all its problems.
Perhaps it will be said that in opposing the system of Diaz I am
opposing the interests of the United States. If the interests of Wall
Street are the interests of the United States, then I plead guilty.
And if it is to the interests of the United States that a nation should
be crucified as Mexico is being crucified, then I am opposed to the
interests of the United States.

But I do not believe that this is so. For the sake of the ultimate
interests of this country, for the sake of humanity, for the sake of
the millions of Mexicans who are actually starving at this moment,
I believe that the Diaz system should be abolished and abolished
quickly.

Hundreds of letters have come to me from all over the world
begging to know what can be done to put a stop to the slavery of
Mexico. Armed intervention of foreign powers has been suggested
again and again. This is unnecessary as well as impractical. But
there is one thing that is practical and necessary, especially for
Americans, and that is to insist that there shall be *no foreign intervention for the purpose of maintaining the slavery*.

In Mexico today exists a nation-wide movement to abolish the
Diaz system of slavery and autocracy. This movement is quite
capable of solving the problems of Mexico without foreign interference. So far it has not succeeded, partly because of the assistance
our government has given in the persecution of some of its leaders,
and partly because of Diaz's threat—constantly held before the
Mexican people—of calling an American army to his aid in case of
a serious revolution against him.

Under the present barbarous government there is no hope for
reform in Mexico except through armed revolution. Armed revolution on the part of the decent and most progressive element is a
strong probability of the early future. When the revolution starts
American troops will be rushed to the border and made ready to

cross in case Diaz is unable to cope with the revolt alone. If the American army crosses it will not be ostensibly to protect Diaz, but to protect American property and American lives. And to this end false reports of outrages upon Americans, or danger to American women and children, will be deliberately circulated in order to arouse the nation to justify the crime of invasion. That will be the time for decent Americans to make their voices heard. They will expose, in no uncertain terms, the conspiracy against democracy and demand that, for all time, our government cease putting the machinery of state at the disposal of the despot to help him crush the movement for the abolition of slavery in Mexico.

INDEX

Acayucan, Veracruz: troops sent against Liberals in, 121, 133, 145
acordada: 119, 126–127, 132, 135
Agricultural Bank: loans made by, 112
agriculture: United States investment in Mexican, 3, 216–217, 224; economics of slavery in, 9–10; practiced by Yaquis, 28, 34, 35, 52; Chinantecos practice, 78; proportion of slave labor in Mexican, 92; free laborers in, 95; size of farms in Mexican, 106–107; loans for, 112; irrigation for, 114; laws regarding, urged, 150; Mexican Herald on labor conditions in, 196; laborers for, in Sonora, 272; lack of machinery for, 284–285
—, plantation: henequen, 6–8, 13, 24–25, 92, 190, 213; tobacco, 57, 65–66, 76, 77, 78, 82, 85, 92; coffee, 70, 195, 226; rubber, 188–189, 226; cotton, 194; sugar, 195
Aguascalientes: newspaper in, suppressed, 142; Anti-Re-electionist demonstrations forbidden in, 165; mechanics' strike in, 176
Aguila, El (company): directorate of, 114
Aguilar, Rafael: lands of, confiscated, 108
Aguirre, Lauro: attempted extradition of, 236; accused of violating neutrality laws, 255
Ahumada, Governor: real-estate holdings of, 107
Alameda: Democrats at meeting in,

arrested, 155; boy kidnapped from, 198, 199, 201
Alamos, Sonora: arrests in, 164
"Alley of Death, The": construction of, 124
Alvarez Soto, Ramon: arrested, 160
American Cordage Trust: buys Mexican henequen, 224
American Magazine, The: first chapters of *Barbarous Mexico* published in, 187; letters to, on Turner's articles, 188; Whitaker's article in, 189; attempt to bar, from mails, 191–192; halts Turner articles, 205–206; Powell articles in, 206–207 n.
American Mine Owners: newspaper of, 192
American Peace Society: honors Diaz, 263
American Sugar Trust: Mexican interests of, 222
Ancona, Abelardo: death of, 143
animals: mules, 5, 17, 20, 41, 203; cattle, 10, 36, 41, 73, 184, 216, 217; burros, 36, 41; oxen, 40, 77, 89; hogs, 51, 217; alligators, 64, 79; dogs, 179, 180, 181; sheep, 214, 217
—, horses: theft of, 35; Yaqui exiles not allowed to ride, 41; routes for, into Valle Nacional, 56; Turner travels by, 73, 75; Turner abandons, 89; Mexicans compared to, 169, 291; on Hearst ranch, 216, 217; Cahuantzi furnishes Diaz with, 268; Diaz' father breaks, 270; price of, 285

Circulo de Obreros, El: founded, 170; officers of, executed, 173

Citadel, The. SEE Ciudadela, La

Citizen, Tucson: Hall's article in, 192

Ciudadela, La (movement): crushed, 265

Ciudad Porfirio Diaz, Coahuila: arrests in, 166; union headquarters in, 175

Clark, —— (General Manager): agreement of, with Union, 176; asks aid from Diaz, 177

clothing: of Merida women, 9; of slaves, 18, 45, 63–64, 93, 199, 201; price of, in plantation stores, 18, 63–64; Yaquis seek, 34; of Yaqui exiles, 39, 40; of Chihuahua laborer, 94; taken from runaway slaves, 193; fabrics for, 209; distributed to Mexico City workmen, 274

Club Anti-Re-eleccionista de Obreros: imprisonment of board of directors of, 165

Club Democratico (Guadalajara): newspaper of, suppressed, 157

Club Reyista (Torreon): secretary of, arrested, 155

Coahuila: long period in office of governor of, 118; *acordada* subchief in, 127; Liberal uprising in, 145, 146, 236; governor of, compelled to resign, 162; arrests in, 164; Anti-Reelectionist demonstrations forbidden in, 165; Madero from, 272

Cole-Ryan mining combination: acquires Cananea mines, 182

Colima: executions in, 133, 156

Congo: American attitude toward, 214, 220

Congress, United States: investigates persecution of Mexican Liberals, 257

Conner, J. Torrey: on Mexican slavery, 196

constitution, Mexican: inoperativeness of, 3; illegality of slavery under, 14; similarity of, to United States constitution, 137; antichurch provisions of, 140; Juarez father of, 275

Constitution, United States: Mexican constitution compared to, 3, 137; principles of, 250

Contreras, Angel: death of, 197

Cooper, C. V.: on peonage, 190–191

Cordoba: slaves escape toward, 55; distance of Valle Nacional from, 57; story of labor agent in, 61, 62; Turner sees slaves, at, 69; train from, 70; Valle Nacional escapees captured in, 73; selling of political offices in, 111; Gomez brought to Rio Blanco from, 174

corn. SEE plants

Corona, Ramon (General): death of, 139; sent against Diaz, 265

Corona Flour Milling Company: head of, jailed, 153

Corral, Ramon (Vice President): long period in office of, as governor of Sonora, 29; real estate holdings of, 107; on Mexican army, 120; visits Belem, 128; nomination of, 150; expected triumph of Reyes over, 151; actions on behalf of, 152; opponents of, contest state and local elections, 156; Reyes fails to act against, 161; re-elected, 166; warns Vera, 177; Greene's connections with, 181; troops in Cananea under orders of, 185; stirs up Yaqui war, 223–224

Correo de la Tarde, El: editor of, driven out of Mazatlan, 158

Cortez, Celso: imprisonment of, 154

Cosio, —— (Governor): real estate holdings of, 107

Cosmopolitan Magazine: defense of Diaz in, 193–194, 207; on writers, 208

Libertad, La: suppressed, 157

Limantour, Jose Yves (Minister of Finance): real estate holdings of, 107; role of, in railroad merger, 228, 229

Linares, Nuevo Leon: newspaper suppressed in, 157–158

Lincoln, Abraham: admiration for, 214; Diaz compared to, 262

literature: lack of Mexican, 269; of Spain, 288

London: Dr. F. S. Pearson's combination in, 113

Lopez Portillo, Jose: deposed from Senate, 152

Lopez Portillo y Rojas, Jose: imprisonment of, 155

Los Angeles, California: Mexican revolutionaries persecuted in, 4, 215–216, 236, 246–249, 252–253, 255; Mexican consulate in, 241; Liberal hideout in, 245–246; defense efforts in, on behalf of Mexican Liberals, 249–250; De Lara's extradition hearing in, 251–252

Lummis, Charles F.: on Mexican education, 285

Luna, Francisco A.: beating of, 143

Macedo, Pablo: role of, in railroad merger, 228

Maderists: parade of, 163–164

Madero, Francisco I.: becomes Democratic leader, 162–163; nominated for president, 163; open letter of, to Diaz, 164, 165; imprisonment of, 165; on order for deportation of Yaquis, 272

Magdalena Bay, Baja California: Root seeks arrangements in regard to, 274

Magon, Enrique. SEE Flores Magon, Enrique

Magon, Jesus. SEE Flores Magon, Jesus

Magon, Ricardo Flores. SEE Flores Magon, Ricardo

Maldonado, Calixto M.: charged with "provocation of rebellion," 158

Mancera, Gabriel: on board of merged railroads, 229

"Mangos, Los" (farm): Yaqui slaves at, 85–86

Mansano, Aaron: position of, in Liberal Junta, 245

Martinez, Angel (General): Yaquis hanged by, 32–33

Martinez, ——— (Governor): long period in office of, 118; newspaper articles exposing, 142

Martinez, Dr. Ignacio: death of, 139

Martinez, Margarita: imprisonment of, 131, 173; leads looting of store, 172

Martinez, Paulino: newspapers owned by, suspended, 159–160; escapes to United States, 161; imprisonment of, 173; on Tizapan strike, 179

Martinez, Mrs. Paulino: imprisonment of, 160, 161

Martinez, Rosalio (General): leads troops against Rio Blanco strikers, 172

Martinez Carrion, Jesus: death of, 143

Martinez de Arredondo, Manuel: imprisonment of, 155

Martinez del Rio, Pablo: loses in attempted railway merger, 229

Masons: Diaz heads, 274

Mata, Filomeno: imprisonment of, 159

Mata, Filomeno, Jr.: imprisonment of, 159

Maxey, ——— (Judge): denies extraditions, 236; on neutrality laws, 256

Maximilian: Yaqui contributions to struggle against, 30; overthrow of, 102, 223, 264–265

Nichols, William H.: on National Railways of Mexico board, 229

Nuevo Leon: governor of, 118, 139, 151, 161; newspaper suppressed in, 157; Anti-Re-electionist demonstrations forbidden in, 165

Oaxaca (city): Daniel T——'s dealings with officials of, 62; cigar factory in, 78; authorities of, engage in slave traffic, 84, 90; shipment of women from, 87; selling of political office in, 111; San Gabriel labor contractor in, 189; Diaz' childhood in, 270

Oaxaca (state): Valle Nacional in, 56; connections of officials of, with slave trade, 90; slavery in, 92; Democrats fired on, 156; Diaz commands troops in, 265; massacre in, 271

Oaxaquena (plantation): Juarez learns of his destined job at, 201

Oaxaquena Plantation Company: contract laborers for, 198

Obregon Gonzalez, ——— (Governor): 118

Olivares, Juan: escapes to United States, 173

Olmos y Contreras, Jesus: death of, 142–143

Opatas: deported to Yucatan, 35, 40

Oregonian, Portland: article in, on peonage, 190–191

Orient railroad. See Kansas City, Mexico and Orient

Orizaba, Veracruz: selling of political offices in, 111; shootings during strike at, 133; arrests in, 164; historicity of strike at, 169; prices in, 169; massacre of, 273

Otis, Harrison Gray: financial interests of, in Mexico, 106, 216

Overland Monthly, The: defends Diaz, 211

Oviedo, Manuel M.: imprisonment of, 157

P———, *Senor*: Turner interviews, 89–90

Pachuca, Hidalgo: slaves from, 71–73; authorities of, engage in slave traffic, 84; selling of political office in, 111

Pacific Ocean: penal colony in, 155; railway to, 195

Pais, El: on Tehuitzingo executions, 132–133; on jail shootings, 134

Paladin, El: suppressed, 160

Palmer, Bradley W.: on National Railways of Mexico board, 229

Palmer, Frederick: on land taxes in Mexico, 109; imprisonment of, 154

Papagos: De Lara one of, 51; lands of, confiscated, 106

Papaloapan River: and geography of Valle Nacional, 56, 57; water power from, 66

Papantla, Veracruz: executions at, 109, 133

Pardo, Rodolpho: receives money from slave trade, 62, 90; gives Turner letter of introduction, 69; Turner meets, 73

Patino, Enrique: imprisoned, 160

Pearson, F. S.: investments of, in Mexico, 113–114, 222

Pearson, S., & Son, Limited: investments of, in Mexico, 113, 114, 222

Pearson's Magazine: Creelman's interview with Diaz in, 148, 259; Creelman leaves, 211

Pena, Juan de la: death of, 143

Pena, William de la: death of, 153

Peniche, Alfonso B.: imprisoned, 158–159

tobacco. SEE agriculture, plantation; plants, tobacco

Tomosachic, Chihuahua: massacre at, 109–110

Tomosachics: lands of, confiscated, 106

Toro, Luis: death of, 143

Torre, Juan de la: sent to San Juan de Ulua, 132

Torreon, Coahuila: cotton fields of, 95; criminal from, as spy, 145; arrests in, 155, 157, 164, 166

Torres, Lorenzo (General): Yaqui lands given to, 31; "Yaquis" on, 40

Torres, Luis (General): brings troops to Cananea, 185

Torres, Luis (Governor): rotation in office of, 29; on Yaqui surrender, 34

Torres Delgado, Ramon: accused of violating neutrality laws, 255

transportation: by mule car, 17, 20; by gunboat, 31; by ship, 36, 37, 38, 39, 42–43, 153, 157; by streetcar, 96; by wagon, 56, 284, by canoe, 56, 61, 73; by horseback, 56–57, 75; by launch, 72; by *balsa*, 89; by automobile, 183, 239, 246; by carriage, 278

—, by railroads: of Yaqui workers, 29, 33, 35; of slaves, 38, 43, 59, 60, 70, 71, 72; of army troops, 145; of strikers' bodies, 173

Treasury Department, United States: reinstates Dowe, 241

Tresgallo, ———: 73

Tres Marias Islands, Nayarit: penal colony on, 155, 159, 185

Trevino, Bruno: sent to San Juan de Ulua, 131; deported, 237

Trevino, Leocadio: imprisonment of, 255

Trout, E. F.: on Yaquis, 28

Trowbridge, Elizabeth D.: Manuel Sarabia marries, 254

Trueno, El: suppressed, 157–158

"Truth About Mexico, The": publication of, 192

Tucson, Arizona: Manuel Sarabia's printing plant destroyed in, 240–241

Tuztepec, Oaxaca: stray travelers in, 57; police and *rurales* in, 57, 74; Daniel T——'s dealings with officials of, 62; Turner travels to, 69; *jefe politico* of, 71, 90; slaves taken to, en route to Valle Nacional, 72; slaves escaping to, 73, 89; Turner interviews labor agent in, 89–90

Ugalde, ———: 132

Ulibarri, ———: 215, 250

Ulloa, Ambrosio: imprisonment of, 153

Ulua. SEE San Juan de Ulua

United States: Mexican revolutionists jailed in, 4; Indians of, 8, 28; henequen purchased by, 21; slaves in, 25; Lelevier editor in, 32; Mexicans as wage laborers in, 93; compared to Mexico, 99, 263, 289; threatens move against Diaz, 103; financial interests from, in Mexico, 113, 209, 221–223, 229–230; elections in, 117–118; Diaz hints at invasion threat from, 120; Liberals deported from, 131, 237, 257; Constitution of, 137; political refugees flee to, 138, 161, 166, 173, 179, 243; Cadena attempts to flee to, 139; Liberal uprisings staged from, 144, 145; persecution of Liberal Party in, 146; nearness of Cananea to, 181; Greene's influence with government of, 182; involvement of, in Cananea strike, 183–185; organized labor in, 186; comment in, on Turner's articles, 187; government reports in, on Mexican slavery, 202–203; Diaz' influence on press of, 204, 206; Hearst's political

arrests of Democrats in, 156; lack
of trusts alleged in, 208
—, slaves of: and population, 6, 7; nationalities of, 8–9; price of Yaqui, 10;
recruitment of, 11, 12; conditions of
life for, 14–20, 43–53; separation of
families of, 26; Yaquis shipped to be,
27, 28, 33–37, 38–43, 192, 224, 272;
death rate of, 54; compared to Valle
Nacional slaves, 55, 57; and rest of
Mexico, 56, 92; Arnold and Frost on,
189; Thompson on, 190; articles corroborate existence of, 192; United
States government report on, 202–
203; Stevens on, 210; Tabor and
Frost on, 213
"Yucatan, the American Egypt": suppression of, 213

Yucatan Nuevo: suppressed, 158
Yucatan Peninsula: geography of, 6;
dependence of, on henequen kings, 8
Yzabal, Rafael (Governor): rotation
in office of, 29; orders Yaquis' hands
cut off, 33; meets Arizona invaders,
184; troops in Cananea under orders
of, 185

Zacatecas (city): Cadena killed at, 139
Zacatecas (state): death of governor
of, 139
Zaragoza, Coahuila: arrests in, 164–
165
Zelaya, ———: 134
Zwickey, W. F.: affidavit sworn to by,
249